THE PR CRISIS BIBLE

THE PR CRISIS BIBLE

Robin Cohn

HOW TO TAKE CHARGE OF THE MEDIA WHEN ALL HELL BREAKS LOOSE

T·T

TRUMAN TALLEY BOOKS

ST. MARTIN'S PRESS ❧ NEW YORK

To the two MCs

LIBRARY OF CONGRESS CATALOGING-IN-PUBLICATION DATA

Cohn, Robin.
    The PR crisis bible : how to take charge of the media when all hell breaks loose / Robin Cohn.—1st ed.
        p. cm.
    "Truman Talley books."
    Includes index.
    ISBN 0-312-25230-7
    1. Crisis management.   2. Corporations—Public relations.   3. Mass media and business.   4. Disasters—Press coverage.   I. Title.

HD49 .C64 2000
659.2—dc21

00-040232

First Edition: November 2000

10 9 8 7 6 5 4 3 2 1

Contents

Acknowledgments

It's a little-known fact that the unsung heroes behind every book are the families and friends of the author. These folks are forced to bear the brunt of moans and groans, yet they manage to get through the process without shooting the author. Not that this happened in my case. . . . However, I would like to thank everybody I know and love for letting me live.

I am deeply grateful to my agent, Martha Jewett (www. marthajewett.com), for her patience, invaluable guidance, and hard work. A heartfelt thank-you goes to Lynne Kemper for her time and razor-sharp input, and grinning appreciation is extended to my charming cartoonist, Curtiss Calleo. I'd also like to acknowledge all the executives who gave me terrific material, both those who are mentioned in the book and those who preferred to remain anonymous. My appreciation also goes to my editor, Mac Talley, and editorial assistant, Jill Sieracki, for their direction, and to my dear friends, thank you for easing the way.

A very special thank-you goes to the effervescent Minna Cohn for her support, and for spending her birthday proofreading my manuscript.

And, thank you, Dick Tracy.

Introduction

When this book was scheduled for its press run, the biggest PR crisis since the Exxon *Valdez* oil spill erupted—the Bridgestone/Firestone tire recall. Here's a brief rundown on its key aspects.

In August 2000, Firestone, a unit of Bridgestone in Japan, recalled 6.5 million Firestone-brand tires after they were linked to fatal accidents, primarily involving Ford Motor Co. Explorer sport-utility vehicles. Until that time, the company had failed to address months of allegations linking the tires to more than a hundred deaths and hundreds of accidents in America, and at least forty-seven deaths in Venezuela. To make matters worse, the company was woefully unprepared to meet the demand for replacement tires. The day after the recall announcement, thousands of panicked vehicle owners showed up demanding replacement tires, but few were available. (As of September, approximately 2.2 million of the 6.5 million tires were replaced.) As Firestone was its supplier, Ford also found itself on the hot seat because it could not supply enough replacement tires for Explorer customers. War broke out between the two companies. Ford went on the offense, pointing the finger at Japanese-owned Firestone.

After the tire recall was announced, documents surfaced indicating that the tire company and, perhaps, Ford already knew about the problems with Firestone-equipped Explorers in the late 1990s, but had neglected to tell consumers or safety regulators. The crisis continued to snowball as congressional hearings were held. Damaging testimony and documents were disclosed, and legislators blasted both Firestone and Ford.

The congressional hearings brought another Ford problem to light. According to information released by congressional investigators, based on company documents, Ford knew that a defective ignition system (T.F.I. module) had been installed in thousands of cars during the 1980s and 1990s, but failed to alert regulators and consumers.

A Morality Tale

One of the most significant early lessons of the tire-recall crisis points directly to top management. It shows what happens when companies believe legal settlements will cost less than fixing problems. When problems become public—and they do—companies face a much bigger hit to the bottom line. Think how much money an earlier recall would have saved Firestone. In fact it's hard to put a price tag on the irreparable harm the company has done to itself by inaction.

A CEO has to choose between short-term profit and responsible behavior. But beware: Consumers are concerned with their own well-being, not the company's. Remember what happened to the now-defunct Ford Pinto and the Dalcon Shield.

When a company discovers it is making a defective product and orders a recall, it is taking responsible action. When a company is caught hiding a problem, its response is perceived by press and public as "damage control"—the focus is on self-defense instead of the customer's well-being. Consumers never reward bad corporate behavior.

Firestone failed to put customer safety before its own interests: It tried to hide the bad news, did not respond fast enough when the story broke, and was clearly unprepared for a recall. These mistakes snowballed into an explosive situation that could have been contained. Constant blunders brought on the "Seven Plagues of Unhappy Repercussions," discussed in Chapter 4. In fact, you can see how Firestone's missteps fit neatly into the diagram of a mismanaged crisis to be found in the same chapter.

Breaking the Rules

Trouble begins when a CEO makes the decision to bury a problem. Then the crisis ball begins rolling.

- Bad news can't be hidden. There are too many people and ways a problem can be leaked; the information usually winds up on a reporter's desk. Disgruntled employees and competitors are especially prone to spilling a company's secrets. Once the news gets out, the company becomes a bigger villain.

- The faster the response, the faster the story dissipates. To say Firestone's response was too slow is to put it mildly. While it's not clear how long the company was aware of the problem, Firestone failed to respond when the defective tire story broke in February 2000. A National Highway Traffic Safety Administration (NHTSA) investigation began in May and became public in July, further raising customer fears. Still no company response. Shortly afterwards, Sears announced it would stop selling Firestone tires. Deluged by negative media coverage, the company finally acted two weeks later. The longer a company remains quiet, the more the story expands as reporters, lawyers, and consumer groups keep digging for damaging information.

- Finger-pointing diminishes stature. While it wasn't Ford's fault that the tires were defective, the fact remains the tires were on Ford vehicles. Therefore, the company, in the eye of the public, is ultimately accountable. Blaming Firestone was unnecessary; the public already knew which company had supplied the defective tires.

- Heed warning signals. Firestone documents show that claims of tread-separation began to grow rapidly for tires the company had made after 1992. According to the *Wall Street Journal,* in 1999, 62 percent of the company's costs from tread-separation claims involved tires made at its Decatur, Illinois, plant. Think of what Firestone might have avoided had it heeded the warning signs.

- Cultural differences impact a crisis response. Firestone's was originally managed by its Japanese parent company, Bridgestone. That company might not have understood the recall's impact on American consumers. A crisis has to be addressed according to the culture and mores of the country where the problem occurs.

- Crisis planning is a must. It's the only way a company can respond rapidly and well. Firestone's botched recall indicates that a plan wasn't in place. As the company scrambled to supply replacement tires, Bridgestone, in Japan, announced it was sending tires by air to the United States. That's the kind of action that should have been triggered as part of a worst-case recall scenario. What's especially ironic is that Firestone nearly went bankrupt after a tire recall in 1978. That alone should have been a wake-up call.

The Final Word—for Now

Perhaps the most significant lesson from the disaster is this: A company can have the best crisis management counsel in the world, but it won't amount to a hill of beans if the CEO pays no heed. Firestone had ignored the advice of an experienced public relations firm (which firm promptly and wisely resigned). CEOs must understand that to contain crisis damage, legal considerations are important but not what the public demands: the CEO taking responsible action.

So, the continuing Firestone/Ford crisis exemplifies every one of the seven deadly "sins" you'll find throughout this book. Read on.

1

It Will Never Happen Here

Is the CEO wearing clothes or not?

A young employee, brought up on computer games instead of fairy tales, overhears an angry employee comparing the CEO with some emperor who wore no clothes. "You can see right through his new suit," another employee agrees.

Thinking this conversation a bit odd, he mentions it to his buddy, an ambitious newspaper reporter. What a scoop! The reporter writes a story saying the CEO lied about wearing new clothes and, in fact, isn't wearing anything. To get a jump on its competitors, his paper runs with the story, based solely on information from an "inside source." Soon, TV cameras and reporters are camping outside headquarters.

The CEO isn't talking to the press, but disgruntled employees are. They say he's running around naked. The CEO's staff, speaking on his behalf, deny the accusation. The media are exploding with sensational reports provided by such "experts" as the janitor.

Why won't the CEO say anything? His silence must mean he's not wearing any clothes. Quick. He's gone bonkers. Sell the stock!

In reality, the CEO was wearing new clothes. He just didn't think it was anybody's business.

And so it goes. With the snap of a media finger, even an innocuous problem can take on a life of its own, becoming a full-blown crisis. The real issue is not the incident itself but the way it is managed. In the suited CEO's case, all he had to do was appear in front of reporters wearing his new clothes. Maybe it was a private matter, but once the "scandal" hit the press, it became a public one. Although it may not be fair, an allegation without a quick response becomes a fact. If he had responded quickly, the news would have been boring: "The CEO Is Wearing a New Suit." So what? In other words, it would not have become a story at all.

It's a Jungle Out There

In today's world, no one is immune to the intense scrutiny of the media. This means a company's image depends on how it responds to a crisis. When a company doesn't perform well and looks bad, its top executives don't look so hot, either. A CEO's reputation, as well as the company's, is at stake. After all, Exxon CEO Lawrence G. Rawls did not pilot the *Exxon Valdez* oil tanker, but he was responsible for the oil spill nonetheless. His actions—or lack of them—became a textbook example of poor crisis management.

Then there was the McKesson scandal. The drug distributor's CEO and CFO were fired after alleged unethical accounting tactics were discovered at an acquired unit even though they were not involved in the accounting problems.

It's bad enough when something goes wrong on your watch. Having an audience makes it worse.

So, what do you do? The answers lie in what you shouldn't do. One can learn a lot from the CEOs in this book who've done an excellent job leading their companies through crises. Then, there are examples of some CEOs' past mistakes and how they could have been avoided or contained. As the cowboys say, "Good judgment comes from experience, and a lotta that comes from bad judgment."

It Will Never Happen Here

The best way to get into trouble is to pretend there won't be any. As a result, it will take a CEO a long time to respond, and he'll look irresponsible. The CEO and his company could even become the brunt of jokes on late-night television shows.

Welcome to the First Deadly Sin: "It Will Never Happen Here." It's the unenlightened executive's mantra. In reality, it's like squatting with your spurs on. The results are painful.

We're Not in Kansas Anymore

News isn't new, but the technology delivering it is, making news faster and more constant. Today, we're living in an "instant atmosphere" with twenty-four-hour news, satellites, computers, the Internet, cell phones, and faxes. Commenting on the immediacy of news, NBC president Bob Wright said, "We're all forced to comment and report on the buzz. . . . We can't be alone or ignorant for a second."

- **This climate has changed the way CEOs have to perform.**
  I was watching a movie from the mid-fifties where the CEO ordered his secretary to get a report to a regional office immediately. She said it would be there by the day after tomorrow. He didn't bat an eye; he even grunted his approval. In those days, that ASAP effort meant getting the report typed (one mistake: start over) and mimeographed, and required employees to run back and forth to train stations.
- **Predecessors had the luxury of a long response time; you don't.**
  Reporters can be on a company's front steps before the CEO knows there's a problem. A CEO has to be ready, fast.

Gone, too, are the days when the media glossed over problems and protected privacy and reputations. For example, take Bill Agee, the married CEO of Bendix. His reputed affair with Mary Cunningham, a Bendix employee whose career he promoted (a lot), garnered as much coverage as his failed raid on Martin Marietta Corporation. Imagine the press they'd get today.

The spotlight on private lives goes beyond sex scandals to personal differences and feuds. Ira Rennert, the CEO and owner of the privately held company Renco Group, wanted to build a massive $100 million home in the Hamptons, a New York playground for the rich and famous. His Hampton neighbors raised holy hell, and the resulting media attention uncovered accusations that went beyond Mr. Rennert's bad taste. Included in the report were scores of EPA penalties and Justice Department suits against some of his companies for record amounts of pollution and toxic waste. The story got even juicier when a gossip sheet claimed that one of his current vice presidents had pleaded guilty to sexual misconduct after being accused of raping a twenty-year-old woman on a conference table (in the company's Rockefeller Center office, no less). Whether this is true or not remains to be seen, but it shows how all kinds of stories come out of the woodwork in situations like Mr. Rennert's. Besides the lesson of not building a home larger than the White House next door to powerful neighbors who object, the story contains an important moral:

- **When a top business executive says "look at me," people do—in bad times as well as good.**

Guilt by Association

There are times an executive's personal problems can put a company in the media spotlight even though the company itself is not involved. For instance, General Electric was dragged into an executive's nasty divorce. The battle between Gary C. Wendt, chief executive of GE Capital Corporation, and his wife turned into a landmark test of women's rights. The divorce raised the issue of whether a wife was entitled to 50 percent of a couple's assets. Mr. Wendt was dumping his wife of thirty-one years with a relatively small settlement. Plus, he still expected her to play dutiful hostess at a corporate Christmas party. The women of America were very unhappy. General Electric wound up in the headlines, appearing to endorse the mean, insensitive executive. So much for bringing good things to life.

Mr. Wendt quickly fell from grace, not only losing his "fair-haired boy" status but his job as well. Mishandling personal crises can get media attention and affect a career.

Pornogate

It comes as no surprise that a married Wall Street banker would have a mistress. It would hardly be considered a crisis except, perhaps, if the wife found out. It wouldn't impact a company— unless the banker was charged with insider trading for passing information along to his girlfriend, a porn star.

That's what happened to respected investment bank Keefe Bruyette & Woods (KBW). It had to scramble to maintain its reputation when former CEO James McDermott was accused of leaking information about potential billion-dollar bank deals to his X-rated girlfriend, who, in turn, passed them along to another boyfriend.

The two men who inherited Mr. McDermott's position after he suddenly resigned months earlier weren't aware of the alleged crime until they were subpoenaed by the Security and Exchange Commission (SEC). Yet they were left with the task of saving the firm's name. Said one co-CEO, "In some people's eyes, we are associated with this scandal even though Jim hasn't been here for six months." He further went on to assure the public that the firm was not under investigation.

Thanks to the porn queen's involvement, the media had a field day. It was even front page news in the mainstream press—unfortunately for the staid KBW. As the co-CEO said, the whole scandal "gave the firm a big black eye."

Ex-CEO McDermott, although charged with securities fraud, was not accused of making any illegal profits himself. However, he wound up being the first Wall Street chief executive charged with insider trading, according to the SEC. With those two words "insider trading," the scandal became the firm's problem as well as Mr. McDermott's.

Family Feud

Here's another story where internal squabbles become public ones: the Haft family feud.

In 1955 Herbert Haft bought a drugstore and turned it into a big regional chain of seventy Dart drugstores. In the 1970s, Mr. Haft and his wife Gloria welcomed their children into the family business. One son, Robert, founded Crown Books.

By 1993, the company's worth was estimated at $500 to $600 million. During this heyday period, The Dart Group included the drugstores, Crown Books, and Trak Auto. However, storm clouds were on the horizon.

A *Wall Street Journal* article suggested the father spent little time at the business and said son Robert had been "the de facto chief executive for the last two years." The father went ballistic, interpreting this as his business obituary.

This was the start of the very public slugfest. Herbert fired his son Robert, replacing him with his younger son, Ronald. Robert, in turn, sued his father, citing his 1993 wrongful termination. In 1994, Robert won a $38 million judgment. Gloria, the wife, who is said to have sided with son Robert, got kicked off the board. Following the suit, Robert took every opportunity to show reporters how the company's sales took a sharp plunge after his dismissal.

The Hafts divorced after forty-six years of marriage. Herbert and his other son Ronald soon parted ways over control of the company, and, at one point, all three children sued their parents for control of their stakes of the company. In 1998, the father gave up control of the Dart Group while the company's worth dropped to $41.6 million.

Due to the massive publicity, the Dart Group was overshadowed by the Haft's feud, not their business prowess.

"Boom Boom" Versus Garden City

Mark Twain once said, "There's a lot to say in her favor, but the other is more interesting." That sentiment has been taken to heart by today's business press.

Partly due to the more personal slant, business has become a lot more popular. Once, newspapers buried business news next to the sports section. Now, business stories often make the front page. In light of intense competition among news organizations, many have shed the principles of objectivity and accuracy. Mainstream press has gone tabloid, including business coverage as the "Pornogate" story illustrates. Smith Barney's Garden City, New York, office was dubbed the "Boom Boom Room" by the media after women in that office filed a sexual-harassment suit. The newspapers reported the juicy allegations of what occurred in the infamous room. After that, would women trust a "Boom Boom Room" broker with their money?

Looking at the blurring between tabloid and mainstream news, talk-show host Charlie Rose noted, ". . . gossip columnists once had exclusive sources. Now, these sources work with network news shows." These "shows" have become so popular (and cheap to produce), they've reached prime-time status, indicating that blurry news makes money.

- **Nothing comes without consequences.**

Today's instant media atmosphere has led to instant judgments by the public. We've lost a kinder, gentler sense of public opinion. Americans once revered business and government, but both are now viewed with distrust. One poll done by The Opinion Research Corporation shows 62 percent of Americans believe that business people will do anything they can to make a profit, even if it means ignoring the public's needs. Small wonder consumers have a limited loyalty span. When a crisis hits, customer defections can begin within the first twenty-four hours.

Now, a company is guilty until proven innocent. We've come a long way but, unfortunately, in the wrong direction.

It's Show Time!

There's a saying that curiosity is the mother of the window shade. Face it. It's human nature to peek. We can blatantly gawk as we're bombarded with "news" involving scandal, sex, and catastrophe. One pundit noted, "One good vice will get you more publicity than a dozen virtues." A nightly news program leading with crime stories wins higher ratings than one leading with important school-board issues. Even though people said there was too much coverage of the President Clinton–Monica Lewinsky scandal, the twenty-four-hour MSNBC recorded an almost 300 percent increase in daily hits on its Internet news Web site when the story broke.

Actually, the shutters of curiosity began flying open like cuckoo clocks when the Gulf War hit. CNN's nonstop coverage of the event played a major role in changing the expectations of news audiences. One TV executive explained, "Five years ago, people had a hope for same-day pictures. Now, they expect same-hour, if not same minute news." CNN's success ultimately led to the explosion of news outlets, which, in turn, led to a volume problem of having to fill more airtime.

- **This glut of information—dubious or otherwise—has turned news into a spectator sport.**

We've become a nation of "watchers." Consider the millions of people glued to their television sets for three hours watching O. J. Simpson's Ford Bronco drive down the L.A. Freeway (although now few admit it).

Thanks to the immediacy of television, we are used to observing a variety of dire situations as they happen. In short, a crisis has become theater. Give the story a bad name, and there will be standing room only. As Will Rogers said, "The theater is a great equalizer; it's the only place where the poor can look down on the rich." For CEOs, this means many enjoy seeing high-and-mighty corporations get their comeuppance.

In this atmosphere, when a problem hits, CEOs play the lead whether they want to or not. After all, facing the media comes with the territory.

Dust Off Your Crystal Ball

One can often predict trouble without even being psychic. The halls of corporate America are filled with the murmurs of warnings. For a CEO, it pays to be a good listener.

- **Studies show 80 percent of potential disasters are people generated and can be prevented.**
- **With few exceptions, people-caused problems leave a trail of early warning signals well in advance of the actual crisis.**

One problem is we tend to overlook the obvious. Although dubious events can come out of left field, the Institute of Crisis Management states 69 percent of business crises are smoldering and 31 percent are sudden.

The dramatic collapse of Barings Bank, once a bastion of

British stability, is a good example of the consequences of not paying attention to warning signals. While rogue trader Nick Leeson brought the bank down with his spending spree, the bank's top management was ultimately responsible. Those folks failed to hear the warning bells—or in this case, gongs. The signs were there: increased trading activity, the extreme use of leverage, escalating trade amounts, and steadily increasing risk. Only no one was watching.

Not all signals are obvious. Sometimes they are subtle; a seemingly random comment can uncover serious problems. For example, at a Fortune 100 company, when the topic of "Dress Down Fridays" came up, one executive mentioned a woman told him she didn't like the casual dress day because she couldn't recognize her supervisor. The client hadn't heard the tinkling of those warning bells. This wasn't about clothes. This was about poor management. If the supervisor had been supervising, the woman would have recognized him regardless of what he was wearing. That discovery helped explain the low morale and productivity within that woman's department.

Actually, it's not surprising. A boss on any level is often the root of a problem. In fact, an Institute of Crisis Management study showed 68 percent of business crises are created by management and only 19 percent are created by employees.

- **That 68 percent means there is a tremendous opportunity to avert problems.**

Unfortunately, some executives are not aware of that advantage. Look at Texaco. Its reputation was tainted when top executives were caught on tape making racially offensive comments and discussing withholding evidence from a long-running employment discrimination lawsuit. The suit mentioned in the tape, which had been pending for two years, concerned the company's alleged discriminatory hiring practices. When the suit was filed, Texaco should have seen it as a warning to act and take such proactive measures as addressing minority recruitment. Instead, it did nothing until the scandal broke. The company had to know minority employees felt they were not being treated fairly. That's what the lawsuit was all about.

Ostrichizing

"When I think of us [sic] human beings, it seems to me that we have a lot of nerve to make fun of an ostrich," commented one pundit. It makes one wonder if an ostrich ever thinks, "It won't happen here."

In any event, let's consider the "It." What is "It" anyway? How about these front-page news stories:

- A twenty-eight-year-old broke into Citicorp's computerized cash-management system, looting customer accounts around the world.
- A Connecticut Lottery accountant stabbed and gunned down four of his bosses before shooting himself.
- A former executive of Sweet'n Low pleaded guilty to making illegal contributions to prominent politicians.
- Two Honda executives were found guilty of accepting $15 million in kickbacks from Honda dealers in a nationwide bribery scheme.
- The opening of the new multimillion-dollar state-of-the-art Denver airport was repeatedly delayed, in part due to software problems associated with the baggage-handling system, resulting in stiff financial penalties as well as adverse publicity.
- A California animal rights group led a protest against

Yoplait yogurt because skunks died when they got their heads caught in empty containers.

You get the picture. From the sublime to the ridiculous, "It" happens.

So why the avoidance? For some, the underlying implication of "it will never happen here" is "I'm going to screw up and look bad." This #1 Sin, "It Will Never Happen Here," becomes a self-fulfilling prophesy. An unprepared company is as vulnerable as a porcupine exposing his belly.

"We know what to do" falls into the same category. This statement is often an assumption rather than reality.

A good example comes from a hospital outside Boston. Hospital administrators thought they were prepared for anything. In fact, they prided themselves on their many triage drills. One day, an Amtrak train derailed, and the injured were taken to that hospital. The event turned into utter chaos. Reporters were blocking the entrance; others walked around the patient floors looking for injured passengers. A reporter and television camera got hold of a crazed emergency-room physician. The result was the hospital looked totally out of control and incompetent. In fact, the attention turned to the hospital rather than the derailment. The hospital had thought of everything except one thing: a crash is news.

- **All of this could have been avoided if the hospital had a security plan, a press room, and an official spokesperson.**

Cleopatra: Queen of Denial

No one wants to be seen as a loser in the business world. The good news is it's possible to avoid or contain problems if one pays attention. Yet it's amazing how many executives are in denial.

The reason seems obvious to some. Intel CEO Andy Grove says denial is a "generic disease." An executive recruiter who has placed many a Fortune 500 CEO believes denial is in many chief executives' DNA.

The same goes for some board members as well. For example, when Mattel's stock lost 70 percent of its value in twenty months, the toy company's board members were severely criticized for being asleep at the switch.

True professionalism lies in taking an objective look at "what ifs," regardless of how bad they may be.

Houston, We Have a Problem

We all hope nothing ever happens, but the reality is something could. Sometimes, it comes out of left field. For example, who would have thought a caller's accusation on a late-night talk show could start a nationwide scare that Motorola's cellular phones cause cancer? Who'd expect McDonald's would be sued over a spilled cup of hot coffee?

Sometimes, another company's problem can become yours.

- The Motorola cancer scare hurt all cell-phone companies as stock market investors began dumping all cell-phone stocks.
- In another case, a misread pap smear at one health laboratory led to a nationwide scare about the accuracy of lab tests. It started when a woman died from ovarian cancer; she could have survived if the cancer had been detected in earlier tests. Her husband went on *Geraldo!* and said the lab's inaccurate reading of her pap smear caused her

"Why in heaven's name would we need an exterminator, Miss Farnsworth?!"

death. The media jumped on the story. All health labora-
tories were suddenly on the hot seat, and their CEOs
wound up testifying before the Congressional House
Oversight and Investigations Committee.

- It became SOS time for the cruise industry when two
cruise lines wound up in big trouble around the same
time. Carnival Cruise Lines disclosed 108 allegations of
sexual misconduct by crew members during a five-year
period. Royal Caribbean Cruises Ltd. pleaded guilty to a
host of ocean-pollution charges. Together, those two
events hurt the whole industry's image. So much so that
the International Council of Cruise Lines adopted a single industry standard requiring on-board crime allega-

tions be reported. In the past, cruise lines reported crimes only when passengers or other victims specifically asked them to.

The whole industry found itself under a magnifying glass. The problems even led to a congressional hearing. Congress warned access to American ports would be restricted unless the cruise lines did a better job of abiding by U.S. laws and insuring the safety of passengers.

The troubles didn't end there. One of the unhappy consequences of getting bad press is it encourages additional focus on the subject. For the cruise industry, it meant an exposé on the harsh treatment of workers, including low pay, poor living conditions, and grueling work hours. As a result, the industry had to develop voluntary guidelines about the rights of crew members to fair treatment. These guidelines were approved after a major newspaper started interviewing cruise lines about workplace conditions.

Then, there was also a big exposé on the inability of cruise ships to handle major medical emergencies, such as heart attacks.

All of this negative attention was caused by the misconduct of two cruise lines.

Getting to Carnegie Hall

Would anyone attend a play if the actors hadn't rehearsed or go to a basketball game if the players didn't practice? It's expected that professionals know what to do. That only happens with planning and practice. Now the question is, when was the last time you practiced for a crisis? Sadly, if you haven't, you're in good company.

Start now. It's in your best interest.

• **Organizations prepared for a crisis recover two to three times faster with significantly less financial and human cost than unprepared ones.**

I'm often asked what a crisis is like. Well, let's put it this way. Time—your most precious commodity—goes into fast-forward, and the atmosphere is chaotic. Nevertheless, a CEO is expected to make major decisions and communicate to the public and a host of other audiences, including board members. At that point, it is too late to begin figuring out what to do. A CEO has to be able to jump into action. Planning is the life jacket to protect an executive in stormy seas.

The result is what I call "crisis mastering"—the successful conclusion of crisis management.

If something were to happen tomorrow, would you be ready? Find out by answering the following:

1. Identify at least ten potential problems that could affect your company.
2. What would be the repercussions of each?
3. What is your primary message for each?
4. Name the people on your crisis team.
5. Have you reviewed your company's liability insurance? Do you know what it covers?
6. Would you know what to do if you were ambushed by a hostile reporter?
7. Do you have a working relationship with the media?
8. Do you think "no comment" is the safest way to answer media questions?
9. How much does your company spend on advertising

campaigns? How much does your company spend on crisis training and planning?

10. Advertising or a crisis: which one can destroy a reputation faster?

Seat-Belting

One of the roadblocks to crisis readiness is superstition: "If I say it, it may happen." Now, just because someone wears a seat belt doesn't mean that person will be in a car crash. Planning for a crisis doesn't mean one will occur. But if it does, a company is protected. I call this process "seat-belting."

After becoming public-relations director at Air Florida, my biggest concern was what to do if there was an accident. The airline had a good emergency procedures manual, but I didn't have a clear picture on what we would actually have to *do*. I began taking all the crisis management seminars I could find. I talked to reporters about their pet peeves when covering disasters. When other airlines experienced problems, I'd think about how I'd manage them. Internally, I pestered department heads about effective action and campaigned on the importance of working with the media.

As a result, Air Florida was prepared when Flight 90 crashed in the Potomac in Washington, D.C. In the midst of the chaos and tragedy, the situation would not have been managed properly if it wasn't for three years of planning and mental preparation. In spite of the circumstances, Air Florida wasn't crucified by the press. The *Miami Herald* later reported, "When Air Florida's Flight 90 crashed . . . the company freely supplied information to the media. That won the airline fair and sympathetic news coverage."

What If?

Not all companies have to worry about airplane crashes. However, that does not mean you are worry-free. No CEO is immune from such problems as:

- Aggressive reporters
- Angry consumers
- Angry shareholders
- Angry vendors
- Berserk employees
- Disgruntled employees
- Executive succession
- False accusations
- Financial problems
- Fire
- Fraud
- Government investigation
- Health-care coverage
- Industry issues
- Internet site crashes
- On-line hacker attacks
- Product tampering
- Proxy contests
- Quotes taken out of context
- Rumors
- Sexual harassment
- Special interest groups
- Trademark infringement
- Unethical behavior
- Whistle-blowers
- Workplace safety

Remember the protection of seat belts. The best way to buckle up a company is to get into the "What If?" mode. Think of all sorts of things that could go wrong and how you'd manage them: "What if we are investigated by the SEC?" "What if we have a defective product?" "What if someone gets shot on the premises?"

The fact is anything can happen anywhere. A man dressed in camouflage and armed with an AK-47 shot his way into a Ford Motor Company plant, killing a manager and wounding three other people as he sprayed gunfire through the building and then outside at a highway. He wasn't even a Ford employee, although his girlfriend worked there.

If anyone needs incentive to begin or review crisis plans, think of Coca-Cola's Belgium contamination scare, which spread through Europe, causing a massive recall. A Coca-Cola senior executive said afterward, "We have a crisis management strategy . . . but the crisis was bigger than any worst-case scenario we could have imagined."

In another instance, Seattle wanted to host the 1999 World Trade Organization meeting to enhance its reputation. Ironically, Seattle's image took a dive after violent clashes between protesters and the police. The National Guard was called in, and many businesses experienced major damage. Afterward, the Seattle police chief, who later resigned, said the city had made intensive preparations to handle the expected thousands of protesters, but had not anticipated that vandals would get out of hand. Neither had the merchants who were vandalized.

Both the Coca-Cola and Seattle examples show what happens when planners don't think big enough. Worst-case scenarios are just that. It appears Coke hadn't planned for a major international crisis, and those in Seattle thought the protesters would behave.

Coca-Cola's crisis also highlights how a multinational company can be like an octopus. Employees at the end of the tentacles might not feel empowered to act without conferring with the headquarters overseas, but the headquarters may not understand the severity of the situation. While a company has the time, it should design crisis plans with all far-flung divisions to determine how incidents will be handled. No matter how intricate and time-consuming, all top managers working outside as well as inside of corporate headquarters have to be crisis-trained. In Coca-Cola's contamination case, its executives in Belgium should have jumped on the problem.

Ready to Roll

"What If" exercises help pinpoint a company's strengths and weaknesses while there's time. Consider the broad scope of operational procedures, external and internal communications, risk management, and the needs of victims and their families.

When you are working with top executives, it's important to know who is responsible for various actions. As scenarios are discussed, learn there are no instant answers. A lot of thought and input has to go into effective planning involving people, operations, facilities—and corporate policies.

- **Crisis planning takes time.**
- **It's nearly impossible to respond well without an established, workable plan.**

In a *Harvard Business Review* article, astronaut James Lovell advises, ". . . contingency plans must be in place to handle a slew of different situations." As part of their rigorous training, for example, astronauts and mission controllers went through numerous simulations to try to make conquering the unexpected as routine as possible.

For Your Own Good

The results of planning can be great for an image. When Hurricane Andrew hit South Florida, Miami television station WTVJ provided crucial information and advice throughout the storm. Not only did WTVJ win national acclaim for its performance, its ratings moved up from third to first place. The station said it had made the decision to be "hurricane-ready" three years before the disaster. In short, the station was "seat-belted."

Seat-belting does not only apply to accidents or natural disasters. Wall Street saw the writing on the wall—or actually, on the computer screen. Facing the Y2K threat of computers not recognizing the first days of the year 2000 after the last days of 1999, the securities industry, among many others, conducted a series of tests to make sure its computers could make a smooth transition. The first simulation in June 1998 lasted ten days and covered stock options, corporate and municipal bonds, and securities. Rehearsal participants included major brokerage firms, all major stock exchanges, and the corporations that clear and process trades for them. This was the first of a number of tests leading to Y2K.

Obviously, it is a lot easier preparing for a known entity. However, planning also means establishing basic principles. One is to grab an umbrella when one sees storm clouds instead of waiting for the downpour.

For instance, a well-known national company under investigation by a state regulatory agency knew it was only a matter of time before the regulators went public after negotiations broke down. The company did nothing until the story broke in a newspaper. Then it assembled a crisis team and prepared a response refuting the claims. The result: the slow response put the company executives on the defensive, and they appeared unethical and unreliable.

- **A prepared company would have begun developing a response as soon as it was notified of the investigation.**

In this case, the company was guilty but had already taken measures to fix the problem. It tried to hide and lost the chance to go on the offensive by telling how the situation had been corrected so it would never happen again. The company also misread the seriousness of the issue, not realizing it would go nationwide.

One large company had a complex method of dealing with issues: different divisions were responsible for managing different problems. The trouble was, no one was clear on which fiefdom managed overlapping issues. When a serious problem occurred:

- **The company was occupied with internal battles, forgetting to focus on the real war raging outside.**

It usually took at least two days to come up with a response. By that time, the company looked like the bad guy regardless of the circumstances.

Welcome to the deadly world of internal bottlenecks. An organization cannot respond externally if its internal ducks aren't in a row. Period. Instead of delivering a comprehensive, coordinated response, everyone is running around in circles.

- **To ensure a successful performance, companies have to operate well internally in order to respond well externally.**

The public is never amused when a company mishandles a crisis—with the exception of late-night comedians. Mattel found this out when it introduced its Cabbage Patch Snacktime Kids doll right in time for Christmas. The doll was supposed to eat little plastic vegetables, but it preferred chomping on childrens' hair and fingers instead, refusing to let go. The child-devouring little cuss did not have an on/off switch. One of the ways to stop it was by taking the battery out with a screwdriver, a tool with which children are especially adept and that they always carry around.

The media had a field day with the story. The doll gobbled its way through at least one hundred alleged accidents. In early January, months after its introduction, Mattel recalled the doll. The company later reported the problems with Cabbage Patch Snacktime Kids reduced sales by $10 million. Talk about an internal control system being asleep at the switch.

Bottleneck Gulch

Large companies are especially response-challenged. Often, divisions don't speak to each other, operating in separate worlds. As a result, divisions release different versions of the company's official script. There can also be a duplication of efforts.

Sometimes, the lack of internal checks and balances leads to serious consequences that go beyond the initial problem. The impact could affect employees, stockholders, and other audiences.

Not to put a damper on things, but what happens if a CEO should die? Because no one wants to think about such things, it's not surprising many companies aren't prepared.

When one company CEO suddenly died, the board had to name a successor immediately. The person they chose was not ready for the position and lacked the experience to run the company; a designated successor would have been groomed and ready to step in. The result was corporate disorganization complete with negative press coverage, a loss of customers and market share, and low morale. Finally, the ex-chairman was called in to help the successor. The company almost went down the tubes because it didn't have a succession plan. As one executive later said, "I think you have to have a recovery plan for not having just lost an individual, but also for the emotional impact on the company and the people they do business with."

Succession planning initially worked for Coca-Cola. When CEO Roberto Goizueta died of cancer in 1997, business was hardly affected. Mr. Goizueta had already designated Douglas Ivester as his successor and was ready to hand over the reins. The result was a sad but smooth transition.

Ironically, Mr. Ivester didn't address the succession subject until 1999. After much criticism, he assigned greater roles to three executives in October, setting up a contest for the top job. Adding a further twist to the saga, Mr. Ivester abruptly announced his resignation that December. The company appointed Douglas N. Daft, one of the three somewhat anointed heirs, as president and chief operating officer. Investors were angered by Mr. Ivester's sudden resignation announcement. One stock analyst said from an investor perspective, Coke used to be all about consistency but hadn't been during Mr. Ivester's tenure.

Mr. Goizueta paved the way for a smooth management transition. In contrast, Mr. Ivester's exit was anything but.

So, if a company doesn't have a succession plan, it had better be added to its "What If?" list.

One more point about succession planning. It's a good idea for a company to utilize talented executives in supporting roles in addition to promoting the CEO. This way, if something should happen to the CEO, especially an ingrained one, the public knows the company is still in capable hands. A case in point is Southwest Airlines and its CEO, Herbert D. Kelleher. The man, who is synonymous with the airline, developed prostate cancer yet refused to designate a successor, to the dismay of many, including Wall Street analysts. The concern was if something should happen to him, there might not be anyone able to run the company and maintain its unique philosophy. In these kinds of cases, a very popular CEO can be a "positive" problem.

Easier Said than Done

When it comes to crisis readiness, the buck really stops, or actually starts, at the top. If the CEO doesn't make it a priority, no one else will. It happens all too often: CEOs assign the crisis readiness task to their lieutenants, who in turn give it to their managers. When top executives find out the CEOs won't be attending the meetings, they don't either, sending substitutes. What's left is a group of middle managers with no decision-making authority.

That doesn't mean top executives should plan in isolation. Astronaut Jim Lovell points out the importance of teamwork in figuring out ways of dealing with a crisis. He should know. In the *Harvard Business Review* article, he emphasized, "Several minds working together are better than one, especially since it is usually necessary to think of new methods of doing things. Those who are so set in their ways that they are unable to innovate are headed for dire straights." He adds that the people responsible for fostering that spirit of cooperation are the leaders of a group.

Whether in space or on the ground, a crisis team has to be in place. It generally includes the CEO/president, chief financial officer, and legal advisor; heads of corporate communications, operations, and human resources; and technical experts. Also, don't forget to designate administrative support assistants.

The team is responsible for assessing the crisis, developing information, initiating control steps, and communicating to the employees, customers, and the media.

- **The command center determines all company action and communication.**
- **Within that team, there has to be a designated chain of command.**
- **Whoever is in line to take over has to have clear-cut authority.**

The top officer might not always be present when a crisis occurs. Often, precious response time is lost in a crisis because senior executives are duking it out for control. At that point, internal cooperation goes out the window, severely handicapping the company's ability to act. The CEO is going to be holding the mismanagement bag, even though he wasn't involved in the action.

For protection from that kind of fate, teams have to practice solving different "What If" scenarios until everyone is comfortable with the response. These scenarios are not just about potential accidents. They can cover any possibility, such as labor issues, product recalls, or a sharp drop in stock value. Once procedures are developed, middle managers should be trained so they, in turn, can work with supervisors. All "players" have to know their roles and practice them.

It's a good idea to utilize tabletop exercises. A scenario is given, and participants talk through their responses. No incident is static; it grows as new wrinkles develop. It's best to have an objective crisis management consultant direct the scenario and add developments as they would occur in real life.

A first attempt rarely goes smoothly—which, in a perverse way, is great. Like any experiments, there are discoveries, even if they're not the intended ones. In some, the players realize one executive can't be in four places at the same time, and responsibilities are reassigned. Sometimes, two departments may be duplicating efforts. Most important, drills often bring out major discussions on corporate policy. These eye-opening experiences also help turn individuals into a cohesive group.

Your Buck

Presidents like Abraham Lincoln, Franklin D. Roosevelt, and Harry Truman owe their reputations to crisis management. History has paid attention to their accomplishments. On the other hand, many presidents have been destroyed by debacles, despite other accomplishments, including Lyndon Johnson (the Vietnam War) and Jimmy Carter (the Iranian hostage crisis).

You might not be running the country, but you are running your business world. Whether it's a U.S. president or CEO, a lot of potential comes with a crisis. It can build a CEO's reputation, as well as a company's—providing that top management knows what to do.

A crisis is any situation that has a severe negative impact on a company's reputation and/or bottom line. It is a turning point in a company's history.

A crisis can be mastered successfully. To find out how, this book provides lessons from CEOs who are star performers. It also points out attitudes that get top executives in trouble. It delves into all the components needed for an effective response, including visual and emotional perception, corporate responsibility, and decision making. Naturally, the media have a starring role.

You will see how problems can be averted or contained. You will also learn how you can maintain your reputation regardless of the problem.

You will discover that proactive readiness takes time up front, but reduces the duration and severity of a crisis. Those with an "it could happen here" mind-set are on a safer plateau because they are on better footing to gain control of an incident.

It is like the story about two politicians trying to solve a problem. One comes up with a simple solution. The other thinks about it, then says, "It will work in practice, but not in theory."

"It Will Never Happen Here" does not work. End of story. Some may call it a theory, but too much is at stake. That is why it's the #1 Deadly Sin.

Chapter **2**

Sin #2: # I Don't Care How It Looks

After mismanaging a crisis, a beleaguered CEO spent a week evading the press. One night he sat in his darkened office with the lights off trying to avoid a television reporter waiting outside. He hoped the reporter would think he'd gone home. Neither budged. As the evening wore on, the CEO remembered when he used to play the game hide-and-seek. He realized he had forgotten the whole point of the game: hiders get sought.

Welcome to the Second Deadly Sin: "I Don't Care How It Looks." Attempting to stay insulated and disengaged during a crisis will undoubtedly exacerbate the crisis. Many a problem has been blown out of proportion because a CEO opted to stay behind closed doors, enabling outside forces to have a field day tearing down the company's image.

As Renaissance "consultant" Machiavelli

pointed out: "It is not reasonable to expect an armed man to obey one who is unarmed."

So true. Executives who insist on hiding have surrendered their weapons to the outside world peering in. As the saying goes: "Tellin' a man to git lost and makin' him do it are two entirely different propositions."

Everybody's Business

Say good-bye to "it's nobody's business." No one wants to air his or her dirty laundry in public. However, it still has to get washed, and once it's out there . . . it's show time! Shakespeare wasn't fooling around when he wrote "the world is a stage."

Like it or not, the public is a large audience that makes judgments based on a company's unfolding drama.

- **You are what people think you are.**

So CEOs have two choices: they can stay insulated, leaving themselves open for inaccurate interpretations, or, they can take charge and direct the show.

Companies play to many publics—the media, employees, customers, shareholders, and lest we forget, friends and family. Like the theater, a company's challenge is to tell its story. The question is, how?

Seeing Is Believing

The first thing to understand is the role of perception.

- **Perception determines the outcome of every crisis response.**

Often, perception is not the same thing as reality. For example, a crisis occurs, and the CEO quickly takes charge internally but does not talk to the press. The reality: the CEO is doing his job. The perception: the CEO is hiding or does not care.

- **Public opinion is formed by perception, not reality.**
- **Regardless of what is really happening internally, the way the public perceives a situation becomes the reality; a company has to address it.**

During the early stages of the Three Mile Island nuclear reactor accident in 1979, the public thought the situation was even worse than it was. A press conference, postponed throughout the day, was finally held by Governor Richard Thornburgh around midnight. It was covered live; the scene was chaotic. Agitated, angry reporters were jammed into a small room, and it appeared that things were out of control. The perception was just the opposite of what the governor wanted to convey.

Pepsi, on the other hand, used images to regain public confidence. In 1993, a man found a syringe in a Pepsi can. Within forty-eight hours, more reports of syringes in cans began coming in from all over the country. Was it safe to drink Pepsi? Who wants to swallow a syringe? Working with the Food and Drug Administration, Pepsi quickly responded. The CEO and other top executives made the round of media appearances. Most effective, however, was a video showing Pepsi's highly automated bottling process. The public could see for itself that at such a high rate of speed, nothing could get in the cans, except the beverage, of course. Then, a Denver store manager produced a surveillance tape of a shopper putting a syringe in an open Pepsi can. That tape was released to the media, showing a can had to first be opened before it could be tampered with. Pepsi cans stopped being scary.

Perception can be deeply rooted. For example, many see a deer and immediately call it Bambi. Smells, sounds, and tastes can take us back to times past. Then, there is the power of a single image. A picture of a dove connotes peace. A swastika evokes hate. Even though some might not be aware of it, these aspects color the way we respond to an event.

Perception has a way of pegging a company to a particular product, even though it makes others. The public sees the Gillette Company as the maker of razor blades even though it is one of the most powerful global consumer product companies, with brands like Braun, Oral-B, Waterman, and Paper Mate. Its identification with blades is so strong, a hiccup in steel prices can affect Gillette's stock—and not for the better.

A company is not a person, but it is often personified as one. Lee Iacocca became synonymous with Chrysler. The same goes for Sam Walton of Wal-Mart, Warren Buffett of Berkshire Hathaway, and Microsoft's Bill Gates. On the other hand, the association between company and leader is not always so great, like Michael Milken and Drexel. The fictionalized character Gordon Gekko in the movie *Wall Street* personified a whole business decade, the 1980s, with his memorable line "greed is good."

Speaking of greed, there are times when an organization is left holding the bag à la "sins of the father." In 1992, United Way of America president William V. Aramony was dismissed and later imprisoned for embezzling charitable money. Contributions dried up. It took six years for United Way to restore its image and reach prescandal donation levels.

Useful Wrong Conclusions

Perception can make us add two and two and come up with five as unrelated events become linked. When Southern Pacific

Railroad ripped up twenty-eight miles of track in Matagorda County, Texas, and shut down operations in the early 1990s, everyone assumed it was because the railroad was tired of frivolous lawsuits. The tale of the disgruntled railroad had been repeated for years. A research center used it as proof of the havoc being wreaked and jobs lost by an irrational legal system.

According to Union Pacific, which merged with Southern Pacific in 1996, Southern Pacific was studying eliminating that line anyway. As a spokesperson said, "It was kind of a coincidence of timing."

It just so happened that traffic was down to one freight car a year.

This is a case where the perceived reason was milked for all it was worth. It became an oft-repeated example used to fight punitive damage awards. A Houston businessman who is a leader of Texas for Lawsuit Reform said he used the railroad story for years in speeches as an example of legal craziness. He said people are horrified.

In this example, perception worked better than reality.

The reality of trends is also questionable. For example, take the "rages": workplace rage, road rage, and air rage. Why is everyone so angry all of a sudden? Why all the violence? Experts in behavior are saying the labels reflect a national penchant for lumping similar but isolated acts of violence into categories. They are questioning whether media coverage is making them seem to be bona fide trends. It also appears more incidents are reported because people suddenly have a name for them.

The Power of Vision:
How to Make It Work for You

Oh, Say Can You See?

- Since a crisis is theatrical, "see" and "hear" are the operative principles of a response.

News has become a spectator sport. The public has expectations of watching a drama. That means a company has to think visually as it responds to a crisis. An empty stage provides room for interpretation, only it's never good.

Although this next example did not take place in a corporate setting, it highlights how quickly a leader's image can plunge in a very short time period. This happened to Britain's Royal Family after Princess Diana's death. The public was in an uproar because Queen Elizabeth and her family did not initially appear in public or display any emotion until they were criticized into doing so. The family's response came almost a week after Princess Diana's death and was interpreted as a public-relations effort rather than a genuine one. But, proving it's better late than never, Queen Elizabeth went public, speaking on live television, paying tribute to Diana and expressing grief.

Although it was an obvious attempt at damage control, the queen's public appearance and show of sentiment did a lot to assuage the public.

This happened through the strength of visual elements: the queen's tribute to Diana—looking and speaking as a sorrowful, kindly grandmother; the Royals walking along the rows of people gathered at Buckingham Palace; and the flag flying at half-staff at Buckingham Palace.

This story brings out an important lesson that applies as much to top executives as it does to queens:

* **People assume a company is uncaring if its leaders aren't out-front and center when crises hit.**

The sooner the better. The Royals' absence was perceived as a sign they were not grieving while the public mourned. No one could see behind castle walls to know how they really felt—just as we don't know what is happening within a company when a problem hits.

Beware of assuming audiences know what a company is doing. Unless they are told by the company, they will rely on unsympathetic sources. In numerous cases, companies that managed crises well still received bad press and negative public opinion because the reality of their actions was not translated for an external audience.

* **A closed-door policy can make a terrible situation even worse.**

Union Carbide immediately comes to mind. In 1984, Union Carbide's Bhopal, India, pesticide plant exploded, killing more than two thousand people and injuring thousands more. It became the world's worst industrial accident.

With the best intentions, CEO Warren Anderson flew to India. However, he was arrested for culpable homicide as soon as he landed. He was released on bail and returned home. This has to be one of the best lessons for CEOs. In most crisis situations, a CEO should stay put at a crisis command center in order to manage the situation and communicate. As soon as Mr. Anderson stepped on the plane, he was out of commission.

If there ever was a time for a CEO to go public early on, show genuine anguish, and pledge responsible action, this was it. Instead, Mr. Anderson was otherwise occupied, and the company sent out press releases. This dehumanized the company even more. Because he was not visible and did not publicly express sorrow, the company fell under intense criticism. As the *New York Times* said, "Union Carbide's defensive posture and faceless approach surely reflects a desire to limit liability in anticipation of lawsuits." Thanks to his invisibility, the CEO made it on to the villain list. Is he a terrible person? By all accounts, no.

Perception *is* in the eyes of the beholder. A 1985 *Wall Street Journal* article, "When a Manager Is Duty-Bound Not to Pass the Buck," written by two management consultants, used Mr. Anderson as a good example of a CEO responding to a crisis. It said his immediate flight to Bhopal "reflected an important management message: No matter how distasteful, disruptive or dangerous some duties may be, certain ones should never be delegated."

That was their reality—even though the CEO wound up helpless in an Indian jail. I would still opt for a CEO staying in the picture, rather than out, when a crisis occurs.

Visual Public Opinion:
How to Win Support

David's Slingshot

The environmental activist group Greenpeace skillfully used images to show how public protest could exert power over big business and government. In February 1995, the British government approved Shell Oil UK's plan to dump the 463-foot Brent Spar oil-storage and loading buoy in the North Atlantic.

Greenpeace launched a protest campaign utilizing/manipulating the media to support its cause. The Greenpeacers came up with a high-profile plan to board the Brent Spar oil rig. They bought satellite communications and video equipment to enable them to transmit pictures while on board. Fourteen activists and nine journalists took over the rig for three weeks until they were expelled. Shell Oil blasted high-powered water cannons to fend off the helicopter carrying the protesters from landing, to no avail. All of this was filmed by a crush of reporters who were crammed into a boat thoughtfully provided by Greenpeace.

Talk about the power of one picture. The public was left with a dramatic image of a huge multinational oil company mustering all its might to bully a band of brave, soaked activists.

As a result, Greenpeace won the public-opinion battle. In fact, because of the negative attention, Shell even lost its political support. The oil industry was viewed as arrogant, secretive, profit-oriented multinationals, not to be trusted. And that's just for starters. One British poll showed a majority of the public was against sinking the platform. In another, a majority of the British public believed Greenpeace should continue with its campaign against the dumping of oil platforms.

Greenpeace's occupation stunt sparked a boycott against Shell, which wound up hurting gasoline sales. The pressure caused Shell to back down and dispose of the Brent Spar on land. After a two-year reappraisal and study of other disposal options, the company said the oil structure would be recycled into a series of rings that would be sunk to form an industrial quayside in Norway.

Fought in public, it was the classic victory of the underdog over big business and government.

- **The visuals won the war.**

The reality? Greenpeace later admitted it erred in assessing the pollution potential of the Brent Spar oil rig.

Say Cheese

A CEO of a Fortune 50 company related his lesson on the power of visuals. A national network evening-news program wanted to feature his company as an exemplary environmental leader. He mistakenly planned to wing it. Luckily for him, a highly experienced Washington political consultant was with him. The CEO was planning to do the interview in his office. The consultant pointed out the fancy wood-paneled office was not in synch with the image of a "paragon of environmental virtue." The CEO was advised to go outside, take his jacket off, and sit on a bench with lots of trees in back of it.

His wife saw the interview. When he got home, he asked her how he did and if he sounded stupid. The wife said he looked good. "You were sitting on a bench with trees all around and it was something about how your company was an environmental leader. It was really nice." He asked her what he said. She replied, "Oh, whatever it was, it was okay, but the overall effect was trees, environmental leader, good company. It was nice, very flattering."

He learned the lesson that news coverage is often about imagery. He noted:

- **"A message is in need of visual impact because the words don't have the substance and the public doesn't listen very carefully."**

During the President Clinton–Monica Lewinsky scandal, news executives realized they had their own image problem after a stampede of camera crews, journalists, and photographers mobbed President Clinton's personal secretary after her Grand Jury testimony. At a media dinner, ABC News chairman Roone Arledge said, "The picture of this poor lady fearing for her life, or at least, for her safety while this whirl of people attacked her has stayed with me."

As a result, five major television networks tried to lower their profile by agreeing to pool coverage, meaning instead of a three-person crew each from ABC, NBC, CBS, CNN, and Fox, only one was assigned to five "staked-out" sites and they shared audio and video feeds.

Spilling the Visual Beans

We've all heard one picture is worth a thousand words. It's true. One of those telling pictures ran in several newspapers showing unhappy passengers on board a cruise ship. Several passengers were holding a huge banner proclaiming "5 Hour Fire, No H_2O or Toilets." It turns out a fire on board the ship damaged a boiler. Then, there were complaints of sewer spills and a lack of water. Plus, the ship was adrift two days in an area threatened by a tropical storm.

The story and picture would probably not have run without the tattletale banner. We wouldn't have known about the poor passengers' woes, and the cruise line could have sailed away without anyone knowing the passengers were ill-treated. The lesson here is to be careful of the visuals poor service creates.

The Audience

Don't Confuse Me with the Facts

After Air Florida Flight 90 crashed in Washington, D.C., in January 1982, the airline filed for bankruptcy protection in July 1984.

While attending an Aviation Disaster conference, one of the speakers was the head of a major airline consulting firm. She was talking about the cost of crashes and mentioned Air Florida went out of business because of its crash. Wrong. The airline went out of business because it grew too fast and couldn't service the debt.

I didn't say anything during the question-and-answer period and talked to her afterward while her eyes glazed over. Regardless of the facts, she had already made up her mind based on perception. The vision of the Air Florida tail stuck in the icy Potomac for a week left too vivid an impression. It didn't matter that the airline continued operating for two years and was flying full planes when the airline filed for Chapter 11—facts easy to check. She could never be convinced.

Winning Over an Audience

In the case of Air Florida, perception became the reality. However, don't loose faith. Just as writers create a script, CEOs have the ability to turn problems to their advantage.

- **Opinion is often formed along good guy–bad guy lines because perception is simplistic, regardless of the problem.**

Issues come in two colors: black and white. There's no gray. (In real life, yes; in perception, no.) In stories, the public can distinguish the good guys from the bad guys by their behavior. This alone becomes a map for crisis planning.

- **People don't judge good guys on whether they've made mistakes but how they've fixed them.**
- **Bad guys, on the other hand, deny problems, won't admit errors, and don't make amends.**

Johnson & Johnson's Tylenol crisis in 1982 is an obvious good-guy example. The company went directly to the public after it was discovered that some Extra Strength Tylenol capsules had been spiked with cyanide. Besides CEO James Burke being visibly in charge, the company immediately recalled the product and reintroduced it in a new triple-seal package.

- **The company took visible moral action.**

Exxon's lack of visual response during the 1989 Valdez oil spill alienated the public. People grabbed their scissors, cutting hundreds of thousands of Exxon credit cards. Masses of other people boycotted service stations.

Suppose Exxon's CEO had quickly apologized and claimed responsibility. Think what would have happened if the company had instead displayed compassion and concern for all affected and had provided employees to help in the clean-up process.

- **Imagine how perception would have changed if we had seen employees in Exxon jackets cleaning poor little oil-soaked birds.**

Or, let's take Shell's run-in with Greenpeace over the Brent Spar incident. Perception might have changed if, instead of using dry, scientific arguments, the company had shown pictures of sunken platform structures that had turned into spectacular reefs. Not only are reefs beautiful, they're important to the ecosystem. It's hard to protest against that.

Johnson & Johnson reacted quickly, following the good-guy formula. Exxon fit neatly into the bad-guy role. Yet, in real life, there's a lot of gray. How many remember that seven people died after taking the spiked Tylenol cyanide capsules? How many know the president of Exxon's shipping subsidiary talked to the press hours after the incident?

- **The presence of the shipping president was overshadowed by the absence of the CEO.**

The same was true with TWA's handling of the Flight 800 crash. The evening of the crash, the airline did a miserable job of communicating with both family members and the media. Without a TWA spokesperson available, New York mayor Rudolph Giuliani, trying to help the families, wound up becoming their spokesperson.

As we did not see any initial display of compassion or action on TWA's part, the perception was that the airline mismanaged the whole crisis. This was true at first.

However, after TWA finally got its act together, the grieving families gave the airline high marks for the way they were treated. Yet, the initial impression of Mayor Guiliani's live criticism regarding TWA's treatment of family members sealed its fate. It left a negative impression that defined the accident.

Rooting for the Underdog

Another branch of the good guy–bad guy interpretation is big guy versus little guy. Big business is not especially popular today. The public is ready to link large companies with the bad guys. A survey by the Opinion Research Corporation shows that one-third of the population believes a company accused of wrongdoing in a lawsuit is probably guilty. Forty-four percent agree a company being investigated by a government agency is probably guilty of some wrongdoing.

As Shell chairman Christopher Fay said after the Brent Spar incident, "Profit remains a term of abuse. The idea that free markets work to the mutual good is being lost beneath the trampling feet of those rushing to blame 'big business' for all the ills of the world—forgetting that everyone with a pension or an insurance fund depends on the profits those businesses produce."

United Parcel Service executives were probably thinking the same thing when the company was hit by a fifteen-day Teamsters strike in 1997. The Teamsters effectively used perception to win public support. Polls showed Americans favored the workers over management in spite of the inconvenience caused by the shutdown. In fact, a Gallup poll found that 55 percent of respondents supported the workers in the strike, compared with 27 percent who backed the company.

There were several reasons for such labor support. The first deals with the public's jaundiced view of how corporations treat employers. There was a strong perception that management was no longer fair and loyal to workers. Polls showed many felt it was wrong for a company with such high profits to insist on hiring so many part-timers instead of full-timers. Part-timers earned too little to support a family.

That view was fostered and reinforced by the union with a

sophisticated game plan, which focused around a single message: utilizing the media and the Internet. When union leaders began distributing $55 benefit checks to striking workers, they showed they understood the power of visuals by printing on each one a message large enough to be picked up by television cameras: "Remember: We're fighting not just for Teamster members, but for every working family in America." This was strengthened with television images of those slim benefit checks being handed out on picket lines and in union halls. Women were used in picket lines whenever possible to soften the union's hard-edged image. Staying away from wearing suits, members wore jeans so they would look like plain, ordinary people.

UPS management was not as quick to the draw. In the past, the company had never had much of a public presence in the media. However, the company came up with its own campaign. It utilized message advertising and asked customers to write to the White House on its behalf. UPS officials insisted the union was mischaracterizing the part-timers' working conditions, asserting they had wrongly led many people to back the union. However, UPS was not as successful or skilled as the Teamsters, who understood how to win public support. The company failed to use simple, visual communication demonstrating its concern for its employees and their future. As a result, the company was unable to offset the perception that it was a big, greedy employer picking on the little guy. In the end, the Teamsters won most of what they wanted in terms of pensions, pay, and the limiting of part-time workers.

Prior to the strike, Americans had not been supportive of unions for some time. During the 1981 air-traffic controllers' strike, the public had no sympathy for the striking workers making $100,000 a year. The public sided with management during the 1982 football players' strike and the 1994 baseball players' strike. In those three cases, the public saw the incidents as guys making big bucks against other guys making big bucks. The UPS case was different. Many Americans knew their friendly UPS drivers, whom they often saw lugging around heavy crates. These drivers were regular folks being unfairly treated by a big greedy company. This case is a good example of perception leading the war.

Only Human?

Often, executives personify the big guy–little guy image. Take Microsoft. The company went from popular underdog in 1975 to mighty giant. When Microsoft CEO Bill Gates first came on the scene as a nerdy computer-software genius, everyone loved him. He became a folk hero out of a Horatio Alger story. Over time, however, he turned into a godzillionaire. His persona changed. Ironically, he is now perceived as a powerful, competitive giant trying to keep little guys away from his turf. The same media that had earlier championed Mr. Gates skewered him during the government's antitrust suit against Microsoft in 1999. Of course, Mr. Gates is still admired. Yet, his image has changed dramatically.

This is not to say big guys can't still have a little guy image. One of the most popular down-to-earth executives around is Warren Buffet, CEO of Berkshire Hathaway, who also happens to be one of the richest men in the United States. His wholesome, "just us folks" image has made him into a true down-home hero. Not only does he make people rich, he listens to them as well. His 1999 annual meeting lasted six hours as he answered all the shareholders' questions. In fact, fifteen thousand attended his annual three-day gathering for investors in Omaha. He also comes out of a Horatio Alger story, but he lives simply. To his fans, he was and still is a little guy at heart.

The Perception of Actions:
How to Use Them Effectively

A Star Performance

The same event can be turned into a good or bad performance depending on how it's played. For example, New York City came out of the World Trade Center bombing crisis with a better image than it had going in.

Why? The police, fire, ambulance, and other emergency units responded rapidly and appropriately. Participating agencies talked to the press, both during the disaster and at the next day's press conference. Officials remained calm, giving the sense that the situation was under control.

During the press conference, the Port Authority quickly admitted the failure of the WTC's evacuation plan, explaining the reasons why and discussing what has to be done to correct the problem.

All departments involved—from fire, police, and rescue personnel, to city and government officials—displayed sorrow for those who were killed and concern for those injured. The city looked like it knew what it was doing. Imagine NYC's image if the police and rescue squads had been incompetent and had run around like the Keystone Kops.

Contrast New York's image to Seattle's after it hosted the World Trade Organization meeting in December 1999. The world watched as neighborhoods were choked by tear gas, stores were looted, and more than five hundred people were arrested by the National Guard and by police clad in black riot outfits. The troubles were dubbed "the Battle of Seattle."

This fiasco turned into a major embarrassment for the United States as well as Seattle, a city formerly known for its laid-back civility. The chaos also led to whopping financial damage. Merchants estimated the vandalism cost at least $3 million and more than that in lost holiday sales.

The Seattle performance also brings up another lesson:

- **Public perception is based on a company's past behavior.**
- **Perception is used to predict future behavior.**

Following on the heels of the WTO debacle, Seattle was facing the threat of a terrorist attack on New Year's Eve. As a result, the mayor of Seattle canceled the city's official New Year's Eve celebration. The perception, true or false, was the city's police would not be able to manage the possible outbreak of violence.

A Change of Mind

File this next one under "better late than never." It shows how a bad decision can still be corrected, especially when the voice of public pressure turns into a dull roar.

In 1987, Chrysler bought American Motors, which came complete with a plant in Kenosha, Wisconsin. The plant employed sixty-five hundred workers in a city of seventy-two hundred. Chrysler said it intended to stay in Kenosha for five years. Remember the word "intended."

In 1988, the town went into shock when Chrysler announced the plant would be closed within a year. At first, the company offered minimal compensation. The next chapter discusses the power of public anger. This is a preview.

The United Auto Workers filed a class-action complaint against Chrysler and the Department of Housing and Urban Development and against the city of Detroit relating to the use of federal funds to help move jobs from Kenosha to Detroit. Then, Chrysler announced its intention to increase production of compact cars in Mexico. That did not go over really well in Kenosha, especially as the Kenosha plant produced two of the compact cars. Anger intensified among employees, their union, and people sympathetic to the fired employees.

Enter the State of Wisconsin. It threatened to sue Chrysler for breach of contract, citing the company's five-year "intention." Thus began a bitter debate between "intend" and "promise," causing Chrysler considerable embarrassment. Finally the governor of Wisconsin and Chrysler agreed the state wouldn't sue if Chrysler stayed in Kenosha for two-to-five years.

There had been strong pressure from the media, social activists, and other interested parties. Chrysler "got religion" and offered impressive social and financial assistance. It tore down the old plant and made the land available for an industrial park and a city park at no cost to the city, and made a $200 million contribution to the community. It provided generous severance pay, set up a trust fund for former employees in financial need, and offered retraining programs. Chrysler also paid a high-ranking executive to help with the development of the area. Since then, at least seventeen companies have relocated from Chicago to Kenosha.

Even if the company responded under social pressure, it wound up doing more than it had to. The company became proactive and reinvigorated Kenosha with new companies, new facilities, and hope. It became a good guy.

- **Chrysler turned its social irresponsibility into social responsiveness.**
- **The lesson here is not about closing a place of employment but rather, how to do it.**

If Chrysler had acted well in the beginning, it would have contained the impact of the plant closing and saved the town a great deal of angst.

A Wrong Turn

Here's another problem that went the wrong way but didn't have to: Intel's flawed Pentium chip. In the summer of 1994, Intel engineers discovered a flaw in the chip that caused mathematical division errors. Deciding the error would occur very infrequently, they went ahead and sold the chip, figuring they could fix it quietly. Months later, the error was detected by a mathematics professor, who posted his discovery on the Internet. When the problem became public, Intel insisted the odds were 9 billion to 1 against the chip causing a mathematical error. In fact, the company initially refused to provide replacements unless users could prove they needed their computers for complex mathematical operations. The problem escalated in December of 1994 when IBM announced it was suspending shipments of personal computers containing the chip.

By not replacing the chip, Intel found itself faced with lawsuits from shareholders and customers; a 37 percent drop in fourth-quarter earnings; decreased share value; three months of bad press; and the loss of credibility with the very market they were cultivating.

This crisis could have been easily prevented; Intel could

have been the good guy. If it had announced the flaw and immediately offered replacement chips, it would have substantially limited negative press coverage—if there was any at all. It would have contained the financial ramifications and enhanced its prestigious image. Instead, Intel became the brunt of jokes:

- **Question:** How many Pentium designers does it take to screw in a lightbulb?
- **Answer:** 199,904,274,017. That's close enough for nontechnical people
- **Question:** What do you get when you cross a Pentium PC with a research grant?
- **Answer:** A mad scientist.

A word about jokes. As one late-night-talk-show host explained, a joke doesn't work if the audience doesn't understand the subject. When a business becomes the target of a joke, it means the problem is big enough to be understood. Jokes exaggerate a mistake. Business life may recover, but people are laughing about what went wrong, not right.

Regardless of how well Intel does in the marketplace, it will never be able to erase an incident that could have been avoided. In a February 22, 1996, *New York Times* article, a customer who complained of the sluggish performance of a new Intel chip and Intel's lack of response said, "One would think Intel would have become a bit more sensitive to acknowledging problems after last year's . . . fiasco." Plus, even though Intel's alive and doing very well, the "flawed" incident has wound up joining Exxon as a business case study of what not to do.

Twenty-Twenty Hindsight

They say experience is something you don't get until just after it's needed. The Intel story is a good "there but for the Grace of God go I" example for CEOs. Often, executives fail to recognize a problem and its effect on the public. In a *Newsweek* interview, Intel CEO Andrew Grove admitted the company had created a mess. Mr. Grove would probably agree he used to be an "it will never happen here" kind of CEO. Perhaps more accurately, "It never occurred to me that something could happen."

In his book *Only The Paranoid Survive,* Mr. Grove talks about how the old business rules no longer work. Referring to the flawed chip incident, he noted, "The trouble was, not only didn't we realize that the rules had changed—what was worse, we didn't know what rules we now had to abide by."

Learning his lesson afterward, Mr. Grove:

- **Encouraged company "Casssandras," particularly middle managers, to pass along potential problems, including those involving disgruntled customers, product development, and employment morale, so the company could respond faster and better.**

In fact, Intel now has a formal process for monitoring and responding to Internet newsgroups.

What really counts is the way mistakes are corrected.

- **Mr. Grove was able to maintain his reputation by admitting his mistakes and fixing them.**

Climate Control

Yet, some of the "it never occurred to me" Intel mind-set still exists, as its Pentium III chip problem illustrates. The good news is Intel has learned how to manage an incident well. Intel embedded a serial number on a new Pentium III processor. Cyberspace privacy activists went nuts. The company was surprised it became a volatile problem. It shouldn't have been. User privacy in cyberspace has been a growing issue. Intel said the numbers would increase security for Internet commerce and would help authenticate E-mail and other documents.

Not so, said privacy advocates, who called for a boycott, saying the serial number wouldn't protect security. It would let direct marketers, data-mining companies, and others track Web surfers more easily.

To Intel's credit, it responded quickly, saying it would work with computer makers to ensure the serial number was switched off by default when personal computers were shipped out to stores and customers.

The saga didn't end there. Enter Zero-Knowledge Systems, a small self-promoting Canadian software company that found a way to make the hidden serial numbers visible again. The company placed a program on its Web site demonstrating the vulnerability—acting in the "public interest."

Intel wasn't ignoring this one. Acting aggressively, Intel hooked up with Symantec Corporation, which makes antivirus software. Symantec agreed Zero-Knowledge's program was dangerous and also found it made a user's computer crash. It added Zero's Web site to its virus warnings.

An Intel spokesman acknowledged there was no perfect way to keep the number hidden, but was working with the industry to build stronger defenses against tampering.

What a difference a proactive response makes. Just to show you it works: One annoyed user sent an E-mail to Zero-Knowledge saying, "My Norton AV (antivirus program) detected a trojan virus when I click on the breaking news link. If you can't even manage your own site, there's no way I'm going to do business with you."

• **Before a company introduces a service, it has to look for downsides.**

It didn't matter if it would be highly impractical to track a user's every activity on the Web using Intel's new identifier. The perception was it could be intrusive. With the firestorm surrounding the issue, Intel should not have been caught off guard.

Great Expectations

We've become a nation of watchers. As the comic-strip character Pogo said, "We have met the enemy and they are us." We all have our own opinions. Our own memories and experiences shade our perception of what's going on.

The day after Monica Lewinsky was interviewed by Barbara Walters on *20/20,* public reaction was interesting. Members of the public interviewed on television had strong, yet varying, opinions about the young woman: "She's a shameless hussy." "She's not a tramp." "She was treated badly." "She got what she deserved." "I feel sorry for her." "I didn't like her hair." There were vast differences in the way she was perceived. Personal backgrounds colored viewers' interpretations. Some viewers paid attention to what she said, others to how she looked.

- Audience members do not necessarily think alike, and that can't always be changed.

Yet, those differences did not keep anyone from wanting to watch in the first place. Advertising rates for the program soared from $160,000 to $800,000 for a thirty-second spot. Forty-six percent of all Americans saw it. In fact, a friend who was in Hawaii said tourists surfed back to their hotels to watch. While I was sitting at an airport waiting for a *very* delayed flight on the night of the broadcast, throughout the gate area the chanting of irate passengers grew louder and louder: "We coulda' been watching Monica."

Intepreting Interpretations

A company has to take a cross section of opinions into consideration when planning a crisis response.

Sometimes, it might not matter what people think, as was the case with the Monica interview. However, there are times when different interpretations of the same event can have serious consequences.

For example, misunderstandings led to a melee in Harlem in 1998 when a notorious agitator held a rally that was supposed to end at 4:00 P.M. sharp. A police helicopter had been sent to be used as a diversion to allow officers to get to the sound system to turn it off at the end of the rally. The officers were wearing helmets and face shields. All stayed peaceful until the event went overtime and the police tried to end it. As a result, there was a clash between police and the crowd.

Conflicting interpretations led to the explosion. For example: the police saw the helicopter as a diversion; the crowd thought it was an aggressive police threat. The police were using helmets and face shields as a precaution; the crowd saw the protective covering as riot gear. This is not a question of who's right or wrong. Rather, that's the way it is. The police and the crowd were speaking in different cultures. In a tense situation, this has to be taken into account. In these cases, it's important to utilize an interpreter who understands both sides of the situation.

Perception and International Culture:
How to Work in a Global World

Getting to Know You

With companies conducting business all over the world, perception can get very tricky. The understanding of cultural diversity extends beyond obvious geographic and language differences to include a knowledge of cultures. Concepts of time, history, personal space, and religious beliefs all come into play.

This being the case, even the best-intentioned plan can turn into a fiasco if you don't do your homework. For instance, a major American airline was launching new service to Tokyo. To celebrate its inaugural flight, attendants gave passengers white carnations as they boarded. Only, in Asia, white is the color for mourning. It was the equivalent of handing out black armbands.

A Japanese company, in turn, found itself in cultural hot water in the United States. Nintendo inadvertently created a hoopla over one of its Pokémon cards. A Japanese-language card appeared to be sporting a swastika. However, it really was a "manji," an ancient Japanese symbol for good fortune. Japanese customers had no problem with it. However, in the United States, Pokémon was in danger of becoming a Nazi. Nintendo quickly—and wisely—halted production of the card even though it had not been intended for the U.S. market.

Advertising messages can also be a bit risky for companies who neglect to use cultural translators. Perdue's advertising campaign in Spain received a lot of attention, but not in the way it intended. Its slogan, "It takes a strong man to make a tender chicken," translated into, "It takes an aroused man to make a chicken affectionate" in Spanish. Pepsi's "Come alive with the Pepsi generation" meant in China, "Pepsi brings your ancestors back from the grave."

While I was meeting the general manager of the Ritz Hotel in Madrid, he asked me how I liked the hotel. I said I thought it was "just beautiful." He grew quite testy and said, "We're more than 'just.'" I apologized for offending him, explaining how I meant "just," but the damage was done.

What's the Problem?

- **Beyond language, cultural differences can lead to misunderstandings with serious consequences.**

Ask Monsanto. The company genetically modifies agricultural seeds, including those that produce many of the protein-rich soybeans Britain imports from America to make food products. The seeds make soybeans, corn, and cotton crops easier to grow.

The problem was Monsanto didn't understand the Europeans' concern for food safety. When the company introduced its genetically engineered soybeans in Britain in 1996, the country was in full panic over mad cow disease. With a lack of public confidence in regulatory and scientific communities, fear spread throughout Europe, impacting Monsanto's biogenetic seeds. The company did not realize the cultural climate was different. Thus began a crisis born on the assumption Europeans would act like Americans. That would change, too (the story continues in Sin #3).

Coca-Cola didn't understand the fear-of-food culture either when its contamination problem was bubbling in Belgium. CEO Douglas Ivester, who felt there was no health issue, didn't recognize Europe's ongoing paranoia about food safety. That is one of the reasons the problem overerupted.

Those two companies are hardly the only ones that are culturally challenged. The perception of American business brashness has offended many a potential foreign partner. Such routine U.S. practices as dismissing employees or cutting costs sharply after a buyout are either definite "don'ts" or illegal in Europe. These misunderstandings can turn into deal killers.

Faux pas are partially to blame for the failure of up to 60 percent of U.S. joint ventures abroad, according to the World Trade Institute. For example, a U.S. buyout firm conducted what it thought was a routine examination of a German business. The German seller misunderstood the process. It accused the U.S. company of pirating information and thought the company's real motive was to obtain competitively sensitive information. Needless to say, the deal didn't go through.

Le Mickey Mouse

The story of the Euro-Disney theme park is a classic case of a company not taking cultural perceptions seriously. When Disney decided to build a theme park outside of Paris, it used good ol' American management styles, American tastes, American labor practices, and American marketing pizzazz. The French stayed away in droves.

In a short time, Disney had managed to alienate every audience upon which it depended. It alienated employees by imposing a dress code, which was perceived as an insult. It alienated customers by overcharging for everything from fast food to accommodations. If that wasn't bad enough, Disney wouldn't permit wine (a staple of French culture). Then, there were the shareholders. They were alienated, too, by Disney's overpromising and underperforming.

Instead of the glowing media attention Disney was used to getting for its theme parks in the United States, most of the prelaunch Euro-Disney coverage focused on all the problems the company was having with its employees. The launch itself was covered by a skeptical press that was more interested in the expense and hype than the glories of the place.

It should come as no surprise the French weren't impressed with what they termed "cultural imperialism." A reporter from the newspaper *Le Figaro* wrote, "Euro-Disney is the very symbol of the process by which people's cultural standards are lowered and money becomes all-conquering. . . . I believe every Frenchman carries in him a notion of the dignity of France and of its past achievements, and that is part of the reason Euro-Disney is less popular than expected. I would be ashamed to go there."

Meanwhile, employees were protesting Disney's dress code, which regulated everything from facial hair, eye shadow, and women's underwear. The company even faced a court battle over the dress code, which the French government said was supposed to be approved by both management and worker representatives.

Visitors weren't happy either. Not only was wine banned,

they hated the long lines for rides and food. A French travel agent explained, "For the French, lining up is like being back in the war." Cultural differences, indeed.

After that, Euro-Disney hired a French president who lowered off-peak admission prices and hotel rates, got rid of the dress code, and brought in the wine. The park began turning around.

The Perception of Gimmicks

Smoke, Mirrors, and Puppies

During early public-relations days, I had to promote boring events. They were the kind that were so dull—forget the press, I didn't want to attend. For those occasions, I tried to think of ways to incorporate a puppy or baby into the event. Quite a challenge when promoting a diabetes and diet class. The reason I wanted puppies and babies was to provide cute photo opportunities that attract reporters and photographers like magnets.

I'm going to let you in on a trick of the trade. There's trouble brewing when you see a public figure with a puppy. Do you think it was coincidence that Buddy, the presidential puppy, suddenly appeared on the White House lawn with President Clinton? The puppy was introduced in mid-December 1997 just as the president was trying to fight off the Paula Jones deposition scheduled for January. Plus, he was dealing with the Monica mess. The puppy should have been named "Red Herring."

Anyway, the nation focused on the frisky rascal. (I'm referring to the puppy.) Little schoolchildren got involved, suggesting names. The puppy saga continued as the president tirelessly worked to resolve the feud between Buddy and the White House cat, Socks. The White House folks were able to divert attention from the growing internal chaos for the rest of December. Socks alone could not do it. He was old news. The question is whether these ploys really work. Well, as an eight-year-old named Randy advises, "Be a good kisser. It makes your wife forget that you never take out the trash." Ploys can be distracting and can soften us up, but they don't hide a problem for long. After all, there's just so much a kiss or a puppy can do. In the puppy's case, it's not his problem. He'll still be cute even if the situation around him gets ugly. The kisser, however, could get in trouble with the "kissee."

This brings us back to credibility. One can't play magician, wave a wand, and make trouble disappear. It's true a magician uses the power of perception to influence our thinking by controlling the environment and directing our attention. Magic also arouses skepticism. We don't enjoy being fooled if we feel someone has pulled a fast one on us.

Entertainment impresario Garth Drabinsky tried to use magic and failed. The wizard who created Broadway extravaganzas like *Ragtime* and *Fosse* enveloped his company, Livent, in an aura of success. Then, the facade came tumbling down when he was charged with cooking the company's books for years, whisking financial facts around like props. Livent lost close to $150 million in market value when the alleged fraud was discovered. He claimed he was too busy producing shows to pay attention to the accounting. However, Mr. Drabinsky did pay attention when he was indicted in the United States, prompting him to hightail it back to his native Canada.

No matter how one tries to divert attention, the problem winds up taking center stage. Therefore, it's far more important to utilize images while fixing the problem, not hiding it.

- There's a difference between "spin" and responsible conduct.
- Spin is the distortion of news.

Don't do it. The goal of a crisis response is to make an emotional connection with the public through tangible, visible representation of a company's actions. A CEO's caring presence in the trenches and employees helping victims' families go a long way in showing contrition as long as the efforts are sincere. These should not be hollow gestures. Again, that's spin. Whatever action is taken should include the wishes of those to whom you are making amends. Ten years after the Bhopal disaster, members of victims' groups in Bhopal were continuing to demand adequate health care and compensation. Union Carbide, on the other hand, was contemplating putting up a memorial for victims in front of their factories. Small wonder a consortium of twenty-five human rights and environmental organizations was demanding Union Carbide CEO Warren Anderson stand trial in India to face criminal proceedings. (Mr. Anderson did not return to India.)

The Days of Reckoning

A national survey by the Scripps Howard News Service and the W. E. Scripps School of Journalism showed 70.3 percent of respondents used local TV news as their primary source of news, followed by network TV news (67.3 percent), newspapers (59 percent), and radio news (48.6 percent). It also showed those between the ages of eighteen and thirty-four watched less news than the rest of the population.

Now, as we happen to be part of those percentages, we can use ourselves as our own guinea pigs. While you're watching and reading the news, notice how you respond and why. On what are you basing your judgments?

Take this a step further and plan your company's responses to various scenarios. Think visually. "How will our actions be interpreted by the public? How will we show we are good guys?" "What do we have to do internally to make sure we can perform externally?"

These are questions New York City police commissioner Howard Safir should have been asking in 1999 when he went on an Academy Awards junket paid for by Revlon. All hell was breaking loose in New York in the aftermath of the shooting of Amadou Diallo, a twenty-two-year-old West African immigrant who was killed by a barrage of forty-one bullets fired by

four white police officers. This tragedy turned national attention on New York and police brutality.

Making matters worse, it looked like Mr. Safir had planned to skip a Monday-morning City Council hearing on police procedures to attend late-night Oscar parties. Whether he had intended to stay in Los Angeles or not, Commissioner Safir scooted back to New York on a late Sunday-night flight to attend the hearing. Critics said he changed his itinerary after being caught on camera at the parties.

Talk about giving the impression of Nero fiddling while Rome burned. Even if he couldn't accomplish anything over a weekend, even if the trip was planned months ago, he should have canceled it. It was plain stupid. The Reverend Al Sharpton was leading the African-American community in fiery public protests covered by the national media. Mr. Safir played right into the protesters' hands. The perception was the police commissioner preferred hanging out with celebrities in Los Angeles to working to combat the problem of police brutality. In New York, he appeared not to care about the senseless shooting. Remember, this is perception. We don't know how he felt.

Until the shooting, the police commissioner had been popular and was credited with reducing crime in the city. He kept a low profile. That one trip damaged his reputation and put his job on the line. All of a sudden, he was under intense media scrutiny. Other not-so-kosher things attracted attention, like Mr. Safir's use of on-duty detectives to provide security at his daughter's wedding.

Critics questioned whether a city official could accept the free trips in the first place. Although a report by New York City lawyers later concluded he hadn't violated any ethics rules, it said he had shown poor judgment. It recommended Mr. Safir pay for the trip, which he did to the tune of $7,000.

Regardless, Mr. Safir shot himself in the foot.

Conduct that would be harmless in normal times could lead to downfall in bad times. When in the midst of a serious problem, remember you're under a public magnifying glass. You have to ask yourself how your actions will be perceived. To be on the safe side, ask others, too.

Show-and-Tell

Crisis mastering is not an exact science. Common sense plays a major role. Many decisions are based on instinct. To determine a response, it's advisable to turn the situation around:

- **How would you feel if you were the wronged party?**
- **As the wronged party, what do you think would be a fair and generous solution?**

It puts the whole problem back in balance, especially if the scales were only tipped by the bottom line.

When a problem occurs, people have questions. They want answers.

- **A crisis response has to answer three basic questions:**
  "What happened?"
  "What are you going to do about it?"
  "How will it affect me?"

This calls for strong, clear, ongoing communication on a company's part, leaving no questions unanswered. Don't forget visibility. As director of the show, CEOs have to emphasize those things that are essential to telling their story. The public has to feel they know and believe the message. That can only be done by being on stage.

Perception and Language:
How to Avoid Traps

Keeping It Simple

As we look at perception, we can't leave out the power of words. They need to be clear-cut, leaving no room for inaccurate interpretation.

It's best to keep messages clear and simple. Those of you who speak in "legal-ese," "medical-ese," or any kind of "industry-ese," beware. People will not understand you unless it is translated into English.

For example, the activist group Greenpeace has been a master at generating outrage by simplifying complex scientific issues and technical information. They know how to turn the information into snappy news items. Typically, their targets' responses—if they do respond—are scientific and cold. This is a sure way to wave good-bye to public support.

Also, be mindful of connotations. Companies tend to take business descriptions for granted, not realizing their underlying negative perceptions. For example, health care, which is feeling the brunt of public anger due to the high cost of patient care, calls itself an "industry." Always remember the human quotient. Patients, customers, and clients are not products. They are people. This is important to realize at all times, but especially when confronting an angry public.

Unfortunately, there are times when words can create a crisis, especially in this scary age of political correctness gone haywire. Take the case in Washington, D.C., of the white city official who correctly used the word "niggardly" when talking about cutting spending on funds he administrated. He was forced to resign because two African-American coworkers took it as an ethnic slur. The story hit the press. After a national outcry, the official was reinstated. This incident could have been nipped in the bud if the mayor had quickly and quietly explained the definition to the offended individuals instead of accepting the official's resignation. There would have been less embarrassment all around.

This is not to say that some words aren't offensive. Slurs of any kind are inexcusable. So is name-calling. And swearing in public. In fact, there is a saying "righteous indignation is the ability to be mad without swearing."

Beware. Inappropriate words can either ignite a situation or make it worse. As top executives, you are entrusted with taking a higher road.

Perception and Credibility:
How to Earn It

Walking the Walks

Effective perception has to be backed by reality if a company wants to remain credible. Credibility takes a long time to build, but it's an enormous asset. Look at it as an insurance policy. When a problem occurs, it serves as a buffer. The public is willing to give a company the benefit of the doubt. Credibility buys time to find and fix the problem in order to maintain and even enhance a reputation. A company that deals with a problem *without* credibility is considered the bad guy. That's not to say it can't act responsibly and change the public's perception, but it starts off with a serious handicap. On the other hand, if a company with a good reputation mishandles a problem, an image that took years to build can tarnish overnight. Therefore, if a company says it's going to do something, it has to do it. When a broken promise is discovered, a company winds up with major egg on its face. Take The Body Shop. The company vowed none of its products were tested on animals. This appealed to socially conscious consumers. The company was personified by cofounder Anita Roddick. Promotional material showed her sitting in a rain forest bargaining with natives to buy their renewable products. She searched for skin creams among the Wodaabe tribe in Niger and for cactus body scrubs among Mexican peasants. The Body Shop became a symbol of a business with a conscience.

Then in 1994 an exposé in *Business Ethics* reported evidence that native peoples supplied less than 1 percent of the company's raw material. Worse, many of its ingredients were tested on animals (although not by The Body Shop itself); and its "natural" products included lots of petroleum. Ms. Roddick's husband, Gordon, issued an angry, detailed rebuttal of the article. However, the publicity impacted perception.

Once the story was out, the company's stock price and sales dropped. Many socially conscious investment houses sold their Body Shop stock. Also, around the same time the article came out, The Body Shop was under investigation by the Federal Trade Commission over its franchising practices. This increased negative focus on the stock.

Here's a case where reality didn't live up to its image, and The Body Shop's financial picture suffered as a result. So did its claims. The company quietly changed product labels from "Not Tested on Animals" to "Against Animal Testing."

Nike also suffered from a split personality. The shoe giant was severely criticized for paying Third World children meager wages to make its sneakers. To improve its image, Nike began its crusade to improve conditions for foreign workers. In 1996, it released an independent study showing its workers in Indonesia and Vietnam had turned into contented consumers. All well and good until Ernst and Young conducted an audit three weeks later reporting unsafe working conditions in Nike's factories in Vietnam. The story became front-page news.

It certainly didn't help when the public learned Nike paid basketball star Michael Jordan $30 million-plus for his endorsement—more than the company paid its nineteen thousand foreign factory workers combined. The perception: Nike wasn't completely committed to its pledge to be socially responsible. However, it should be noted that since that time, strong pressure from advocacy groups has led Nike to change its out-sourcing practices.

- **A company cannot say it is ethical if it does not cut out questionable practices.**
- **Perception reflects on management as well as the actual problem.**

When Bankers Trust merged with Deutsche Bank, making Deutsche Bank the largest bank in the world, a full-page advertisement ran promoting the "integration." With the two bank names on top, the headline proclaimed, "That's a combination of strength and innovation bound to produce results." Further down the page, the ad declared the bank was uniquely positioned to help its customers achieve superior results: "We combine industry focus and creative market insights, financial innovation . . ."

That very same day, that very same newspaper ran an article titled "Bank Officials Investigated in Tax-Evasion Case." The officials were executives from—you guessed it—Deutsche Bank.

According to the article, German authorities were investigating whether the bank helped clients illegally shelter income to avoid taxes. The Deutsche Bank officials included the chief executive and five other current and former senior executives.

As an extra wrinkle, it just so happened that in March 1999, Bankers Trust pleaded guilty to criminal charges of illegally diverting $19.1 million in cash and other unclaimed funds.

It was only a matter of time before the bad news would become public. *Pull the advertisement.*

Yes, they had to promote the "integration." However:

- **There are times when it's better to take a lower profile until the heat dies down.**

The unfortunate timing of the ad highlighted the dichotomy. Saying one is trustworthy doesn't make it true unless the claim is backed up by action.

Perception with a Twist

There's a house in Santa Cruz, California, known as the "Mystery Spot." In this house, balls roll uphill, chairs sit on walls, and people lean over so far they can't see their shoes but they don't fall down.

It turns out a study concluded the reason for all the visual illusions is the house is tilted. A psychology professor said, "You know the house is tilted, but you don't know how much. Everything is tilted. You can't look outside and see a horizon, so you think what you see is right."

Great metaphor. We are such visual animals. The horizontal and vertical are mostly affected by what we see. If the context is screwy, it throws off what we observe. If floors are slanted, people will hang pictures on a slant because the slant is the reality.

• **A company's challenge is to be aware of a perception slant and get it leveled—fast.**

Show Time

Perception affects every step of a crisis response. Regardless of the problem, if a company sets the stage effectively and gives a sound performance, it can still win applause. If not, the public will agree with Groucho Marx, who said, "I didn't like the play, but then I saw it under adverse conditions—the curtain was up."

Stay tuned.

3

Let Them Eat Cake

There was once a CEO who prided himself on his ruthlessness. His company's bottom line was all that mattered. He had legions of lawyers to pulverize any impediment in his way, even if it meant destroying innocent people in the process. One day a photographer caught the CEO kicking an adorable dog who had the bad luck to be in his way. The tabloids gleefully ran the picture on their front pages. Even more gleefully, former adversaries and employees Xeroxed the photo and sent it to their friends and mothers.

A ruthless businessman is one thing. A man who kicks a dog is another. Boycotts were called by so many organizations, there weren't any consumers left to buy his company's products. His bottom line was toast.

We have come to the Third Deadly Sin: "Let Them Eat Cake." This is committed by CEOs who ignore the human (or animal) damage they cause. Leaders are judged by their perceived actions. It is not only what you do, but how you do it.

People react to a situation according to the way their feelings interpret what they see. As a result, the human factor is so important, it gets its own chapter.

- **Public perception is formed by emotion, not reason.**

In fact, many companies get in trouble because they see emotional reactions as irrational and therefore unimportant. Yet, as Mark Twain said way back in 1889, "But that is the way we are made: we don't reason, where we feel, we just feel."

Never underestimate the way emotion controls public opinion. A cold, dispassionate response is not the way to win public respect and loyalty. Think of all those Exxon customers who cut up their credit cards even though they weren't personally affected by an oil spill in Alaska.

The Power of Emotion:
How to Work with It

It Only Takes a Minute

Emotion has tremendous power. In fact, thanks to our visual age, it can be a call to arms to a usually placid public.

Remember every mother's worst nightmare, the English au pair Louise Woodward? She was convicted of murder in the 1997 death of an eight-month-old Massachusetts baby. During the trial, the expressionless young woman was not a particularly sympathetic character.

Then, the verdict. Live television. Global audience. When she was convicted of murder, she began to weep. It was heartbreaking, especially when she said, sobbing, she was only seventeen years old. In an instant, Ms. Woodward ignited public sympathy and support.

This put the judge in a tricky situation. After such a gut-wrenching scene, he didn't want to look like a bad guy in front of the whole world. He reduced the verdict to manslaughter and sentenced her to the 279 days in jail she'd already served.

Think the sentence would have been different if the verdict had not been televised or if Ms. Woodward had not broken down?

Whether the media cover a story on grieving victims, people losing their home or business, or a woman who claims she has been sexually harassed by her boss:

- **The public is going to judge a company by its approach to the problem.**
- **To win support, executives have to come across as caring individuals.**

When it comes to image, CEOs are in the game whether they like it or not. Just as people can't see behind company walls, they can't look into someone's head and heart.

Public Relating

President Clinton's "I feel your pain" kind of empathy for people played a big role in his election. He turned political issues into emotional ones. Compare how Mr. Clinton came across versus his iceberg opponents George Bush and Bob Dole.

CEOs also need to know how to display empathy. They have to know how to replace "corporate-ese" with "people-ese." A good example is the time that a general counsel of a huge company agreed to talk about legal issues to a group of poor women entering the workforce. Many were on welfare. He spoke about estate planning.

Often, the higher the executive, the more isolated he or she becomes. This is not good, internally or externally. They lose touch with reality. As bad as this is in good times, it's very dangerous in a crisis. Top executives do not have to burst into tears and rip out their hair when something bad happens. However, the lack of emotion can be disastrous.

A classic example is how Michael Dukakis self-destructed during a 1988 presidential debate. He was asked a hypothetical question about whether he would favor the death penalty if someone raped and murdered his wife. What an awful question! It made just about everyone shudder, with the exception of Mrs. Dukakis's husband. The man showed no emotion and gave a coldly impersonal answer, saying he was opposed to the death penalty, and he provided examples of how he dealt with violent crime in Massachusetts.

In a *Time* magazine article, "Shoulda, Woulda, Coulda," Calvin Trillin imagines Dukakis thinking back to what he should have said. " 'I'd tear his guts out,' Dukakis says, glancing over at a mirror to see if he looks sufficiently impassioned. 'I'd break his legs with my bare hands. . . .' "

Something along the lines of a shocked "heaven forbid" before answering the question would have sufficed. Instead, his robotic response created a cold, insensitive image he couldn't shake.

• A perceived insensitive act tends to freeze an image, which never melts.

Union Carbide CEO Anderson and Exxon's CEO Rawls will be remembered for what they didn't do. If they had responded with visable compassion and sorrow to their crises, they would have improved their reputations.

Emotion:
How to Avoid Anger

It's Your Own Fault

Perception is not created by images alone. One has to be careful of the buttons that push people to anger. Anger means big trouble.

Audi learned this the hard way. In 1986, customers complained that the Audi 5000S model experienced sudden, unintended acceleration, causing accidents, injuries, and some deaths. The car was further doomed when it was attacked on the killer television show *60 Minutes*.

Audi had a tactful response: drivers were to blame.

Potential buyers shunned Audis in favor of competing models. Once-loyal customers were angered and disappointed that the car's value plunged. As one angry customer said, "Audi couldn't have done a worse job if they had sat back and formulated a strategy to kill the car."

In 1987, Audi complied with a U.S. government request to recall all 1978–1986 5000S cars to correct problems. This came to about 250,000 vehicles.

Seems cut-and-dried, doesn't it? Audi had a defective car.

In reality, it turned out the 1986 *60 Minutes* program attacking the Audi 5000S car used a rigged example. *And*—following a three-year investigation of the model, the National Highway Traffic Safety Administration (NHTSA) concluded the reason for the sudden acceleration *was attributable to driver error.*

Here's a perfect example of perception beating out reality. What really happened was that the car's pedals were placed further to the left and closer together than those in many American cars. It was designed to make it easier to brake in high speed emergencies. However, U.S. drivers tended to hit the wrong pedal.

While European drivers were used to this configuration, obviously American drivers weren't. All Audi had to do was alter the design for the U.S. market and educate customers instead of blaming them. After all, the auto industry finally redesigned cars with right-hand drive for the Japanese market. Would it have cost money? Yup. However, it would have ultimately been cheaper.

The company initially refused to order a recall. As a result, sales fell 20 percent in one year, and they never fully recovered. Plus, the company was saddled with multimillion-dollar lawsuits.

Finally, Audi introduced a modified 5000S model for the U.S. market. Too bad the company was so slow to act.

Biting the Hands That Feed You

Audi isn't the only car company that had a problem realizing their customers do not relish driving safety hazards. Think Ford Pinto. Actually, this is a case of dueling perceptions.

Introduced in 1970, the Pinto was a small car designed to

compete with the growing foreign car market. Problem was, tests showed the Pinto's fuel tank often ruptured when struck from the rear at a relatively low speed (thirty-one miles per hour). The problem could have been fixed by redesigning the tank and its location. Instead, the Pinto wound up causing hundreds of deaths. Ford initially refused to recall the cars. The public perception was that Ford was putting profits before the cost of lives and was showing no remorse. The 1977 Pinto model was redesigned. However, it was too late to assuage the negative perception. In 1978, a grand jury indicted Ford on reckless homicide in a case where three teenage girls died in a fire triggered after their 1973 Pinto was hit from behind by a van.

In 1978, Ford finally recalled all 1971–1976 cars and ceased production of the Pinto.

That's one side of the story. Then, there's Ford's perception of the situation. Ford insiders said the "hysterical" mounting media campaign was "a crusade against us."

Here's the company's take on the story. In a 1977 article in *Mother Jones* magazine, journalist Mark Dowie claimed Ford executives had decided to produce and still were continuing to market the Pinto even after company crash tests showed its gas tank would rupture in rear-end collisions at relatively low speeds. Dowie claimed Ford's cost-benefit analysis said a redesign wasn't justified.

Then Mr. Dowie and Ralph Nader held a press conference in Washington, D.C., which drew national attention to the problem. A day later, the NHTSA began its own investigation.

So far, everyone would agree with these events. Now here's where it really gets interesting. The following are points justifying Ford's actions according to Matthew T. Lee, who presented a paper at a Business History Conference in 1998.

Ford's points:

- The government and the NHTSA were buckling to public pressure based on the Dowie article.
- Starting with 1977 models, cars were only supposed to withstand a thirty-miles-per-hour rear impact. Therefore, Pinto met the minimum standard, and it wasn't fair that the NHTSA said the Pinto was unsafe even though it met the minimum standard.
- NHTSA's test wasn't fair. (Imagine. The gas tanks were filled with gas rather than the nonflammable fluid normally used. The Pinto burst into flames.)
- Ford agreed to "voluntarily" recall the 1971–1976 Pintos even though they were built before the federal standard took effect.
- A few months before the recall, a California civil jury awarded $126 million to a plaintiff (later reduced to $6.6 million), and the company was indicted (but not found guilty) for reckless homicide in the case of the three teenage girls mentioned earlier.

Here are the real kickers:

- According to Mr. Lee, authorities have noted that if Pintos had been built even a decade earlier (1961–1966), neither the criminal trial nor the record-setting civil award would have been likely. In fact, prior to 1976, the federal government did not even have the authority to recall cars.
- Mr. Dowie had released an internal memo that indicated the Pinto was defective, but figured that settling lawsuits would be cheaper than fixing the design. Mr. Lee explains:
  1. "It was written in 1973, three years after the first Pinto was sold, so it cannot be the document" upon which the earlier design decisions were based.

2. "Ford was aware of the outcomes of the court cases . . . cost/benefit analysis showing a proposed standard was not 'practicable' or 'reasonable' could bring about its delay or defeat." In other words, Ford was disputing the identity of the document but not its contents.

3. "Cost/benefit analyses were routinely used by the industry and NHTSA in auto safety debates. *Given the lengthy history of a lack of concern with crashworthiness, industry representatives felt justified in arguing against NHTSA's fuel tank standard.*"

A company has to put customer safety before its wallet. Notice there was no mention of protecting Pinto drivers.

* **If it turns out a product is dangerous, warn customers, recall the product, and stop selling it until it is fixed.**

As the Audi and Pinto examples show, costs will ultimately be much lower.

Arguments like Ford's are the very reason big companies have such a bad image with the public. Instead of complaining about following standards that were inadequate, Ford should have been worried about safeguarding its product.

No matter how you look at it, perception killed the Pinto. Do we know the real story? Was it blown out of proportion? Ford's mistake was not jumping on the problem and fixing it. Their beliefs and perceptions were at odds with the very folks making the purchasing decision.

Anger and Public Opinion:
How to Escape the Impact

Mad as Hell

Clearly, victims/consumers have to be a company's top priority—regardless of the size of the problem. It goes back to biting the hand that feeds you. You need consumers and/or shareholders more than they need you. Perceived misconduct or mistreatment sends a company into dangerous territory.

• **Public anger is news.**

A Texaco discrimination suit was settled quickly because of the financial damage caused by bad publicity. For example, public reaction was strong enough to make the city of Philadelphia sell $5.7 million of Texaco stock owned by its city employee retirement fund in response to the crisis.

After the Union Carbide Bhopal tragedy, one man who lost his sister and his health said, "I wanted him [the CEO] to apologize, be humble. Say, 'We made a mistake. Get treatment, we'll pay for it.' We wouldn't have hung him."

When the 1988 Pan Am Flight 103 blew up over Lockerbie, Scotland, Bert Ammerman, brother of one of the victims, said the families would not have been nearly as *angry* and vocal if Pan Am had better managed the crisis. Families felt they were not treated with compassion and were not considered a top priority. As a result, they were a loud, dramatic thorn in Pan Am's side.

In the case of the restaurant chain Jack in the Box, some children died, and more than one hundred people were hospitalized after eating hamburgers tainted by E. coli bacteria. When the outbreak occurred, the company promised to pay for medical expenses for the victims. However, six months later, parents of the stricken children said the company had not paid their hospital bills. Parents also said they were unable to get the company's assurance to pay in writing. One woman who went to her lawyer because her child's medical bills had not been paid said, "I shouldn't have had to get *angry.*" (It should be noted I was an expert witness for meat supplier Monfort, Inc., in a litigation, "Hamburger Patty Cases," against Jack in the Box.)

Keeping the story alive a year later in January 1994, parents of a two-year-old who almost died said the fast-food chain hadn't paid their medical bills. When the hospital threatened to turn the account over to a collection agency, they turned the matter over to their lawyer, who in turn went to the media.

- **Anger turns victims into powerful enemies.**
- **The public understands that problems or accidents can happen, but what they won't accept is the semblance of insensitivity on the part of its leaders.**

The public perception in each of the foregoing cases was based on what people saw and heard from the victims; they were poignant elements of the tragedies. We didn't see enough caring responses from the companies to balance the negatives.

Hang 'Em High

The power of anger can turn jurors into avenging angels. Twelve people are supposed to make decisions based on hard evidence presented during a trial. Yet, throughout the country, jurors are turning what should be an objective decision into a passionate one. Just ask Philip Morris. The company was slammed with $1.5 million in compensatory damages and $50 million in punitive damages on behalf of a former smoker with lung cancer. The woman's lawyer had asked for $980,000 in compensatory damages and $15 million in punitive damages. After a month-long trial, the jury deliberated only several hours before determining punitive damages.

A Morgan Stanley analyst said, "The most important message of the entire process is that the jury was very, very, very angry."

Philip Morris's lead counsel explained, "We had a jury that either, because of sympathy or emotion for the plaintiff, or out of antagonism for Philip Morris, let those feelings determine how they reviewed and decided the evidence in this case."

Whether or not the punitive damage award is considered excessive and eventually reduced is not the point.

• **If a company can make twelve people angry, think of the ramifications of anger on the general population.**

Today, there are a lot of people minding your business. Many have learned the emotional value of a cause. That's why activist groups have become masters at stirring moral outrage against a company. There are some issues that go straight to the heart and others that don't. Animal rights does, global warming doesn't. A single word can be scary—*carcinogen*, for instance.

As the next example shows, the power of words can whip the public into a frenzy.

When Nestlé Crackled

During the Nestlé's "Baby Killer" fiasco, the company was a big loser in the great "Alphabet Protest." Participating groups

"An angry lynch mob to see you, sir."

included the TWAG, INBC, ICCR, NCCN, WCC, NIFAC, ICIFI, WHO, WCC, and MTF.

Nestlé mismanaged the crisis, and activist groups, who galvanized public support for their position by skillfully using the media, were able to keep the international controversy going for over a decade.

The problem had to do with a link between bottle-feeding and infant diseases and deaths in the Third World. The crux of the matter was infant formula marketed in Third World countries was powder based and had to be mixed with water. The trouble was, babies wound up drinking contaminated formula in areas where there was general ignorance of hygiene and unclean water. Plus, mothers couldn't read the instructions.

Although the problem was brought to the public's attention in the 1960s, the issue exploded when a pamphlet, "The Baby Killer," was published in 1974. The pamphlet, published by

War on Want, a London-based activist group, claimed babies in the Third World were dying because of irresponsible marketing of infant formula by multinational corporations. It berated the way the formula was marketed through the use of saleswomen dressed as nurses, the distribution of free samples, and the association of bottle-feeding with healthy babies to promote the use of infant formulas to mothers who would have been better off breast-feeding.

Then, a German group, the Third World Action Group (TWAG), translated the pamphlet into German with a new title, "Nestlé Kills Babies."

Thanks to the pamphlet, Nestlé was perceived as an evil company responsible for the deaths of thousands of helpless infants. Nestlé, a large Swiss international company making billions of dollars, was ripe for the picking. It had about 40 percent of the infant-formula market in the Third World.

Nestlé sued everyone involved with the translation and publication of "Nestlé Kills Babies." The two-year suit made news around the world. The judge found the thirty members of TWAG guilty of libel. Nestlé won the legal battle but lost the public-opinion war. Unwittingly, the company had given the group a public platform. Having attracted media and public attention, the trial moved the issue to center stage. It legitimized an unknown group and added an emotional dimension to the cause.

The controversy spread from Europe to the United States. A new group, the U.S. Infant Formula Action Coalition (IN-FACT), announced a boycott of all Nestlé products in 1977. Its boycott announcement came complete with a street procession, which included a baby coffin; a major demonstration at Nestlé's headquarters; and appeals to church groups. Many religious organizations sanctioned INFACT and provided financial support.

In response to pressure, the International Council of Infant

Food Industries (ICIFI) was formed to adopt a marketing code of ethics governing competitive standards in the infant food industry.

As Nestlé's infant formula product in the United States was negligible, the American public boycotted Nestlé's candy and other food products.

ABCDEF . . .

The whole story is long and complicated. It lasted ten years. In brief, the International Nestlé Boycott Committee (INBC) joined forces with INFACT. This got the Interfaith Center on Corporate Responsibility (ICCR) going, followed by the Methodist Task Force (MTF), World Council of Churches (WCC), and Nestlé Infant Formula Audit Commission (NIFAC). The boycott was endorsed by Ralph Nader, César Chavez, and labor groups. The controversy eventually wound its way to the World Health Organization (WHO), a unit of the United Nations.

These activist groups scored two major victories. They persuaded WHO to form an international code of marketing of breast-milk substitute. It spelled out rules for companies involved in the sale and distribution of infant formula in the Third World.

The biggest coup was getting Senator Edward Kennedy involved. He jumped in, orchestrating a U. S. Senate Subcommittee on Health and Scientific Research to look into the way infant formula was marketed. There were no experts on marketing or international business on his witness list.

These hearings led to public outrage. A widely viewed *CBS Reports* documentary used images of sick and dying infants to portray the horrors of Third World bottle-feeding. This led to Congressman Ronald Dellums introducing the Infant Nutrition

Act, designed to regulate the sale and distribution of infant formula to and in developing companies.

To say Nestlé botched its response is putting it mildly. When subpoenaed by the Senate, Nestlé said that as a Swiss corporation, they didn't have to testify. Making matters worse, Nestlé finally sent a representative, its Brazilian CEO (don't ask), who didn't understand the American political system. He argued the controversy was propaganda by leftist radicals bent on destroying the free-enterprise system. Although he admitted that the misuse of Nestlé products could result in illness or death, he also said the company had neither the power nor obligation to even attempt to prevent such outcomes. That played real well with the public.

Nestlé just didn't get it. Its strategy was concocted by management in Switzerland who did not have a clue about the U.S. climate. They completely miscalculated the effect infants had on people. Nestlé ignored the major issues, focusing on its belief that antibusiness forces were causing all the trouble. In terms of public perception, Nestlé appeared to be attacking the people who were trying to protect poor innocent babies.

The activist groups were using powerful emotional appeals. Nestlé's response was based on complex scientific facts and devoid of any emotion.

Dollars Versus Sense

Nestlé finally figured out something had to give and changed its tune. In 1981, it created the Nestlé Coordination Center for Nutrition (NCCN) to deal with the crisis. The boycott finally ended in 1984. It took years of negotiations between different groups, complying with the World Health Organization's code, and finally agreeing to change some of the company's business practices. The end of the boycott was announced jointly by Nestlé and the International Nestlé Boycott Committee. The protesters came out the clear winners. As *Newsweek* reported, ". . . scores of religious, women's health and public-interest groups have waged a very rough and costly boycott against the Swiss-based Nestlé company. . . . Last week, after spending tens of billions of dollars resisting the boycott, Nestlé finally reached the accord with protesters."

INFACT realized it would be difficult to motivate public support by focusing on scientific issues such as whether infant formula is a good substitute for breast milk. Instead, it changed the issue to a human one involving good guys and bad guys. The victims were helpless Third World babies. The culprits were large multinational corporations whose products were killing these babies.

What did not come out was that some of the groups' sensationalized information was inaccurate. Plus, nobody mentioned the adverse effects of poor conditions on infant mortality in the Third World, regardless of the method of feeding. It didn't matter because no one was effectively pointing out these facts. The "Alphabets" were adroit at galvanizing public support. Nestlé was not.

After all the time and money spent, Nestlé did not win a positive image. It was forced into changing its marketing practices. It would have been a whole lot cheaper had the company negotiated at the outset.

Nestlé could have responded quickly by focusing public attention on the broader scope of malnutrition and the infant mortality problem in the Third World. It could have worked in concert with legitimate groups to save babies, spearheading a campaign to educate mothers. If Nestlé had moved rapidly, it would have cut other groups off at the pass.

The crisis began in earnest in 1977. Nestlé is still considered the bad guy in Great Britain. Trying to rebuild its image there, its chief executive, Peter Brabeck, held a press conference in London in May 1999 announcing 1998 financial results. This was the first time a top Nestlé executive had talked to British media since 1988. Mr. Brabeck signaled a new course of action by confronting the issue head on.

Emotional Activism:
How to Manage It

Minding Your Business

Most issues can be turned into emotional ones. Greenpeace understood the human element and used it in the infamous Brent Spar oil-rig protest. Shell saw sinking the oil rig as a scientific and financial problem. Miscalculating the power of grassroots pressure, the blind oil giant shook the proverbial bean stalk. Shell did not realize it's not nice to shoot water cannons at people, especially in front of cameras. The oil rig didn't get sunk.

In another case of hitting human buttons, the Sierra Club and other environmental groups used fear to ignite public concern about the chemical industry. They issued a report charging that 99 percent of chemical facilities contacted had no plan to reduce the hazards they pose to local communities. Notice how the activists turned the dry subject of chemicals into a story about personal health risk. The word *chemical* isn't comforting to begin with. Think Bhopal. Working off public concerns, these groups claimed chemical exposure could have long-term health impacts.

The efforts of these activists have resulted in new restrictions on plant sites, the cancellation of entire product lines, and regulatory pressures.

Animal rights is another button-pusher issue. Once peripheral, the activist group People for the Ethical Treatment of Animals (PETA) has gone mainstream with an organized lobbying force. It has confronted and affected a number of industries, including pharmaceuticals, cosmetics, and food. Look at its dramatic impact on the issue of wearing fur. It has become a social taboo for many.

Scary Food

Sin #2 talked about Monsanto misreading Europe's fear-of-food climate when it tried to introduce gene-modified seeds. That's not the end of the story. In fact, the introduction of the seeds was only the beginning of their problems. The credibility of the environmental activists had soared in Britain because many had prophesied the link between mad cow disease and people's illnesses. Protest groups took one look at genetically modified foods, assumed battle stations, and went on a campaign to unmodify them. Part of their audience was Britain's press. British newspapers had largely ignored the environmentalists before. Now, they paid attention. They called Monsanto the "Frankenstein food giant" and the "biotech bully boy."

A member of parliament proclaimed the company "Public Enemy Number One." One civic group representative said, "Many people here really hate Monsanto. The rest of us are just scared." The fallout spread across the Continent.

Monsanto decided to mount a public-relations campaign to fight the negative press by promoting biotechnology as a means of feeding the world more effectively. Again, they misread the culture. European companies do not use corporate-backed issue campaigns. "Public relations is seen as a species of corporate lying," explained the director of a watchdog group. Monsanto's campaign flopped. Before the British campaign, 44 percent of British consumers surveyed said they had negative feelings about genetically engineered foods. By the end of the campaign, the figure had climbed to 51 percent.

Afterward, Monsanto's vice president of communications admitted they looked at it "too much through a U.S. lens."

Activists whipped Monsanto's missteps into an opportunity to arouse public anger and fear. Some food retailers pledged not to carry the genetically modified foods. One store said it received twelve thousand phone calls in a single month from worried shoppers.

Remember, these are the seeds that Americans farmers loved. This shows, again, how perception is in the eyes of the beholder. However, note the word "love" is in the past tense.

Scarier Scary Food

The antibiotech hysteria story is far from over. A global world means a global sharing of human fears and emotions. The concern over the issue jumped across the Atlantic and landed in the United States.

By 1999 in the United States, 55 percent of the soybean crop, 35 percent of the corn crop, and 39 percent of the cotton crop were derived from genetically engineered seeds. Then, environmental groups began lobbying and running full-page advertisements to warn against genetically modified foods. Federal lawmakers introduced legislation requiring the labeling of food made with genetically modified crops, and regulators began reevaluating everything from food safety to the effects bioengineered crops might have on monarch butterflies.

American companies that had been thanking their lucky stars that biogenetic engineering wasn't an issue in the United States suddenly found themselves under attack in their own backyards. Caught unaware, the industry joined together to form an alliance to fight the growing campaign against biogenetic food. One representative from Du Pont explained, "Public concern has been aggravated by the *perception* that we in the industry have often acted as though public fears are not legitimate and are the result of ignorance."

As the issue grew, Gerber and Heinz baby foods announced they would not use genetically altered corn or soy ingredients. More companies joined them in banning such foods, leaving farmers holding the proverbial crop bag. With a loss in European exports and the growing concern in the United States, many have wound up deliberating whether to continue growing these crops, thus seriously affecting the biotech industry.

Active Activists

Here's how American consumer awareness of the biogenetic issue began. Environmentalists from twelve countries met in the United States and began an all-out assault on the biotech-food industry. Several of the participants had helped orchestrate previous campaigns against the industry in Europe. Although they conceded that any real risks to people are unknown, they argued the biotech industry was treating people as "guinea pigs."

Utilizing planning and focus, the protests from public-interest groups were able to get the world's attention during the 1999 World Trade Organization meeting in Seattle.

The advocates' campaign to raise public awareness and concern was successful because they turned the "unsexy" topic of biogenetics into the good-guy-versus-bad-guy formula by planting the perception that big greedy companies don't care about the safety of ordinary people. Although most people probably don't understand what a biogenetic seed actually is, they do take notice when they hear it could hurt them. In today's world, companies have to realize scary issues travel—fast. Negative public opinion has become contagious and no longer needs a passport to arrive on a CEO's doorstep. As a result, a company has to respond swiftly, addressing false accusations, showing its concern for the public's well-being, and highlighting the positive aspects of the issue. This has to be communicated through the media, the Internet, and meetings with concerned audiences.

It's never too late to begin altering or reversing strategy in order to build public support. However, nothing is instant and a campaign may take a while, as in the case with battle-weary Monsanto. The company hired a public relations firm to help build a grassroots campaign in the United States to counter the attacks from environmentalists and consumer groups. This time around, Monsanto focused on the human factor of the issue, utilizing such slogans as "biotech saves children's lives" and "biotech equals jobs." Supporters have been prepped with such arguments as:

- Biotechnology can develop crops that may help feed the growing populations in sub-Saharan Africa.
- Farmers benefit by utilizing crops that have been engineered to produce their own pesticides.

The biogenetic issue is one that will be with us for some time. The field is too new; scientists don't know about long-term effects. Advocacy groups have supplied examples of how their campaigns have been successful by utilizing emotion against big business and science. Companies would be wise to study their efforts and apply them to their own responses. Action, however, has to be based on a company's sincere commitment to social accountability.

Can't Run, Can't Hide

What right do others have to tell you how to run your business? Well, the reality is that we are now living in a world defined by social conscience. Today, companies have to be nimble and integrate social concerns into their business. For example, in terms of perception, if Nestlé had spearheaded efforts to fight child malnutrition or similar problems, it would have displayed strong corporate responsibility. The public is not going to be angry at a company working to save babies.

It all boils down to corporate morality.

• **If executives are doing the right thing or willing to make changes, they can solve or minimize a problem.**

British Petroleum-Amoco is a good example. CEO Sir John Brown established a policy of developing socially responsible programs in emerging markets, such as community-building programs, training workers, and building transport systems. What's key here is that BP-Amoco executives are responsible for insuring these things get done and their success is a determining factor in their pay.

There are times when changing a policy can lead to surprising results, like a glowing advertisement from an activist group. The Rainforest Action Network took out full-page ads thanking Home Depot for "recognizing that ancient trees are worth more in the forests than in their stores." Home Depot, the largest lumber retailer in the world, said it would stop selling wood products from endangered forests by the year 2002. Home Depot's policy change turned out to be a public relations bonus as well as an environmental one.

Turning the Tables

A savvy company can turn the tables when threatened unfairly by interest groups. That is what Mo Siegel, chief executive of Boulder, Colorado–based Celestial Seasonings Inc., was able to do when confronted by a New York City gay activist group. The activists threatened a "tea party" to dump the company's herbal teas into New York's East River to protest a Colorado amendment banning local laws that protect homosexuals from discrimination. We're talking about a Colorado amendment; Celestial Seasonings had nothing to do with it. In fact, the company opposed the amendment but said it has a policy of not getting involved in political issues.

However, New York City is the company's largest market, and if successful, the boycott could have seriously hurt the company. So, Mr. Siegel flew to New York to meet with Boycott Colorado, the group that was boycotting all consumer products from that state.

The upshot: Mr. Siegel said the group demanded the company go on record as opposing the measure and donate $100,000 or else face a boycott.

In a counterattack, Mr. Siegel went to the press. In a *New York Times* article, Mr. Siegel was quoted saying, "It was outright extortion. They told me that if I didn't put up the money they would destroy me."

By going on the offensive and reporting the group's threats, the company hurt the group's image and ability to mobilize support. Extortionists don't come across as sympathetic, especially when the targeted party has nothing to do with the actual issue. The group denied it had made demands and said it was going to boycott anyway. Just as bad. It's hard to look noble while threatening an innocent party who has not done anything wrong. As a result, the East River remained herbal-tea-free.

In another example, Nike Corporation fought back when Operation Push threatened to boycott the company. The group claimed Nike was exploiting American blacks. Nike enlisted the support of other civil-rights groups after convincing them that Push's charges weren't valid. The company said sales of its sportswear didn't fall during the boycott.

Just to reiterate:

• **A company should not give in to pressure if it has not done anything wrong.**
• **It's another matter if there is any validity to the claims.**

If a company is doing something wrong, the problem has to be addressed. And fixed.

Stating the Issue

The Internet, in addition to being effective in disseminating news in a crisis, can be used proactively to communicate a company's message on a particular issue.

The Web site www.camisea.com was created and managed by Shell Oil in 1998, but it's not about the company per se. That's why the name isn't prominent. Instead, it's about the issue of drilling for oil in a part of the Peruvian rain forest

Camisea. It involved a multicompany effort with local Mobil operations and an engineering consortium including Peruvian and Brazilian partners.

Shell's external affairs manager in Peru said they put up the site to provide accurate information, noting it was raw. He meant readers could look at the environmental impact assessment in its original form. Realizing they were treading on a sensitive issue in a CNN kind of world, the manager said, "The best way to live in that world is to show everyone what you're doing, and the Web is the best way to do that. You can incorporate words, pictures, media in any combination, and people can visit the parts that interest them."

Interestingly enough, the E-mail generated by the site initially came from job-seekers. Then, members of Rainforest Action Network. The Shell person said they had included a link to the group. "They've been hypercritical of us in the past. We knew from the outset that we wanted to do this project differently. Transparency and objectivity were our goals from the outset."

Special-interest groups have become very sophisticated in using the Internet to their advantage. When Greenpeace battled the French government over nuclear testing, the group's home page registered nearly 500,000 hits in one week. It enabled Greenpeace to communicate its key, passionate messages to a global audience with a blow-by-blow description of the event.

Strike Out

Franklin Roosevelt told a story of two Chinese coolies arguing heatedly in the midst of a crowd. A stranger expressed surprise that no blows were being struck. The reply was, "The man who strikes first admits that his ideas have given out."

Companies who skip the arguments and go straight to blows rarely win. The other party might not win either, but both are left with scorched earth. No matter what happens, the process winds up costing a fortune in public opinion as well as dollars. Although business disagreements involve money, economics isn't a sexy topic. It doesn't stir up passion, and a dry subject gets little support.

- **Realize that when confronting a major problem with such groups as activists and unions, the other side is going to hit human buttons.**

This means when facing self-proclaimed underdogs, think in "underdog-ese." We know big is usually associated with bad. If we look at successful labor strikes of the past, we find that the unions were the underdogs, even though they had millions of dollars in their war chests.

The reason is that many companies show no sign of humanity or concern for their own employees. All the public sees is the front of a building. No people or sensitivity.

A company has to focus on an issue's impact on its audiences, not on its own balance sheet. Take an employee with a family of four. That worker is far more concerned about his or her ability to feed them than how a company's bottom line is affected.

Let's say a company is knocking heads with a union. Members are threatening to strike, thereby shutting down the company. At this point, the company is perceived as uncooperative and elitist.

Now, what if it were to say publicly, "Obviously, we have some serious disagreements, and we need to continue negotiating, but please don't use our employees as hostages."

The tables have just been turned. The company cares about

its employees, and the opposing party is the one hurting them. Yes, a company wants to keep operating to avoid a financial loss. A working business means employees continue getting paychecks.

The Sound of Music

The New York City Ballet (NYCB) took a graceful leap to counter a strike by musicians and kept its balance with aplomb. The ballet orchestra members turned into Scrooges during Christmas, of all times. They refused to play during performances of *The Nutcracker* because they didn't like the attendance rules. It was the first time musicians had walked out of *The Nutcracker*, which the NYCB has performed annually since 1954. The ballet went on with taped music—which is what most ballet companies use.

The NYCB's response was as lithe as its dancers. In addition to talking to the media, the ballet's board chairman took out a full-page advertisement to explain the situation. The beginning of the ad turned the tables:

- It noted the importance of music and stressed the orchestra consisted of highly skilled musicians who play beautifully and enhance the dancers' performance.
- It said the ballet believed the musicians cared deeply about their art and the company thought it was tragic they weren't playing the glorious music.

Then, it continued, explaining the issues:

- Rehearsals were not mandatory for the musicians, so many were unrehearsed for performances.

- No dancer ever appeared without rehearsing a role.
- NYCB was proposing to pay more money to musicians who adhered to conventional performance rules, and those who didn't accept the new work rules could receive their current compensation.
- A pay increase would be more costly, but they were prepared to incur the expense to assure consistent quality performances.

It's hard for strikers to generate support against a company extolling their virtues. Plus, public opinion was not swayed in favor of musicians who made $66,000 for twenty-three weeks and complained about rehearsing.

The union also chose the wrong ballet to mess with. *The Nutcracker* is a beloved Christmas tradition that attracts an audience full of, among others, little girls in velvet dresses. The strike did not endear the musicians' cause to parents, especially as they had paid top dollar for their tickets and wanted the whole shebang.

In the end, the strike had little effect on ticket sales. It lasted two weeks, and the musicians agreed to new rehearsal rules.

The NYCB took a high road by not attacking its orchestra. It went on the offensive and presented facts that spoke for themselves. At the same time, it focused on its commitment to artistic quality and was able to promote the fact that NYCB utilizes a live orchestra while most other companies don't.

Say What?

There are times when killer underdogs come out of left field. However, a polite offensive stand can keep a problem under control. One large boycott was started by a major activist group that became publicly upset because it did not like a company executive's innocuous quote in a magazine article. The company was able to contain the problem because top executives showed a willingness to discuss the issues on the table. In some cases, the protesters' complaints about the company were valid; others were not. Because the company solved some of the problems, consumer anger turned into disinterest. It's hard to complain about something that has been fixed. The boycott never officially ended. It just faded away. The damage was negligible.

That's not to say the company gave away the store; it stuck to its guns on some issues. But it also came up with some ideas that went beyond the group's demands. The chagrined boycott leaders had not anticipated the response. They had figured the company would ignore their concerns. Their chances for media exposure came and went after the initial volley. The story of a company cooperating is not news. Fighting, yes. Working together, no.

Leadership:
How to Utilize Emotion

I'm in Charge Here

To be effective in a crisis, a company must be aware of emotional reactions as well as responses.

Think of the day President Ronald Reagan was shot and Secretary of State Alexander Haig stood in front of the cameras barking out the immortal "I'm in charge here." It appeared as if a military coup had just taken place. This is not an approach to use.

When something happens, a company can be humanized through a powerful response that appeals to emotion. The first step begins with a CEO giving a compassionate public statement soon after the incident occurs. Sensitivity is the key. You want the public to know you're in charge. At the same time, you want them to know you care about what happened. Also, you are going to find out what went wrong and fix it.

I've just advised you to take charge while castigating Secretary Haig for doing it. Remember, it's not what you say, but *how* you say it. The difference is in the perception. Secretary Haig's "in charge" sounded like he was taking over the country. Your "in charge" means taking control of a problem. You want to calm the public, not shoot it.

Part of crisis mastering lies in understanding an affected public's concerns about its safety. Is the company treading on issues affecting public health or safety? How about the environment? These are all valid concerns and must be treated with sensitivity as well as responsibility.

Being at the helm is a must. One of the biggest mistakes made in the TWA Flight 800 crash was the long absence of the CEO after the accident. The excuse was he was in London at the time. Doesn't matter. He still could have made a statement to the press in London. The result of his absence—and that of other high-ranking executives—was TWA looked like a cold, uncaring company with no one in charge.

People who are hurt or scared need to be reassured, not ignored.

Now that leaders can be seen face-to-face, the electronic media have changed the way they are perceived. We want them to respond with feeling. So much so that the way emotion is perceived has changed. Think of public tears. During the 1972 presidential race, Senator Edmund Muskie cried in public while defending his wife against unkind newspaper editorials.

His loss of emotional control was perceived as a disabling personal weakness, ending his front-running lead for the Democratic nomination. The shifting attitude toward acceptance of public emotion was illustrated in the 1987 movie *Broadcast News* when a television reporter faked tears during a human-interest interview to show sensitivity.

Utilizing Compassion

Xerox provided an excellent example of corporate concern and leadership when seven Xerox employees were shot by another employee at its warehouse in Hawaii.

Within hours of the shooting, the company put out a statement expressing sorrow and concern. Later that day, Xerox Hawaii's vice president and general manager held a press conference, noting the company's priority was to provide aid and comfort to the families of the victims and to help all of its employees deal with the grieving process.

Then Xerox CEO Rick Thomas arrived the next day and met with employees a few hours before holding a press conference. During the conference, Mr. Thomas spoke of the impact of the tragedy on the victims' families and employees. Here's an excerpt:

Obviously this is a situation we have never faced before. But as we speak, a team of Xerox people is working on a series of items that are designed to ensure that emotionally, and financially, we take care of the victims' families. They're part of our family, too.

He went on to say the assistance included the creation of a policy providing for the financial needs of the families of the victims. He also added that he had met with his employees and told them of the company's grief for what they had gone through, as friends, colleagues, and witnesses to this crime. This is a model response. It demonstrates how:

- **The actions of a company and CEO can be perceived as positive, even under tragic circumstances.**

Loving Care

Connecticut state officials also showed what kindness and compassion can do. In 1998, an employee at the Connecticut Lottery methodically shot four of the lottery's top managers to death, including the president. The employee then killed himself.

Connecticut state officials' humane response is one to emulate. The tragedy occurred on a Friday. Here's what they did over the weekend to try to ease a painful transition for returning employees:

- Grief counselors were stationed throughout the lottery headquarters building.
- A new entrance was built so the workers could avoid the doors they ran through in terror to escape the shooting.
- The killer's desk, chair, and cubicle were taken away.
- Bloodstained offices were sealed, and hallways were reconfigured, to soften the sadness felt by those who missed their supervisors, mentors, and friends.
- Flowers were left on every desk.
- When workers returned, they were personally greeted by the head of security, who had been injured in the shootings.

- Buses were provided for those who wanted to attend two of the funerals, and a lunch was catered for them afterward.
- The state said all employees could have a week off if they wished.

State officials said they understood their efforts couldn't erase the workers' memories and grief. Yet, their response was swift, and they did everything they could do try to comfort the workers.

Internal Coping

Like the story of Xerox, Connecticut Lottery's story is also a model for crisis planning. A responsible company has to include procedures for internal trauma. Talk about the power of emotion. It has a direct impact on a workforce. Employees with post-traumatic stress disorder tend to exhibit a range of reactions, including emotional numbness, social withdrawal, irritability, fearfulness, depression, sleep disturbances, medical problems, substance abuse, and marital problems.

If these issues aren't dealt with, companies will face the cost of increased Workers Compensation claims, high turnover, lowered productivity. . . . You get the point.

CEOs are not immune to being affected by a crisis. Executives have to know they could have feelings of responsibility and guilt as well as some of the other reactions of post-traumatic stress disorder.

A *New York Times* column on how the workplace treats grieving employees elicited dozens of letters, E-mails, and calls from readers. The gist was business relationships are permanently changed by the way bosses respond.

One important point that came out was:

- **Individual bosses, more than any employer policy, set the tone for the workplace response to bereavement.**

One reader wrote, "I would suggest the following title to your article. Some managers can be jerks to a grieving employee, no matter what efforts a company may make to create a sensitive workplace." This is a major point. Companies must ensure their commitment flows down through the ranks.

On the other hand, if business executives treat employees in mourning with sensitivity, they take on larger-than-life dimensions. One man wrote that an executive vice president of operations attended his wife's funeral— "a man I wasn't particularly close to, but one I now have a great deal of respect for."

Evoking Feeling

The Xerox and Connecticut Lottery tragedies show how a company can actually enhance its image by *showing* compassion.

In the Connecticut Lottery example, look at what the placement of flowers on a desk said. Physical action lies not in the act but in what it evokes: conditions, circumstances, and feelings. For example, the scene in *Macbeth* where Lady Macbeth is trying to wash a spot of blood off her hand is not about her quest for soap. Her physical action is interpreting her inner conscience.

Ms. Macbeth shows us how, in real life, many moments of emotion can be revealed by some ordinary, small movement. A CEO caught looking at his watch during an important meeting with employees gives the impression he would clearly like to be somewhere else; a CEO looking at his watch during a press conference during a crisis implies he understandably has much to do.

Curtain Call

Successful crisis mastering lies in realizing the drama of a crisis. It requires a sincere, powerful response that appeals to emotions.

If a company does nothing, it's not doing anything right.

Chapter **4**

Sin #4:

It's Not Our Fault

There was once a CEO who made shareholders and employees ecstatic with his company's outstanding financial performance. He could do no wrong. In fact, admiring the CEO's Midas touch, a reporter asked the CEO to "touch his pen."

However, matters weren't as rosy inside the company. The CFO was getting very nervous about "accounting irregularities," but the CEO had assured him no one would ever know. Then, the SEC became suspicious and discovered the phantom profits. It turned out, not only was the company broke, it had wiped out the money from the employee pension fund. Employees were left with nothing. So were shareholders. Lives were ruined.

Sitting in prison, the CEO continued to claim none of this was his fault.

Welcome to the Fourth Deadly Sin: "It's Not Our Fault," the fatal mistake of not taking responsibility for a problem. This sin is the main reason companies and CEOs lose their reputations. If you think reputation doesn't matter, read on. If you know it does, please read on anyway.

It seems "success always occurs in private and failure in full view." Failure is the by-product of bad behavior. It's hard to fail if you're good.

Corporate Responsibility:
How Right Makes Might

Honest to Goodness

From the time of our Founding Fathers, truth has been held up as a major virtue. When we were little, we learned that George Washington cut down the cherry tree and admitted it with the immortal words "I cannot tell a lie." (The fact that the story may not be true is another matter.)

However, the George Washington story has withstood the test of time. Also, we have Honest Abe. No one has to say Abe who?

The point is we are all taught honesty is the best policy. So how come companies are so afraid of the truth? The public expects accountability. A study by the Henley Centre shows customer loyalty is actually greater toward a company that had a problem and fixed it than a company that hasn't had a problem at all.

Makes sense. Let's say you buy an appliance that is somewhat erratic, working more on inclination than demand. You take it back to the store, and of course, it works.

If the store refuses to take it back, you will not be happy and will most likely take your business elsewhere. You'll probably tell your friends about it, too. In fact, according to the Henley Centre, a consumer's bad service experience will be told to nine other people, and five will be influenced by the story. On the other hand, if the company immediately replaces it without question, not only will you become a loyal customer, you can milk the story at cocktail parties.

The same concept applies to crisis management. When a company is facing a problem, taking responsibility is not only the right thing to do, it's the easiest and produces the best results.

A company doesn't necessarily get off scot-free when it manages a crisis well. There are consequences. The bottom line and the stock could take a hit, and there could be lawsuits, but the damage is relatively short-term in contrast to a poorly managed problem. (See the diagrams on pages 112 and 113.)

A mismanaged crisis brings on the dreaded *Seven Plagues of Unhappy Repercussions:*

Plague #1: Extended duration/negative press.
Plague #2: Angry customers and shareholders.
Plague #3: Lawsuits.
Plague #4: Government investigations.
Plague #5: Public interest groups.
Plague #6: Low employee morale/productivity.
Plague #7: Drop in stock price and earnings.

Each plague begets another. The longer a story is covered, the bigger hit to the company's reputation and bottom line. Screwing up is expensive. Doesn't seem worth it, does it?

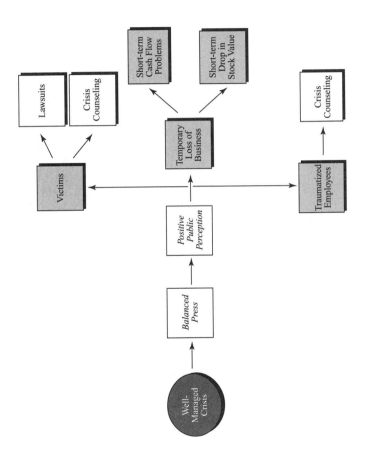

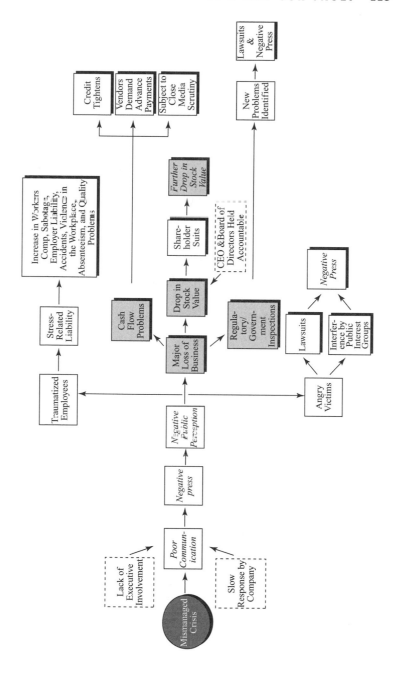

No One Has to Know

The first way to botch a crisis is by trying to hide a problem. "Don't get caught" falls under this category as well. For those who think they can keep bad news from getting out—forget it.

- **The media don't need a company's consent to do a story.**
- **Behind every bad story stands an eager source.**

It may take time before a hidden problem comes to light, but eventually it does. Information leaks like faucets. Such sources as disgruntled employees, competitors, and spouses—all with their own agendas—can and will spill the beans. And don't forget lawyers.

Today, when stories break, we're not just talking about media coverage. People are now venting their anger on the Internet, accurately or otherwise.

- **Caught trying to hide a problem, a company looks even worse for not disclosing it.**

Drip, Drip

Leaks can come from unexpected sources. Take the case of an ex-fiancée of a Philip Morris worker who gave damning files to an antitobacco group in 1996. The woman's former boyfriend, then a Philip Morris researcher, stored boxes of documents in her basement. Falling under the "hell hath no fury . . ." category, after their breakup, the woman turned the documents over to lawyers representing plaintiffs in a class-action suit against

Philip Morris. The lawyers in turn gave the papers to the *Wall Street Journal* and the Justice Department.

Speaking of tobacco, a former top manager at the R. J. Reynolds Tobacco Company secretly told federal regulators in 1994 that the company manipulated nicotine levels in some products to give them more "oompph" and "pizazz," according to a transcript that would up in the *New York Times'* hot little hands in 1998. Of course, we know the transcript beamed itself into the *New York Times* newsroom all by itself.

What Discrimination?

In another case, Richard A. Lundwall taped Texaco executives discussing plans to destroy evidence in a racial discrimination suit. They also made disparaging remarks about minority employees, calling them "black jelly beans" and the "n" word. Mr. Lundwall, then a senior coordinator of personnel in the finance department, was angry when Texaco shoved him into forced retirement during a reorganization. So, he handed the tapes over to the plaintiffs' lawyers of the aforementioned discrimination suit. His action detonated a national furor about Texaco's unfair treatment of minority employees. Texaco wound up paying $176 million to settle the discrimination suit in 1996, a record sum for a bias suit at the time. Legal problems didn't end there. To avoid a discrimination lawsuit by the government, Texaco agreed to a settlement with the Equal Employment Opportunity Commission, giving the EEOC power to scrutinize every detail of the company's hiring and promotion practices for five years.

A human-resources specialist for Texaco was sent down to some godforsaken place to conduct sensitivity training with a bunch of burly oil riggers, who watched her with bemused expressions while they chewed and spit tobacco in her direction. It was not one of her most successful efforts. It isn't easy to change corporate culture, especially with one training session.

Corny Intrigue

Next, we go to Archer Daniels Midland (ADM). This is a real cloak-and-dagger story of how the company's price-fixing practices were discovered. One of its executives, Mark Whitacre, the former president of ADM's BioProducts Division, told the FBI about an illegal price-fixing scheme. He became an informant for more than two-and-a-half years.

The Justice Department was investigating whether ADM conspired with domestic and foreign competitors to rig prices of three corn products: lysine, high-fructose corn syrup, and citric acid.

Once Mr. Whitacre's whistle-blower role became public, ADM fired him, accusing him and three colleagues of embezzling at least $10 million. Mr. Whitacre confessed he personally made about $6.4 million in tax-free money from bogus invoice schemes. He just forgot to mention this to the FBI. The Justice Department chief witness wound up being a crook with a credibility problem.

Meanwhile, the price-fixing probe got very long and complex, involving the CIA, the FBI, the Japanese, and South Koreans. The investigation turned into claims of sabotage and conspiracy. Apparently everyone was eavesdropping on everyone else. ADM wound up pleading guilty to two criminal charges of price fixing and paid a record $100 million fine.

ADM executive vice president and heir apparent Michael Andreas, son of politically connected CEO Dwayne Andreas, and Terrance S. Wilson, head of the corn-processing unit, were found guilty of a worldwide conspiracy to fix the prices of lysine. Michael Andreas was forced to relinquish his title and board seat, and Mr. Wilson "retired."

Mr. Whitacre was found guilty as well, and both Mr. Andreas and Mr. Wilson were sentenced to two years in prison and fined $350,000 each. Dwayne Andreas stepped down as chairman and handed the reins over to his nephew G. Allen Andreas.

The point of this saga is that Mr. Whitacre had secretly taped thousands of hours of conversations and meetings discussing price fixing at ADM and handed over these incriminating video and audiotapes to the government. These tapes also swayed the jury to convict Mr. Andreas and Mr. Wilson.

It may take time for a leak to get out. Mr. Whitacre told the FBI about the company's dubious practices in 1992. The scandal went public in 1996. The same thing with Texaco. The infamous taped meeting was held in August 1994. The story also broke in 1996.

So if anyone's hiding a dubious deed, don't get too comfortable.

A Flood in Cyberspace

The Internet has become the patron saint of the disgruntled. Now a major source of leaks, the Internet often beats the media to the punch. Mentioned earlier, the flawed Intel chip story broke on the Internet. The Clinton-Lewinsky scandal became public, courtesy of gossip Matt Drudge in his infamous on-line "Drudge Report." Public interest groups, unhappy workers, and angry customers are taking out their vengeance on their own Web pages. An address usually ending with "sucks.com" or starting with "Ihate" is a clue someone's mad at a company. In fact, there are so many of these Web pages, there's now a name for them: hate sites. Thanks to our instant age, employees who were once afraid of getting caught leaking company information now have anonymity in cyberspace. Another blow to "no one has to know."

Shooting Oneself in the Foot

One more thing about leaks. Companies can be their own worst enemies. Be careful what you put in writing, on paper, or in cyberspace. Do not write sensitive E-mail messages if you don't want them made public. That's been one of the biggest lessons of the Microsoft antitrust trial. Damaging Microsoft E-mails wound up being introduced into evidence by the government. Bill Gates wrote an internal E-mail message asking his managers to come up with a survey showing 90 percent of developers believe putting the browser into the operating system makes sense. In another E-mail he added he'd like to have the survey before his Senate appearance on March 3. In subsequent messages, employees explained how they would phrase questions to elicit the responses Mr. Gates wanted. Computer geniuses should know E-mail can't be erased. Even after this fiasco, they continued E-mailing sensitive material.

Microsoft introduced a host of new evidence to show the Netscape browser was still healthy and thriving despite its all-out assault on the browser market. This was undercut when a government lawyer produced an E-mail message that indicated the company had selectively produced data to support this point of view.

In the E-mail message, a Microsoft public-relations executive asked others at the company: "What data can we find right away, showing that the Netscape browser is still healthy? The government is introducing a bunch of data showing Netscape headed down big time and Microsoft way up. . . . It would help if you could send me some reports showing their share healthy and holding." Later, a group manager E-mailed back, saying, "All the analyses have pretty much come to the same conclusion, which is that Netscape is declining and Internet Explorer is gaining."

A half-hour later, a director of Windows marketing said he had found one survey showing "us very close on Internet Explorer share. . . . This is for the trial, so let's provide the more negative analysis." After the government lawyer read it aloud, the judge chuckled and shook his head.

Next time, talk face-to-face.

It's Not Our Fault

The worst mistake companies make in a bad situation is putting their own interests before the interests of those affected. Don't do this. Not only is it morally wrong, it's bad for business. A poll conducted by Porter Novelli found 71 percent of the public are upset when companies put profits ahead of public interest. Just think about what all those unhappy folks could do to a bottom line.

Look at A. H. Robins. The company had problems with its intrauterine device, the Dalcon Shield, from the start but ignored and denied evidence that it caused injury and death. When it lost a major lawsuit, a federal court judge summed up public opinion by saying, "You have taken the bottom line as your guiding beacon and the low road as your route. That is corporate irresponsibility at its meanest."

The public agreed; the company went out of business.

In another example, a jury fined CSX Corporation $3.4 billion because it refused to take responsibility for a fire that burned down half of a town. A leaky, unattended rail car filled with thirty thousand gallons of butadiene (used to make carpet backing) caught fire and burned for a day and half in a mostly black neighborhood in New Orleans. Residents in a two-hundred-city-block area had to be evacuated in the middle of the night. The railroad refused to take responsibility for the fire and initially turned down the mayor's frantic plea for help. CSX said it would be improper because residents were already filing suits against the company. The mayor said he had to scream and curse to get CSX to help bring in fire-fighting experts.

Ten years later, in 1997, the case went to trial. The jury decided CSX had to be held accountable to the tune of a billion dollars, not millions. They made no bones about saying they wanted to spur change and send a message that business can't ignore people. One juror explained, "The punishment should fit the crime. . . . It was just a bunch of people being greedy."

The next day, the Louisiana Supreme Court blocked the verdict from taking effect until all the injuries received by all eight thousand victims could be documented. This will take years. However, the jury's message remains clear.

Deadly Beer

An international public affairs expert was called in to assist a foreign brewers association, a group made up of brewing-company presidents. There seemed to be a health problem among some heavy, mainly beer drinkers centered in blue-collar areas. The "health problem" turned out to be a dreadful euphemism for death from severe myocardial infarction.

At first, it had seemed those who had died or were deathly ill had tended to drink an inordinate quantity of beer a day, with little or no food. They also tended to lead rough-and-tumble lives and were not generally in the best of health.

After some hemming and hawing, the association finally told

the consultant there had been some changes in the brewing process. For centuries, gum arabic has been used as a foam stabilizer in the making of beer. But going back several years, a brewery chemist in Denmark had come up with the idea to use cobaltous salts as replacement because it was cheaper, would work more effectively, and perhaps give beer a longer shelf life. So what was the problem?

To try to figure out what was really wrong, the consultant talked to a Ph.D. molecular biologist who had just been awarded a postdoctoral fellowship at the Cavendish Labs in Cambridge. The scientist explained that while cobalt is an essential part of livestock diet, *it is toxic to humans.*

It seems that brewers had played around with cobalt change several years before, but had experimented with it only with their African licensees. Documentary evidence showed numerous deaths had occurred in Africa shortly after the change was made. Beer-guzzling blue-collar workers leading rough-and-tumble lives were becoming deathly ill, too.

The consultant advised the association the best approach was to come clean about the cobalt. Instead, the association wanted to blame the beer drinkers for overdoing it. After all, it did not want to be sued. He told them they were going to be sued anyway, so they might as well get as much goodwill as possible by going public. They said their equivalent of the U.S. FDA had approved the change in additives and thus would have to share the blame. Had the association talked with them about the present deadly situation? Well, no.

There were also outbreaks of the health problem in Ohio, but it was unclear whether domestic U.S. beer or imports were the cause. By this time, the problem was beginning to get international media attention. Falling into the "shoot-the-messenger" category, the association blamed the consultant for the bad press and sent him packing.

Shortly afterward, the dominos began to fall after the first brewery went bankrupt. For some reason, the customers had little sympathy for the beer producers.

Cruising for a Bruising

Sadly, greed can raise its ugly head in the best of companies. The world's most famous luxury liner, the *Queen Elizabeth 2* (QE2), was in the midst of a $45 million refurbishing. In 1994, although the renovations were not completed, the ship set sail on a transatlantic trip. Ticket prices at that time ranged from $2,100 to $8,760.

Because of the premature sailing, five hundred passengers were left behind in Britain because their cabins were not ready. The six hundred remaining passengers were subjected to faulty plumbing and repair problems, which turned their vacations into a foul-smelling fiasco complete with brown water in toilets and dangling electric wires. Adding to the ship's woes, it encountered rough weather at sea and arrived in New York behind schedule.

When it did arrive, the Coast Guard held the ship at the dock for thirty-seven hours to correct safety violations before it allowed the ship to sail on a Christmas Caribbean cruise. Adding to the embarrassment, the QE2 folks had planned to show off its new face-lift at a luncheon for hundreds of dignitaries, travel agents, and the press. Instead, the QE2 came in late and in great dishabille.

The media had a field day. When the ship docked, the press was out in droves interviewing irate passengers. The company refused to talk to the media.

As a result of the ill-fated cruise, the ship's parent company:

- Paid $11.8 million in compensation and free trips to angry passengers.

- Faced litigation from 120 aggrieved passengers seeking $100,000 per person in compensation and created a $50 million fund for any future health problems they may suffer as a result of the ship's condition.
- Took a $22.6 million pretax loss for the first half of the year.
- Accepted the resignation of the cruise line's chief executive officer.
- Received damaging negative publicity and ill will.

This is a classic example of a company being penny-wise and pound-foolish. Clearly, the ship was not ready to sail. It would have cost far less to cancel the cruise than suffer the tangible and intangible consequences that followed. It appears some high-ranking bean counter put the company's financial well-being ahead of its passengers' comfort. This is especially ironic for a luxury liner known for its first-class service. While canceling the trip would have meant refunding money and disappointing passengers, the cruise line could have protected its reputation and bottom line by going out of its way to take care of its passengers—providing alternative transportation, sending a token gift along with sincere apologies—thus maintaining its reputation as the Queen of the Global Seas.

So Long

Notice how the QE2's CEO got the boot for mishandling the mess. For those at the top, one of the ramifications of screwing up is not only embarrassment. Think job loss.

Going back to the TWA Flight 800 crash, Jeffrey H. Erickson, CEO of TWA at the time, "quit" three months after the accident. Most attribute his departure to his botched crisis performance. In fact, analysts believe the way Mr. Erickson and the airline mishandled the tragedy probably compounded the problem of slumping ticket sales.

Ironically, prior to the accident, Mr. Erickson was widely lauded for reviving TWA's financial health as he guided the airline through six consecutive quarters of operating profits.

In another case, Coca-Cola CEO Douglas Ivester announced his retirement about five months after the Belgian contamination/ recall crisis occurred. Although the perception is the crisis caused his downfall, other problems occurred during his reign as well. Coca-Cola was unable to clear government hurdles to acquisitions abroad. It experienced slowing sales, and the stock lost more than 11 percent of its value. The high-profile European debacle was the last straw. That misstep is all the public remembers.

As these examples illustrate, no top executive is invincible. Even Michael Andreas, the boss's son, was kicked out of Archer Daniels Midland.

So, for those who think taking responsible action in a crisis is a bunch of hooey, think again.

Shifting Blame:
How to Prevent Escalating Damage

The Dog Ate It

To look really bad, try blaming others. A Porter Novelli poll of more than one thousand adult customers showed 76 percent of consumers are angry when companies refuse to accept blame for problems. We learned what happened to Audi when it blamed its customers for getting into accidents—even though the drivers were ultimately at fault.

After the Bhopal incident, the Union Carbide CEO said safety was the responsibility of those who ran the plants. The parent company in the United States wasn't responsible. At one point, the company even said the plant had been sabotaged. This reminds me of the cowboy guide rule "If you find yourself in a hole, the first thing to do is stop diggin'."

Former Sunbeam CEO Al Dunlap blamed Sunbeam's earnings problems on El Niño. "People don't think about buying grills during a storm," he explained.

He failed to mention his alleged "bill-and-hold" scam of recording the sale of goods but holding them in the warehouse. This combo is forbidden unless a customer has taken bona fide ownership of the goods and has requested they be stored.

The Jack in the Box hamburger crisis is a classic example of how a company made a bad situation worse by trying to shift the blame through finger-pointing. The company, which served beef contaminated with E. coli bacteria, blamed its meat supplier for the tragic consequences. No doubt about it, the supplier provided contaminated beef. However, the State Department of Health said the bacteria would have been killed if Jack in the Box had cooked the beef at the correct temperature.

Jack in the Box management insisted the company was the victim, blaming not only the meat company, but the State Department of Health and the U.S. government as well.

Jack in the Box executives said they never used the word "blame." In a national television interview, the president claimed the Health Department was inept and the product was the reason for the crisis, not undercooking. The restaurant's television ads said its supplier was responsible for the tragedy, and in a conference call with investors, the CEO said he believed the company was the victim, not the culprit.

Whether it actually said "blame" or not, the perception was the company was blaming others.

When you get a hamburger from Burger King, do you think of it as a Burger King hamburger or the meat supplier's? Most of us don't know where the meat comes from, nor do we want to.

• **The buck has to stop where it lands last.**

Compare a "not our fault" attitude with a statement made by an America Online vice president when the entire system blacked out for nineteen hours. Declining to name the vendor of the routing software, he said, "This was our problem, and we take responsibility for it."

AOL's computer-outage problem wasn't nearly as serious as the Jack in the Box crisis, but it still shows how a company comes out looking better if it comes forward and takes responsibility.

This goes back to how to handle a question without inferring blame. Using the Jack in the Box "who is your meat supplier?" query, there are three choices:

1. XYZ is our meat supplier.
2. XYZ is our meat supplier; it's their fault.
3. XYZ is our meat supplier; however, the buck stops here at Jack in the Box.

It's all a matter of taking control of the situation. The third answer implies moral responsibility and begins shaping the story. Also, it's on the record. The first answer, though accurate, is open-ended, leaving itself open to interpretation. The second answer speaks for itself.

When Regulators Regulate

If another source is to blame and a company is left holding the bag, it should try to let another party say it. It will have more credibility and will look better for it. For example, in the Jack in the Box's case, the contaminated beef issue would have been addressed by the State Department of Health and the FDA anyway.

It doesn't make sense for a company to alienate the very people who regulate and make public statements about it. In the

"That's him! That's the culprit."

Jack in the Box case, blaming the regulators led the regulators, in turn, to fire back. For example, one Health Department inspector said point-blank, "If they had followed the standards, no one would have gotten sick."

A bad situation can be contained when a company works with regulatory officials. When a Russian IBM subsidiary pleaded guilty to illegally exporting advanced computers to a Russian nuclear weapons laboratory, U.S. prosecutors made it clear there was no evidence that IBM's American executives were aware or involved in any way. "IBM acted in a highly responsible manner by cooperating with the government," said the assistant U.S. attorney who prosecuted the case.

Then, there is the Schwan's ice-cream crisis. When bacteria were discovered in its ice cream, Schwan's cooperated with the Health Department throughout the investigation, and the local officials helped the company reestablish its reputation. The company held an ice-cream social to celebrate the reopening of its plant, with the governor of Minnesota (pre Jesse Ventura days) in attendance.

Just goes to show what a concerted effort can do. True, there are times a company has no choice but to fight—only if all peaceful possibilities have failed.

Mitsubishi was another company that made a bad situation worse by picking a fight with a government entity. The Equal Employment Opportunity Commission had charged the company with the largest sexual-harassment suit in its history. To protest the agency's actions, Mitsubishi staged a march and demonstration in front of the Chicago EEOC office. "Stage" is the operative word here. Employees who participated got a day off and a full day's pay. The whole Mitsubishi story is a doozie (continued in Sin #6). The company's attempt to discredit the EEOC backfired, making matters worse.

There's nothing wrong in wanting to show employee loyalty,

but it has to be employee inspired and held at an appropriate time and place.

Bully for You

Microsoft didn't score a lot of points for its combative stance against the government prior to its antitrust trial in 1999. A "take-no-prisoners approach" to fighting the Justice Department is not the most diplomatic or successful route to take. Microsoft officials publicly characterized the Justice Department's antitrust division as "little more than the unwitting dupes of Microsoft's rivals." An executive vice president was quoted as saying "to heck with [Attorney General] Janet Reno."

It's like going in for an operation you don't want to have and announcing to the world beforehand that your surgeon is a jerk.

One legal expert said, "Microsoft has gratuitously made high-octane statements that may make their people feel good at the time. But in the end, those kind of tactics work against Microsoft."

Microsoft's insulting remarks and belligerent stance against the Justice Department backfired. The media, covering the trial, gleefully reported Microsoft's missteps and embarrassments in the hands of the government's lead trial lawyer, David Boies, one of the "unwitting dupes." It's usually the government who's portrayed as the bad guy in the press. Ironically, thanks to Mr. Boies, the government wound up looking like David versus the Microsoft Goliath.

At the same time, Intel took a low-profile route when it was under investigation for antitrust practices. Intel was accused of violating the patent rights of three other computer makers. Regardless of how management really felt, Intel was careful not to antagonize the court. As a result, the company managed to escape an unflattering image in the press.

While the Microsoft circus was going on, Intel settled its antitrust suit. It agreed to stop withholding technical details about its chips when it becomes mixed up in patent disputes with its customers.

"Although we have different interpretations regarding Intel's market position and the legality of our past actions, the compromise provides a framework for resolving future intellectual property disputes with our customers," Intel president Craig Barrett said. He gracefully made the point that Intel didn't agree with the Justice Department, but he did not insult the players.

As for Microsoft, it appears to have seen the error of its ways. The company toned down its rhetoric and became much more respectful during the trial.

Politics in a Crisis:
How to Prepare for the Inevitable

It Will All Blow Over

When a crisis occurs, that's just the beginning of a company's woes. The problems grows, thanks to help from the outside. Crises fall into the "everyone-into-the-pool" category:

- **Crises become ripe for political picking.**

Like moths to a flame, the media attention garnered by a problem brings out all sorts of people who have their own agendas. Expect this to happen.

Opportunity Knocks

For instance, after the TWA Flight 800 crash, politicians and federal officials swooped down on the site to get their share of the spotlight. Here's who showed up (not counting National Transportation Safety Board members, FAA officials, and the FBI, who were there doing their jobs):

* President and Mrs. Clinton
* New York governor George Pataki
* New York senator Alphonse D'Amato
* Congressman/House Speaker Newt Gingrich
* U.S. congressman Charles Schumer
* New York mayor Rudolph Giuliani
* New Jersey senator Frank Lautenberg
* Pennsylvania governor Tom Ridge
* New York congressman Michael Forbes (Long Island)
* New York congressman Ben Gelman (Peekskill)
* Suffolk County executive Robert Gaffney
* Federal Emergency Management director James Lee Witt

Keep in mind, they all held news conferences after their visits, and some released premature or erroneous information. Their presence also meant rescue workers and investigators had to arrange tours, taking time and manpower away from more-crucial efforts. The politicians, however, got their fifteen minutes of fame and kept public attention focused on the story.

In another example, after the tragic Columbine High School shooting near Denver in 1999, many politicians visited the grieving community, including Vice President Al Gore. Sarah Ferguson (Fergie), the duchess of Windsor, also showed up.

This is the very same Fergie who claims the press has taken advantage of her.

Emotional issues open the doors to various activist groups who use events to attract visibility they would not receive otherwise. This is another way a story grows. Such examples are:

* A Federal sexual-harassment suit against Mitsubishi attracted protests by the National Rainbow Coalition, Operation Push, and NOW.

* The Texaco scandal brought out the National Urban League, the New York State division of the NAACP, as well as the Reverends Jessie Jackson and Al Sharpton.

* Nestlé's "killer" baby formula turned out War on Want, the International Nestlé Boycott Committee (INBC), the Infant Formula Action Coalition (INFACT), the Interfaith Center for Corporate Responsibility (ICCR), the World Council of Churches (WCC), Ralph Nader, and Cesar Chavez.

* A World Trade Organization meeting in Seattle attracted Greenpeace, Friends of the Earth, the Sierra Club, Public Citizen, anarchists, and steel workers.

For the media, the activist angle is manna from heaven because it gives them something new to report. The front of a building is not newsworthy, but protesters in front are. This kind of visible element is lively and keeps a story from getting stagnant.

* **If a company is taking responsible action, there's little to protest against.**

Quick, Find a Scapegoat

There are times when a crisis gets caught in a political cross fire. ValuJet is a prime example. On May 11, 1996, a ValuJet plane crashed in the Florida Everglades, killing all 110 people on board. The accident was caused by illegally stored oxygen generators that caught fire in the cargo hold. ValuJet's maintenance services were handled by SabreTech, an independent company responsible for the packaging and loading of the generators.

The airline, once praised for its low fares and fast growth, was now blamed for its cost-cutting and safety practices. Following the accident, ValuJet hired a "safety czar" and resumed flying about 50 percent of its schedule while its fleet was inspected by the FAA. However, the airline was subsequently grounded by the FAA for safety and maintenance practices. That essentially killed the airline. The climate had turned, and the perception was that a no-frills airlines compromised on safety in order to offer low fares. ValuJet eventually resumed service and merged with Airtran, assuming the name.

This is a case of politics and perception. USAir (now US-Airways) had five crashes in five years. Yet, the FAA didn't shut it down, and the airline stayed in business after every accident.

Why ground ValuJet?

The airline got caught in the midst of a political slugfest. At the time of the tragedy, the transportation inspector general leapt into the media spotlight. Making the most out of her fifteen minutes of fame, she set up a media tour and went on a tangent about FAA incompetence. She pummeled the agency for certifying low-cost carriers and commuter airlines. She fanned her flame against the FAA and low-cost carriers in a *Newsweek* article, saying, "I avoided flying on ValuJet." Well, this whipped the public and politicians and other regulators into a frenzy.

The FAA's back was to the wall. As a result of national waves of criticism, the FAA had to do something. So it grounded the airline for more than three months. ValuJet became the scapegoat.

ValuJet appeared to have had a good chance of making it back to preaccident levels if the FAA hadn't shut it down. Lots of airlines continue flying after accidents. While the inspector general was saying how big carriers were safe and low-cost carriers weren't, there was no mention of USAir's track record, or TWA's, or Northwest's, or United's, or American's, or that of any other major airline that has experienced accidents.

ValuJet also provided opportunities for additional players. It became a convenient excuse for other low-cost carriers facing financial difficulties. Claiming the publicity hurt all small carriers, little airlines like Kiwi International, Frontier Airlines, and JetTrain said they lost summer business in the wake of the ValuJet crash. Some didn't have the business anyway, but it's always great to have an excuse.

Yes, ValuJet had safety violations prior to the crash and disgruntled employees. But they didn't warrant a shutdown. Inspection, yes. The longer the airline stayed grounded, the longer the story hung around. Its resumption of service brought another onslaught of press. Extensive media coverage. Political agendas. A deadly combination.

No Anniversary Present

There are other ways a story is extended. For starters, anniversaries are a great way to have mistakes rehashed. The first anniversary of a crisis is a big story. Major crises like the Oklahoma City bombing and the TWA Flight 800 crash get noted annually. Then, there are milestone anniversaries. For example, there was a lot of hoopla over the tenth anniversary of the Exxon Valdez oil spill. Not only did we get reruns of the accident in the media, new issues came to light. There were reports Exxon's oil tankers were caught speeding in Prince William Sound. Exxon was also raked over the media coals because there were claims its clean-up crews weren't prepared for another disaster.

Anniversaries are hell on companies whose crises have slipped out of the public's mind. It's like parents who finally get their screaming babies to sleep, praying a noise doesn't wake them. A company with a past crisis tiptoes around, and just as it thinks it's safe to breathe easily—WHAM. The press wakes up. Happy anniversary.

Made-for-television movies are also known to keep a crisis going. Not to mention political recognition. President Reagan brought up the Air Florida crash during a State of the Union address. The Pan Am Lockerbie crash led to years of trials and tribulations in getting the terrorists out of Libya to be tried in the United States.

A company can't prevent an anniversary story or a movie from being made, but:

- **It can be ready with a compassionate statement concerning the incident if asked to comment.**

It's All Relative

Also to be considered are story-related incidents. Like lawsuits. At one point, a reporter from the Associated Press called at 2:00 A.M. for a response when the first lawsuit was filed against Air Florida after the Flight 90 crash.

Month after month, the press would call every time a suit

was filed, stringing the story along. They all received the same answer: "As with any tragedy, the suits were expected." They never gave up asking. The only good news is they called during the day.

Another example of a related incident involved the TWA Flight 800 crash. In one case, two freelance "investigative journalists" snuck into a government hangar and stole two small pieces of seat fabric from the plane's wreckage. The couple was using them to back up their theory that the plane was brought down by a navy missile. Hundreds of FBI and National Transportation Safety Board investigators spent millions of hours of their time putting zillions of pieces of the airplane back together to figure out the cause, and these two came to their conclusion with mere scraps of fabric. The duo was later convicted of conspiracy and aiding in the theft of government property.

Sin #1 mentioned the Keefe Bruyette & Woods story about a banker who passed along insider trading tips to his porn star girlfriend. The story, since dubbed the "Stocks and Blondes" scandal, continued making headlines, to the obvious dismay of the staid banking firm. Put money and sex together, and you've got a lot of gleeful reporters with an ongoing story.

Also, in terms of story extensions, attorneys are very good at getting press attention for their clients. If you have noticed, the media stories about complaints are usually the results of clients going to their lawyers.

They'll Sue Anyway

Law and morality are not always synonymous.

- **Some actions that are legally acceptable may be morally unacceptable.**

Legal considerations play a vital part in a company's response during a crisis; however, they should not be the determining factor.

- **The CEO is the one who has to make the choice between profit and responsible behavior.**

Choosing profit is not all that profitable if a company's image is tarnished. There doesn't seem any point to winning in a court of law if a company no longer has any customers.

This applies to any problem, especially when money is involved. For example, an important customer of a famous, ritzy auction house bought a pair of ruby-and-diamond earrings for $132,000 in 1987. He said the auction house told him at the time he could resell them for a great deal more than he had paid. Flash-forward to 1998. The customer had the rubies tested by the Swiss Gemological Institute. One of the stones was not genuine. It had been thermally enhanced and contained artificial residues. He was left with one ruby worth less than a fraction of what he had paid for the pair. So, he asked the company to compensate him for the difference.

You wouldn't think there would be a problem. There was. The auction house wrote the customer saying 1987 testing methods weren't as advanced as they are now and that, anyway, the limited warranty of six years had expired. It said that at the time of the sale gem labs didn't disclose heat treatment nor was it a practice in the industry to do so. Cloaked by legality, the company said it was not until 1998 that the Gubelin Gemological Laboratory, the recognized authority on precious stones, disclosed heat treatments in its reports. It wrote, "U.S. regulations governing the disclosure of heat treatment were not promulgated until 1996."

In other words, the auction house said, "Tough. We sold you fake goods, but technically, we're not responsible."

- **Just because something is legal doesn't necessarily make it right.**

Here was a good customer who happened to be very wealthy and influential. Yet, the company sought to hide behind legal protection. How much would it have cost to compensate the customer? Certainly a lot less than the issuing legal costs and bad press, not to mention the loss of credibility and business. It's doubtful the customer will ever buy another bauble from them.

Handle with Care

The public has expectations of moral business conduct whether we're talking about products or lives. The A. H. Robbins and CSX examples bring that point home. Both companies chose to put profits ahead of people. That choice ultimately wound up being very expensive.

A company has to be protected, but at the same time, it has to provide a public response.

- **To avoid dangerous missteps, get fights about legal requirements and communication out of the way before something happens.**

There's no time to debate once all hell breaks loose.

When a problem occurs, spokespeople need to know what they can say and what they can't. The "can't" is especially important; otherwise someone could inadvertently spill the bad beans.

The following advice was given by two attorneys, John Buckley and F. Samuel Eberts III, who represented Schwan's Sales Enterprises when dangerous bacteria had been found in its ice cream.

Acceptance of responsibility without acceptance of liability is possible. You need not admit liability when publicly pronouncing you are sorry your customers have been injured, you are doing everything to discover whether your company has a role in such an injury, and in such a case, you will do everything in your power to cure the problem. A well-timed apology and promise to get to the bottom of the matter can often defuse a potential crisis or lessen its intensity.

That is the essence of effective crisis management. Explained by lawyers.

Actually Schwan's did a great job managing the problem. What happened was the Minnesota Department of Health told Schwan's there was linkage between its ice cream and an unusually large number of reports of salmonellosis. Schwan's immediately stopped production of the ice cream, held onto further shipments, and recalled all of its ice cream. The company publicized the information and alerted its customers.

Schwan's also set up a toll-free telephone number to receive and record customer complaints. This hot line later became the basis of Schwan's legal solution—settle the claims to satisfy the customers. By the time plaintiffs' class-action lawyers could get organized and obtain a hearing on class-certification issues, Schwan's had resolved more than 80 percent of the claims made to the phone bank. Schwan's then settled one class-action suit encompassing a national class of its customers, which prevented the need for any further large-scale litigation.

According to Mr. Buckley and Mr. Eberts:

- **Schwan's actions minimized the damage to customers and maintained the loyalty of its customer base.**

Those two attorneys aren't the only ones who have discovered victims are more likely to settle than sue if treated well. In a presentation at The Risk and Insurance Management Society, Inc., conference, litigation attorney David B. Zoffer recommended the following steps to prepare for a company response to disasters. According to a Rand Corporation Institute for Civil Justice study, these procedures led to a 30 percent reduction in the overall cost of resolving claims and shortened the time of claim resolutions by 50 percent. Procedures include:

- Dealing effectively, promptly, and reasonably in providing care and assistance to the injured, their families, and the immediate relatives of any deceased.
- Coordinating rescue efforts with police, fire, emergency medical services, and other city, state, and federal agencies.
- Providing accurate and timely information.
- Assisting appropriate investigating agencies in fact-gathering and analyzing the circumstances surrounding the accident accurately and completely without impairing the company's legal position.
- Responding promptly and effectively to media questions and public concerns.

These are classic rules by which to live. Mr. Zoffer went on to talk about other actions, but in a nutshell, he was saying:

- **A company is going to be in better shape acting responsibly.**

It goes without saying those affected will be, too. Mr. Zoffer said the procedures work with any kind of major loss.

Mum's Not the Word

Ironically, while we have attorneys who've learned to utilize the media, there are those who believe in taking the "don't say anything" route. This is not to say a company has to spill its guts, but it can't close up like a clam.

One international resort was facing two lawsuits from women claiming to have been raped by employees at different locations. The story wound up in the tabloids, with big headlines.

Within days, the resort's reservations department was bombarded by calls from concerned customers. Travel agents had their hands full as clients began canceling their reservations. Bookings went down. Employees didn't know what to say to public queries and wondered why management wasn't sticking up for the company.

One would think the story had to be true or the company would have denied it. Wrong.

This is a story that got out of hand, thanks to legal tongue-tying. It turns out both claims were "without merit," meaning they were bogus.

One claim came from a woman who got mad when a resort employee spurned her advances. Luckily for the accused, there were lots of witnesses who saw her storm off to her room as others watched him falling off a bar stool when the deed was allegedly done. This woman happened to be neighbors with a disgruntled resort employee who had been fired and boasted how she was going to "get" the company.

So the women went to one of the tabloids. When the first reporter called the company, the lawyer's advice was not to say anything. As a result, the article only had the women's version.

The coverage grew. The two women, looking so sad and vulnerable, seemed credible, while the resort appeared to be cold and heartless.

Then, a reporter from a national television show called. That woke up the company. Over the lawyer's objections, a crisis consultant was called in.

The company told its side of the story to the television reporter and, with the consent of a few of the witnesses, invited the reporter to call them. Naturally, because they were available, he didn't.

The flame was doused. The reporter went back to the women's lawyers. The result was a lukewarm story. Meanwhile, the accusers knew the jig was up, and that was the end of their media campaign.

None of the reporters went back and wrote the company had been wrongly accused. However, the story died a sudden death, and business got back to normal.

The company could have nipped the story in the bud by telling the first reporter it didn't want to embarrass the women in public but their claims were not true. It could then have briefly explained why. That would have made the company look sensitive and responsible. Even if it didn't want to go into the details, the company could have offered general information. Plus, it could have invited the reporter to cover the trial.

- **A company that doesn't talk is immediately suspected of wrongdoing.**

One that does, isn't. In many cases, reporters are on fishing expeditions. When a company is saying it has nothing to hide, a story often tends to dry up.

Due to the sensitivity of the issue, the resort needed to not only deny the accusation, but show its concern for the welfare of its guests. "No merit" doesn't cut it. In fact, it's devoid of emotion. Albeit belatedly, the company president sent a letter to travel agents and employees. He explained the situation and stressed the company's main concern was the safety and well-being of its guests. He also apologized for the company's slow response. Scripts were provided to relieved reservation and customer-service representatives, who finally knew what to say to those calling about the allegations. Chapter closed.

It's important to stress the delicacy of these matters.

• **True or false, sexual-harassment and sexual-misconduct claims must be treated quickly with sensitivity and concern, or the accused company's reputation is going to suffer.**

Ask Carnival Cruise Lines. The company reported in court papers that its crew members were accused of sexually assaulting passengers and fellow workers aboard its ships sixty-two times in the five years ending in August 1998. The cruise line was forced to produce the numbers in connection with a lawsuit filed against the company by a former crew member who said she was raped and sodomized by an officer aboard a ship. According to the suit, the woman immediately told ship security that she had been attacked and identified her attacker but was persuaded not to file a report. Carnival said she didn't file a report and maintained the sex had been consensual, which she has repeatedly denied.

The company appeared unprepared for the resulting media onslaught. First, when the papers were filed, the company's spokesperson said he wasn't aware of the assault figures and referred questions to Carnival's lawyer, who served as Carnival's spokesperson. Where were Carnival's top executives? There didn't appear to be any in sight.

The lawyer did all the talking; he showed up everywhere in the media. He rationalized the numbers instead of expressing the company's concern for safety. On ABC's *Good Morning America,* he attacked the woman who had filed the suit. If the woman hadn't been a sympathetic victim before, she became one.

Two weeks later, Carnival released new figures to the media, raising its tally of reports to 108, but said there were only twenty-two rape allegations and most of the cases were less serious than previously indicated. The majority of the "less-serious" cases involved accusations of unwanted touching and kissing, and other inappropriate advances. It's questionable whether most women would consider those offenses minor.

However, Carnival put the figures into context, noting the cruise line had carried 6.5 million passengers during those five years. That response could have been even more effective if the company had used it while addressing passenger safety concerns when the story broke.

Sexual assault is an emotional issue, not one based on facts. It needs to be addressed quickly. It appears the cruise line finally saw the light. Carnival's president said, "Even one allegation is one too many." Good statement, but late. That is what should have been said at the start. By that time, the damage in terms of perception had been done.

Wanting to hide is understandable, but top executives must be the ones to respond in public under these kinds of circumstances. Sexual assault is a very scary subject, and consumers want to know what a company is doing about it. Any number reported would have caused an emotional reaction. It was naive to think the figures would not turn into a full-blown crisis. The company should have been ready to respond before the papers were even filed.

- **If public documents containing explosive information are filed, a company has to expect media attention and prepare for it.**

The lawsuit that ignited all the problems was quietly settled out of court.

Responsible Companies in Action:
How to Enhance a Reputation

The Crisis Masters

No company has been criticized for acting responsibly. A company has the opportunity to diffuse or lessen a problem's intensity. There's a hackneyed expression that happens to be so true: "Out of crisis comes opportunity." The right response can enhance a company's image regardless of the nature of the incident.

Luby's Cafeteria crisis is a good example. Luby's is a chain of restaurants in the southern United States On October 16, 1991, a gunman drove his pickup truck through the front window of Luby's Cafeteria in Kileen, Texas, shooting and killing twenty-four people.

Luby's CEO, Ralph Erben, left his San Antonio office immediately upon learning of the tragedy and personally directed all operations with investigators and families for the next four days. He stopped Luby's stock from trading on the New York Stock Exchange. When it began trading two days later, its value went up more than one point.

During the crucial first twenty-four hours of the tragedy, Mr. Erben:

- Offered the city of Killen a $100,000 trust fund for victims.
- Met with local employees and made sure the rest were accounted for.
- Requested Luby's employees attend a prayer session the morning after the murders.
- Offered long-term psychiatric care to any employee who needed assistance.
- Assured employees they would receive full pay until the restaurant reopened.

Mr. Erben also offered to close the site if local residents wanted him to, but they wanted it to be reopened. When the restaurant did open in March 1992, there were lines waiting to get in.

After the crisis, Mr. Erben said he had utilized Luby's crisis-management plan, written a year earlier. Although it dealt with food sanitation and issues other than violence, he said the fact that he had a plan, had thought in advance of the myriad decisions inherent in a crisis, helped him respond.

- **Mr. Erben's actions show how advance planning and empathy turned his actions into a textbook case of effective crisis management.**
- **It's better to be recognized for doing something right rather than something wrong.**

Sober in Cyberspace

Fortunately, there are still a lot of responsible executives out there. After the terrible shootings at Columbine High School in Littleton, Colorado, America Online (AOL) took a lot of heat. One of the gunmen had a Web page that included instructions on how to build pipe bombs, a picture of a creature holding a shotgun while standing on a pile of skulls with a knife, and the song lyrics: "What I don't do I don't like. What I don't like I waste."

AOL was criticized for letting that kind of page be posted. In a *New York Times* Op-Ed article about the roles of the NRA and AOL in the shootings, *Times* columnist Thomas Friedman called AOL's CEO, Steve Case. He said he expected Mr. Case to say AOL had nothing to do with this story. Instead, Mr. Friedman found Mr. Case was truly wrestling with the issue of free speech and censorship. "I share the outrage that everyone feels about this incident," Mr. Case said, "and to the extent that there is an Internet connection . . . it is alarming and troubling. This is especially hard for me because I have spent most of my life building a medium that I want to be used for the better."

He went on to talk about how the Internet has given people unlimited choices and unlimited power to make them. He urged parents and teachers to pay more attention to what their kids were doing.

Mr. Case could have taken an "it's not our fault" position. Instead, his willingness to talk about the issue showed moral concern. He was able to discuss the realities, good and bad, of the Internet without blaming anyone. He brought out the need for adult supervision, but he wasn't passing the buck.

Mr. Friedman was clearly impressed that Mr. Case didn't brush him off. He, like so many of us, assumed CEOs in his situation would stay behind closed doors. Look how Mr. Case's acknowledgment changed the perception. His explanation probably went a long way in generating the sub-headline in Mr. Friedman's column: "Guns kill, Webs don't."

All the Right Moves

The Ashland oil spill occurred one year before the Exxon Valdez crisis, yet one rarely hears about it. CEO John Hall came out a winner even though one of Ashland's storage tanks had exploded, releasing nearly 1 million gallons of diesel fuel into the Monongahela River near Pittsburgh. Within days, the oil flowed into the Ohio River all the way to Louisville, Kentucky. The crisis affected seventeen communities and killed two thousand birds and eleven thousand fish.

- **Ashland's response was immediate and visible.**
- **Ignoring legal advice, Mr. Hall took full responsibility for the accident, admitting actions that had clear legal implications.**

To survey and clean up the damage, the company hired contractors, utilized Ashland employees, alerted the Coast Guard, and mobilized boats, helicopters, and planes.

Mr. Hall and other top executives worked with a number of concerned agencies and the media and took officials on tours of the spill area. The company also brought in temporary piping to provide communities with clean drinking water. It began its own investigation and also hired an outside firm to look into the explosion. Although both reports were damaging, the company released them. According to *CEO Brief,* employee morale was maintained, and the rumor mill was contained within the company by keeping employees informed of the company's actions throughout the crisis.

As a result, the company won such news coverage as "Oil spill response gets good ratings," *Pittsburgh Post-Gazette;* "Ashland getting praise for candor . . . quick action on spill may boost Ashland Oil's image," *Louisville Courier-Journal.* A positive *Wall Street Journal* article on crisis management was subtitled "How Ashland's (CEO) John Hall handled the fuel spill."

Compare this to how Exxon's oil spill was managed and perceived.

A Reliable Recall

In another example, Proctor & Gamble took ethical action when its Rely tampons were associated with toxic shock syndrome. The product, introduced in 1977, was quite successful. It was made with two new fibers that worked much better than cotton. Then, bad news. Close to nine hundred cases of toxic shock syndrome had been reported to the Center for Disease Control in Atlanta. The cause was a complete mystery until researchers discovered the common element in most of the cases was the use of Rely tampons.

P&G acted rapidly to recall the product.

- **It made the recall decision even though there was no evidence directly linking Rely and toxic shock at that time.**

In fact, it wasn't until 1985 that scientists discovered the cause was attributable to the new fibers in the Rely product.

P&G didn't have to do anything. It could have played victim and said the toxic shock syndrome wasn't the fault of their products. Instead, the company studied the available information and decided there was a connection. As a result, P&G showed its commitment to protect its customers.

Not only did the decision save lives, it also saved the company from the enormous expense of product liability suits that it would have incurred if the product hadn't been recalled. That's not to say there weren't any suits, but there were substantially fewer than there would have been.

Rolling Along

Here's another story of how a company turned a problem around. Hewlett Packard (HP) discovered its popular inkjet printers made at its Vancouver plant sometimes failed to grab the top sheet of paper in their feeder trays.

They had a choice:

- **Pretend the problem didn't exist or turn it to an advantage.**

HP chose the latter. The company decided to take control of the problem before most customers learned about it. It wound up developing an easy-to-use roller-repair kit for people who bought any of the one-and-a-half million affected printers. It sent the free kits to all registered owners of those printers and asked everybody else to call a toll-free number to ask for the kit.

One customer was so pleased with HP's roller-repair kit, he posted a note applauding the company on an on-line bulletin board. What a contrast to the Intel customer's flawed chip complaint, which also ran on the Internet.

The problem had not been a snap to fix. The company committed forty full-time engineers to develop a remedy.

Small wonder HP has a strong reputation for reliability and

customer service. Bob Weiss, general manager of HP's Vancouver division, said, "It goes back to the values you manage business by. Customers always come first in our value set."

Piping Down

When talking about corporate responsibility, one can't ignore Tiger Electronics, a unit of Hasbro Inc. The company made it easier to shut up a Furby, an electronic talking toy. The Furby craze started during the 1998 Christmas season, and sales continued strong. The original little creatures chattered incessantly, giggling, burping, and demanding attention. Why not just shut it off? According to the designers, the Furby didn't have an on/off switch because real pets don't have one.

Activated by touch, sounds, light, or nearby movement picked up with a motion sensor, Furbys are preprogrammed and vocalize via a voice microchip. Thanks to those hi-tech guts, the poor misunderstood Furby was accused, falsely, of stealing defense secrets, disrupting medical equipment, and teaching bad words to children.

Tiger Electronics engineered a new version that stops Furby's endless babble. Conceding Furby was driving adults nuts, it came up with a compromise to suit both parents and kids. It now has to be turned upside down and back again before it launches into its relentless chatter.

Good Is Not News

Going back to the Hewlett Packard example, notice how we've heard a lot about the Intel pentium chip problem and little on HP's.

- **The "trouble" with managing a problem well is that it doesn't get much media attention.**

No news is no news. J&J/Tylenol is used as a good example of crisis management because it's one of the few that's been publicized. This means when things are managed successfully, a company might not receive public kudos, but the results are happy customers and a protected bottom line.

The next example came by word of mouth, namely via a friend who had a special model coffeepot designed to fit under a shelf. (The company requested anonymity.) One day, she received a big box in the mail. The manufacturer said it had detected a slight problem of exploding coffeepots. (I'm paraphrasing.) There had only been a few incidents, but they didn't want to take any chances with their customers' safety. So, they asked that the perhaps-defective pot be returned in a postage-paid box. The pièce de résistance was they had also sent another coffeepot because they didn't want their customers to be without their coffee. Some months later, customers received a redesigned coffeepot.

After that, those who knew about the manufacturer's actions became devoted customers.

The coffeepot company could have decided it was cheaper to settle lawsuits than order a recall. It certainly didn't have to provide free coffeepots. However, it would have never earned loyal lifetime customers. Moral action has that kind of effect on people. Also—if the pots had become deadly, the company would have been assailed by the *Seven Plagues of Unhappy Repercussions*, which were introduced in the second chapter (Sin #2).

Oh, Build Me a Home

Home Depot escaped those plagues when it faced major community opposition. The home-improvement store had bought fourteen acres of land in downtown Tulsa in early 1993. Building its store meant tearing down all the structures on the property, including a landmark building with an art-deco tower and facade. Architects, historians, preservationists, and local residents were up in arms. Home Depot was bombarded with complaints from the American Institute of Architects, the Tulsa Preservation Commission, the Oklahoma Main Street Program, Downtown Tulsa University, Route 66 Association, and various chapters of the Art Deco Society. Even members in Canada and Boston joined in.

Home Depot could have ignored the complaints, figuring the residents would get over it. However, the enlightened company was listening and met with the concerned groups.

In September, Home Depot announced it would preserve the art-deco facade and tower of the landmarked building to the tune of up to $2 million. The structure attached to the facade was torn down and replaced with a new retail strip, which was leased to other businesses. To say the community was happy is an understatement.

As for the store? It was built five hundred feet behind the landmark/retail center. After the company announced its plan, local news coverage and editorials extolled Home Depot to the high heavens. The company was flooded with thank-you letters.

Instead of the condemnation Home Depot would have received if it had gone ahead with its original plan, editorial pages sang the company's praises: "Let's hear it for the management of Home Depot," "Welcome to the neighborhood," and "Not all corporate giants are heartless, money-oriented organizations."

- **You can't buy that kind of positive exposure.**

Responsibility is truly part of Home Depot's corporate culture, and it shows. After Hurricane Andrew hit Miami, Home Depot became the patron saint of home-rebuilders. After the disastrous storm, lumber, plywood, and other building materials were in incredible demand. Companies shamelessly raised their prices sky high. Not Home Depot. Within thirty hours, they had a tent operation going. They rerouted materials from other parts of the country and kept their prices down. The Home Depot people also provided invaluable free expertise to a grateful, shell-shocked public. Executives later explained they were not in it for the short term; they wanted a long-term relationship with customers. They got it. Just goes to show you:

- **Doing the right thing can be very profitable.**

Learn by the Mistakes of Others—You Can't Live Long Enough to Make Them All Yourself

Errors provide significant lessons.

- **Executives aren't mean people. Rather, they're unprepared.**

CEOs must have the knowledge to ask the right questions to insure their companies are protected. A company has the responsibility to identify risk and be crisis-ready.

- **Crisis planning takes time.**

There are certain businesses where the risk is easily identifiable by the nature of the industry. Obviously, in the airline industry, accidents can happen. That's what made TWA's slow response to the Flight 800 tragedy even more surprising. When a TWA spokesperson tried to explain the reason for the airline's poor performance, he said it was because there hadn't been an accident in a while. That is not a valid excuse for blundering, nor is "it's never happened to us before."

Xerox never had an employee go on a violent shooting spree, yet it skillfully managed the unexpected tragedy. So did Luby's when a gunman killed twenty-four people. Even if a crisis plan doesn't cover all contingencies, the basic premise of taking responsible, accountable action should be applied to all problems. The key to practicing "What Ifs" is utilizing that premise to develop responses.

Front and Center

We tend to think big companies will know what to do when a problem hits. That's not always the case, as we saw when Coca-Cola stumbled and fell during its contamination crisis in Europe, making a bad situation worse.

Before continuing with the Coke crisis, I'm going to digress a minute to talk about Kikkoman Foods, Inc. Malcolm W. Pennington, a Kikkoman director, stated the company hadn't lost a (product) batch in two hundred years. "That's because we really worry about every batch," he explained.

In addition to having stringent internal procedures and an excellent product recall plan in place, the company also has a sincere commitment to acting responsibly. As I peppered him one afternoon about various crisis scenarios, he summed up the company's policy by saying, "If the product has our name, we're responsible." He added that if the product didn't have the Kikkoman name but it was the cause of the problem, the company would again be responsible. (Soy sauce is used as an ingredient by other food manufacturers.) When asked about whether the company had legal concerns about that policy, he gave an "are you crazy?" look and said, "Not taking responsibility is not an option."

I thought of Kikkoman when the Coca-Cola story broke. The problem should have been managed and ended quickly by Coca-Cola's Belgium managers. Instead, officials in Belgium and France repeatedly complained the company didn't provide information fast enough. When people are scared, they want— and need— answers. A German scientist from a government-financed Consumer Center said, "We couldn't get any information from the company until we had made scores of calls." By that time, the crisis was out of hand, and the CEO should have visibly taken charge. He said he didn't take a high-profile role because Belgian health officials didn't want him to respond. He claimed the health minister had ordered, "Don't manage me in the press."

All well and good, but Coca-Cola was responsible for the problem, not the government, and it should have been showing consumers the company took it seriously and was fixing it. Instead, Coca-Cola's lack of action made the company seem insensitive to the safety of its customers. Ironically, it became the government's problem because Coca-Cola's response was unresponsive.

Not Chicken

Contrast Coke's acts to KFC's approach to a health scare. Around the same time in Belgium, the fast-food giant discovered it was using Belgian chickens contaminated with carcinogenic dioxins. The company swiftly withdrew all Belgian KFC products and went on a PR offensive.

The next day, a newspaper headline read, "Poison alert, KFC bans danger birds." As the story broke, KFC's managing director appeared on several evening news programs to reassure customers. KFC nipped the crisis perception problem in the bud and received little press, except to say how well the problem was managed.

Remember the Audi lesson in Sin #3? When perception is stronger than reality, then the perception is the reality. The perception of Coca-Cola's arrogance grew as the company implied the government and consumers were overreacting. Even if they were—again, remember Audi.

As a result of mismanagement, Coca-Cola's European bottler, Coca-Cola Enterprises, lost $103 million in the second quarter as a result of the product recall. Back in Atlanta, Coca-Cola Company's second-quarter profits fell 21 percent.

No One Is Listening Until You Make a Mistake

The only good thing about a crisis is it teaches lessons. Jack in the Box's slow response was deadly. Like TWA, it did some things right, but not fast enough. It was too late to change the initial perception.

The Health Department first alerted Jack in the Box to the contaminated meat problem via a phone message late on a Friday afternoon. Understandably, it could have been missed. Also at that point, no one knew which company was serving the deadly hamburgers.

So we'll call Saturday Day One. On that day, case reports started coming in, and the health inspector called with information of possible linkage. A doctor, knee-deep in sick children, also called to tell them to stop cooking hamburgers. On Day Two, the Health Department sent out an E-coli advisory to the media. Jack in the Box held its first crisis meeting in the afternoon of Day Two and stopped cooking hamburgers on Day Three.

- Lesson #1: When safety is at stake, don't take chances. Jack in the Box should have stopped selling hamburgers on Day One, especially after the doctor called. It makes one wonder how many illnesses could have been prevented if they had.

Even if you think someone else's product is the culprit, stop selling yours until you are certain. Lives are worth more than a few days of revenue. Even if another restaurant was selling the infected beef, Jack in the Box could have earned kudos for demonstrating its concern for customer safety. The same holds true for Coca-Cola.

- Lesson #2: When confronted with a possible life-threatening situation, a crisis team has to go into action when the company begins receiving serious warnings. Emergencies cannot be left in the hands of middle managers who do not have decision-making authority. They should be encouraged to warn their bosses when serious problems are detected.

In this case, it would have been smart for all of the crisis-team players to begin monitoring the problem on Day One. Even if it was a false alarm, the only thing that would have been lost was a weekend.

- Lesson #3: When a story breaks, a company has to respond in public rapidly. The story broke on Day Three; Jack in the Box held its first press conference on Day Six. Too late. It should have held the conference on Day Three. When asked why a news conference was not held earlier, the president said they didn't want to speculate. "We're very sorry" is not speculative.

- Lesson #4: A company must release information to all of

its audiences at the same time. The company made matters worse when it held a conference call to investors the day after the story broke, prior to holding a press conference. Management wondered why the public thought the company cared more about its financial health than the health of people. The release of information will be covered further in Sin #5.

• Lesson #5: A company should determine policies and procedure, and be aware of its liability coverage in advance so it can hit the ground running when something happens. The company did provide a telephone hot line and announced it would pay for the victims' medical care. The problem is it took about a week to get this information out. It should have been announced during the initial press briefings.

A commitment to provide medical care should be a no-brainer. So is the toll-free hot line. Crises are chaotic to begin with; advance planning prevents unnecessary complications. At the press conference, the president said the first thing they did at the crisis meeting was decide they would take responsible action. That should be a given.

Besides the embarrassment, Jack in the Box got hit by the *Seven Plagues.* Initial sales dropped nearly 40 percent in the first two weeks after the outbreak. The stock went from a pre-crisis $13.62 per share to $7.5 two months later. For that year, it lost $44.1 million compared to earnings of $21.9 million the prior year. A shareholders' class-action suit was filed against the company, the parent company chairman, and Jack in the Box's president. Numerous franchisees filed an action against the company claiming damages from reduced sales and profits. A settlement was reached with most of the them to the tune of $44.5 million. Jack in the Box also got hit by suits from victims, and a congressional hearing was held with activist groups who also got in on the act.

The good news is a company can turn its negative perception

into a positive one if it fixes a problem. Jack in the Box has since recovered. Its successful turnaround is discussed later in this chapter.

Sea Sickness

Back to the QE2 incident. The objectives are to have passengers leave with a better impression of the company and to contain negative press. Here's how the problem could have been contained (given the fact the ship set sail when it shouldn't have).

- Instead of clamming up, the highest-ranking cruise line executive should have responded immediately to the press, taking responsibility for the situation. The company's concern for its passengers' well-being should have been especially stressed. For instance:

  > We truly apologize to our passengers. They clearly didn't get the kind of service they expected and should have received. We hope they'll give us a second chance by being our guests on another QE2 cruise. We guarantee the experience will be far more enjoyable. We do understand, however, that this won't make up for a spoiled holiday, and we will try to do whatever we can to make amends.
  >
  > If hindsight was twenty-twenty vision, we would have canceled the cruise. Ironically, we didn't want to disappoint our passengers.

- Customer-service personnel (preferably wearing company jackets) should have been dispatched to work with the disgruntled passengers in person when they arrived in port. Also, other executives needed to be visibly present to talk to passengers because seeing is believing. Those affected—and the public—should know the company cares.

Dog Gone It

Although it is important to take appropriate action when there's a problem, beware of overdoing it.

Burlington Coat Factory discovered it had been duped into buying men's parkas trimmed with fur from dogs killed in China. Once the problem was discovered in mid-December 1998, the store stopped selling the remaining stock. The story received press, but as major coverages go, it had a short duration. The company didn't have to do anything else except refund the sold jackets and beef up their inspection process. At that point, *leave the story alone.*

The company didn't let it go. Although the incident was traumatic for them, it wasn't to the public. (On the other hand, it would have been if the company had knowingly sold the dog-hair coats without telling the public.) Instead of thanking their lucky stars the story was going away, the store kept it literally front and center.

When a friend went to his local store in February, he saw a table at the entrance with a sign something along the lines of "Help us put through legislation that will stop the importation of dog and cat fur." A petition was on the table.

People who read the sign laughed and shook their heads; shoppers saw it as an obvious PR scheme. The store's attempt to show itself as a victimized, yet responsible, company was heavy-handed and obvious.

According to the company's third-quarter results ending February 28, 1999, sales were up 2.5 percent. It says coat sales were adversely affected by mild weather, but there's no mention of the dog-hair incident. There was no reason for public self-flagellation.

Get Real

In the real world, corporate cultures and CEOs don't change with a snap of the fingers or because they're told to do so. It takes time to instill and reinforce ethical values. Also, top executives don't have control over everything that happens in a company. For example, a CEO didn't know his marketing department designed a cereal box with a "fake" Internet address. He found out about it via the media when the address turned out to be a pornographic Web site discovered by a wide-eyed twelve-year-old.

A CEO might not know a division is doing something illegal. He/she may not be aware of racial discrimination or sexual harassment practices going on somewhere within the company. The CEO could be surrounded by people who keep bad news from the boss.

That's the point. Once reporters show up, it becomes the CEO's problem, and he or she needs to know how to take care of it.

- **The commitment to responsible conduct has to start at the top.**

One has to mean it. And, once is not enough. It has to be reinforced. And enforced.

There are a lot of codes of ethics out there that don't address violations. Perception is usually black-and-white and when it comes to moral responsibility, there is no gray for those in leadership positions—even though that may be the reality. A CEO is either a trustworthy leader or not. This goes for all senior executives.

As management expert Peter Drucker wrote, "The rhetoric of profit maximization and profit motive is not only antisocial. They are immoral."

After the Exxon Valdez incident, someone in Exxon's public-relations department said he knew the company should have been communicating but was afraid to say anything. A middle manager was scared to do his job the right way. What a legacy for the CEO.

Taking Your Medicine

Those who have gone before and made mistakes have provided guides for what not to do. The good news is enlightened executives like you are paying attention and heeding the message.

Among two full pages of newspaper advertisements, which ran nationally, one is from Colonial Pipeline Company, which carried the big headline "WE APOLOGIZE!" The second is an open letter from the Sara Lee Corporation.

Colonial Pipeline Company said it had pleaded guilty to one count of criminal negligence for a June 1996 discharge of approximately 1 million gallons of diesel fuel in the Reed River in South Carolina due to ruptured pipelines. It went on to say while the company conducted a prompt emergency response, the discharge violated the Clean Water Act. Then, it said the company "accepts full responsibility for the incident and offers its sincere apology." It talked about the preventative action it would take, and concluded that it was striving to learn its lesson from the accident and "earn the reputation of being a responsible neighbor."

It turns out Colonial's advertisements were part of its plea agreement. The paragraphs were spelled out word-for-word in the deal, but the company said it chose to add the eye-catching headline. According to a spokesperson, the company really did want to acknowledge it had done wrong and was committed to seeing it didn't happen again.

The Sara Lee Corporation advertisement is an open letter addressed to consumers and trade customers. It talked about its voluntary December 1998 recall of hot dogs and packaged meat products, thanking everyone for responding swiftly. It went on to say the recall was still in effect (January 20, 1999) and named the affected products and urged they be discarded or returned to a grocery story for a full refund. It provided a toll-free telephone information number and concluded, "Our primary concern continues to be the health and well-being of our consumers."

It was signed by John H. Bryan, chairman of the board and chief executive officer, and C. Steven McMillan, president and chief operating officer.

These are classic textbook responses that need to be communicated through all channels. As I learned once from a wise and crafty man, go on the offensive, never the defensive.

- **Companies score points for telling the truth.**

Once a company has made a mistake and admitted it, it's time to move on. Here's a great example provided by the Warner-Lambert Company after it was rocked by scandal when it pleaded guilty to charges of hiding manufacturing processes from the FDA in 1995. A company spokesperson handled the incident with dignity:

We regret that the violation ever took place, and we have put in place strict practices to assure that this type of activity will never take place again. Mistakes were made. But we are glad to have this problem behind us.

Book 'Em

Paying attention to criticism doesn't hurt either. Amazon.com learned that lesson when the press reported the on-line bookseller was offering "cooperative" advertising packages to publishers. Meaning, whoever paid lots of money could get a prominent display for a book on Amazon's Web page. Publishers could also pay for books to be placed in its "Destined for Greatness" section and on its "What We're Reading" list. Maybe a lot of those great books weren't so great. How was a customer to know? They weren't told about the pay-for-placements offer.

The news created a brouhaha. The day after the story broke, Amazon.com back-pedaled fast, announcing it would tell customers which displays were bought and paid for. Amazon founder and CEO Jeff Bezos swore on a stack of cyberspace bibles that no book got a good review unless it deserved it.

Amazon said it was offering full refunds for any recommended book. "It doesn't matter how dog-eared or worn it is. Even if you ripped out the pages because you thought the book was so bad, you can still return the pieces to us for a full refund," said Mr. Bezos. (Amazon's usual policy is it won't take books back unless they are in new condition.)

Amazon goofed, took its punishment, proclaimed a new, fairer policy, and said it was sorry. End of story.

The Perils of Assuming

We all make mistakes, but sometimes, a seemingly little misunderstanding can cause severe damage. It brings to mind the following story:

A young executive was leaving the office late one evening when he found the CEO standing in front of a shredder with a piece of paper in his hand. "Listen," said the CEO, "this is a very sensitive and important document here, and my secretary has gone for the night. Can you make this thing work?" "Certainly," said the young executive. He turned the machine on, inserted the paper, and pressed the start button. "Excellent, excellent," said the CEO as his paper disappeared inside the machine. "I just need one copy."

- **Many a mistake has been made by an assumption.**

Management experts say one of the reasons companies make mistakes is because of the failure to communicate. This often occurs because people feel they understand each other too well.

If we're lucky, we can learn from our mistakes, or even better, others'. What separates the men from the boys is what you do about them.

For example, twelve German companies established a fund estimated at $1.7 billion to compensate victims of the Nazis. So far so good. Then, when making the announcement, German chancellor Gerhard Schroder said the main function of the fund was to "counter lawsuits, particularly class-action suits, and to *remove the basis of the campaign being led against German industry and our country.*"

So much for demonstrating moral duty and mending fences.

The chancellor was actually saying the companies were establishing the fund because they were forced to rather than because they felt an obligation to do so.

He could have said, *"The fund is one way for us to take moral responsibility for the past. We realize no amount of money will erase the horror of what happened, but we hope this demonstrates our profound sorrow and commitment to see that it never happens again."*

It doesn't change the way the money would be used. The difference is the intentions would have seemed sincere.

Positive $$ Returns

Sometimes responsibility means taking a higher road even though one doesn't like the path. If that's the case, of course venting is permissible. In private. Remember, actions can be turned into an opportunity. Call it enlightened self-interest.

Once, exploding gas tanks or polluting rivers were viewed as financial issues. Then, along came the flower children of the 1960s, who became consumers in the 1980s, and the problems turned into moral ones.

Social conscience has become smart business. Look at the cult following of Ben & Jerry's. Many were skeptical when Ben Cohen and Jerry Greenfield, the two ice-cream entrepreneurs, introduced their policy of charitable largess. Their unique form of "caring capitalism" includes giving 7.5 percent of pretax profits to charity and helping such causes as saving the rain forest and helping the homeless. When the Vermont-based ice-cream company announced it had received inquiries from several potential buyers, Vermont was sent into a tailspin. The governor, congressional representatives, and the general public begged the company not to sell out to the big (implication bad) guys. Ben & Jerry store owners protested, saying a corporate takeover would threaten the company's socially responsible image. As one owner explained, "I got involved with Ben & Jerry's because I liked the way they mixed business with their social mission."

The importance of social responsibility and consumer action was shown in a 1999 Cone/Roper study. It found 64 percent of Americans surveyed said they would be likely to switch brands or retailers to one associated with a good cause, when price and quality are equal. Two-thirds of the respondents reported having greater trust in companies that support a cause they care about.

A reputation also determines investment choice. The president of the Social Responsibility Investment Group said:

- **"If I don't invest in companies with actual or potential social and environmental liabilities, I'm reducing my risk of owning a company that suddenly owes huge fines or settlements in damage suits."**

He also added those companies won't be hit by boycotts or bad publicity, all problems that affect the bottom line.

Investors' and analysts' enthusiasm does tend to dampen when a company misbehaves. An NYU Stern School of Business study took a look at the market impact of a reputational crisis with a one-week window around the event. Archer Daniels Midlands' price-fixing crisis led to a $1 billion loss in market value. Exxon's oil spill caused a loss of $3 billion, and Texaco's was $1.1 billion. Yes, their market value bounced back, but who needs the grief?

Making Amends

The concept of honor was ingrained in us just as honesty was. However, some executives lose the concept on the way up the ladder. When a company has really messed up, the crisis does not end with "I'm sorry." In fact, an apology kicks off a new phase of going forward. This means taking concrete steps to insure the problem doesn't happen again. For example, Tylenol introduced a tamper-proof cap on its medicine bottles to demonstrate its commitment to customer safety. In its full-page ad, The Colonial Pipeline Company, the folks with the leaky diesel fuel pipeline, said it would "develop and implement a prevention and detection program to prevent and detect discharges of pollutants from the pipeline to U.S. waters. . . ."

Phoenix Rising

A crisis doesn't have to doom a company forever if it has the right mind-set and makes a concerted effort. An example of a successful turnaround is provided by Jack in the Box. Five years after its hamburger crisis, Jack in the Box made a profitable comeback with record earnings. The company focused on improved service and fresh quality. The CEO brought in an expert to work on a food-distribution-and-preparation system that now sets the industry standard and has become a model for other chains. "Town hall" employee meetings were held to discuss the crisis as well as the employees' concerns about their jobs and the company's future. The CEO also met quarterly with franchisees. A human-resources executive noted the company now asks what others in the company think before implementing a new product or program.

Perhaps most significantly, the CEO said the crisis taught him ". . . we should have recognized you've got to communicate." (Direct quote)

Quite an about-face. Reminds me of Thoreau's "things do not change, we do." In another example, Nike's image was badly hurt when a prominent critic blasted the company for unsafe conditions at one of its factories in Vietnam in 1997. In 1999, that same critic went to the press praising Nike for its work on improving the working conditions. This positive exposure also gave Nike the opportunity to talk about improvements made at its other factories in Asia.

Personal reputations can also be restored as well. New York City's police commissioner, tainted by the Revlon/Academy Awards scandal, received widespread praise and a national pat on the back for the flawless management of New York City's massive New Year's Eve Millennium celebration.

It's Not Our Problem

Either responsibility is taken seriously, or it's not.

- **Success or failure usually depends on a company's attitudes and corporate culture.**

Take Texaco. The secretly taped executives had no problem discussing illegal, let alone unethical, action. After the embarrassing tape was leaked, the chairman quickly apologized and said he hadn't been aware of the behavior. It reminds me of the movie *Casablanca*, in which the corrupt Captain Louis Renault says he's "shocked, shocked" to find gambling there as he asks for his winnings at Rick's Cafe.

The words taped during the Texaco meeting had to be a part

of the corporate language, or someone would have been asking what the speakers meant by such words as "jelly beans."

Royal Caribbean Cruises Ltd. has insisted on sailing into instead of out of trouble waters. In June 1998, the company pleaded guilty to the then-largest criminal case of ocean pollution ever. Five of the cruise line's ships were discarding contaminated waste water into the Pacific Ocean and trying to hide the records. This plea bargain came after the company first tried arguing that its ships operated outside U.S. jurisdiction because the company is incorporated in Liberia.

As a result of the agreement, the company was supposed to institute new environmental regulations aboard its ships and install new pollution-control equipment to reduce its discharges below international and U.S. requirements. Positive.

But a year later in March 1999, Royal Caribbean pleaded guilty again. One of its ships was concealing the fact it was discharging oily waste water from one of its ships. (That's a criminal charge.) The ship's record books had lots of false entries trying to hide the fact that its pollution-control equipment wasn't working.

The saga doesn't end there. In July 1999, Royal Caribbean agreed to pay a record $18 million fine and to plead guilty to a whole bunch of ocean-pollution charges. The fine is the biggest environmental penalty ever imposed on a cruise line. The second-biggest penalty was also paid by Royal Caribbean.

The Miami cruise line admitted to routinely dumping waste oil from its fleet of cruise ships over a wide range of ocean. It also acknowledged it deliberately dumped various pollutants, including hazardous chemicals from photo-processing, dry-cleaning, and printing equipment, into U.S. harbors and coastal areas. The plea covered twenty-one felony charges ranging from making false statements to the Coast Guard to violating the Clean Water Act by knowingly discharging pollutants.

The first time around, when it pleaded guilty to dumping oil at sea, Royal Caribbean had the opportunity to take a strong lead in the effort to fight ocean pollution. This would have put the company on the road to good-guy territory. The second fine of $1.5 million and the lawyers' fees could have been put to much better use. So could the third.

In a statement following the July 1999 plea, the president said, "We are profoundly sorry that a group of our employees knowingly violated environmental laws and our own company policy."

Notice he blamed his employees without taking any responsibility. This is the third time the cruise line pleaded guilty to polluting the ocean. This says something about management.

After the settlement, the cruise line wound up getting Justice Department prosecutors really mad when its press release suggested that many of the violations involving the illegal dumping of "gray water" (water from cabin, sinks, and drains) were inadvertent violations. This led the chief of the environmental crimes section to say, "It's of concern to me because we thought there was a problem with the corporate culture."

Top executives are not supposed to distance themselves from a serious problem. A corporate culture emulates the behavior of its top management. The mind-set sweeps through the company like a tidal wave.

Dishonor Among Thieves

The following stories help explain why business people are still three times more likely than other professionals to be criminals on television shows.

Cendant was the result of a merger between CUC International and HFS in April 1998. CUC operated a discount shopping-club business. HFS owned such companies as Avis rental cars and Ramada Inn hotels. Walter Forbes, from CUC, was named chairman of Cendant. After it was discovered there were "pervasive" accounting problems to the tune of $500 million, then-CEO Forbes said he had no knowledge of the accounting irregularities, which wiped out $14 billion of stockholder value. Shades of *Casablanca*.

The scandal came from the CUC side. An audit report said CUC accrued $500 million before taxes of fictional profits for the past three years. This included inflating operating income, decreasing expenses, and adjusting its balance sheet "particularly to show a greater balance than the company actually had

". . . and so Mr. Willard comes up to me, and he says, 'I would be happy to take the fall, sir.'"

on its books." A merger reserve was used to cover $597,000 of private airplane expenses for which Mr. Forbes had paid and requested to be reimbursed.

Paul R. Brown, chairman of the accounting department at the NYU Stern School of Business, said there had been many cases of companies using one or two of these techniques, "but to see an organization use a combination of many of them is somewhat amazing." He also said that the "tone at the top set by senior company officials affects behavior at all levels."

Mr. Forbes, claiming he had no responsibility for the problems, said he had "absolutely no knowledge" of the "accounting irregularities" and "the actions of a few have profoundly hurt us all."

Mr. Forbes resigned in July 1998 and went away licking his wounds with a severance package worth more than $35 million. Nine board members associated with CUC also resigned. This happened after forty-four executives wrote a letter to the company's board asking them to fire Mr. Forbes. "We're all accountable for our performance," said an executive vice president for strategic development. "We can't work for someone who isn't held to the same standard."

Irate shareholders who were left holding the significantly devalued bag didn't care whether Mr. Forbes knew of the problem or not; it happened under his watch. "Someone must bear responsibility," said a substantial Cendant stockholder. When the news about the CUC funny-business broke, the stock lost more than $14 billion in a single day.

The audit committee report, which came out in August 1998, said Mr. Forbes had failed to create a corporate culture intolerant of inaccurate financial reporting, failed to put in place appropriate controls and procedures to catch such problems, and failed to adequately inform himself about the sources of the company's profits.

After the report was released, Mr. Forbes said in a statement that the investigation "found absolutely no evidence that I had any knowledge of or involvement in the accounting irregularities. Any suggestion that I should have known, is completely unfounded. There is no way I could or should have known about the fraud and I never did or ever would condone any improper conduct under any circumstances."

The lawyer representing Cosmo Corigliano, the former CUC chief financial officer, said his client was "shocked that certain Cendant employees have apparently admitted making improper financial entries and that those employees would falsely attempt to implicate him in their wrongful conduct."

Whatever those executives did cost Cendant additional billions. The company wound up settling a fraud suit filed by stockholders to the tune of $2.8 billion in December 1999. At the insistence of pension-fund managers, Cendant agreed to several changes in its corporate structure to create a more independent board and prevent executives from increasing stock-option benefits without consent of shareholders.

While Cendant might not be a household name, some of its operating companies are. In situations like this, the media tend to use familiar names. In this case, such headlines as "Parent of Ramada and Avis Agrees to Settle Fraud Case" ran. With a stroke of a settlement pen, those two companies were woven into the story, even though neither was involved in the case.

So much for the fictional Gordon Gekko's declaration of "greed is good" in the movie *Wall Street*. Among many lessons, this story shows what happens when a company's board of directors turns a blind eye to illegal activities.

Clueless

Whether a top executive likes it or not, he or she is holding the proverbial buck when unethical practices are discovered. Otherwise, an executive looks even worse when the problem comes to light. Ask Roche Holding A. G.'s chairman and chief executive officer. In May 1999, the Swiss pharmaceutical giant was found to be part of a sophisticated cartel to fix worldwide vitamin prices. Chairman Fritz Gerber and CEO Franz B. Humer claimed they never knew about the decade-long price-fixing scheme, even though some of their senior executives were involved.

At a press conference, Mr. Humer said, "You will understand that this was not part of our responsibility. . . . It is certainly not easy to understand the reasons for actions of employees who in secrecy organized a conspiracy of this kind."

Roche paid $500 million to settle antitrust charges with the Justice Department. Two of its top executives resigned, and one served a four-month prison sentence in the United States. The company also faced class-action lawsuits that could wind up costing up to $1 billion.

BASF AG of Germany, another participant, settled by paying $445 million in fines. The other cartel member, Rhone-Poulenc of France, wasn't penalized after it provided vital information to prosecutors.

This was not the first time Roche was implicated in a price-fixing conspiracy. In 1997, the company paid a $14 million fine for its involvement in fixing the price of food additives citric acid and lysine with Archer Daniels Midland. In fact, the vitamin cartel case grew out of that ADM investigation discussed earlier in this chapter (see pages 116–117). All the while, the guilty Roche executives who participated in the scheme kept their jobs as the company was vowing to clean up its act.

After that episode, Mr. Humer insisted the company had "never tolerated practices of this kind." He also said he'd start a "vigorous" information campaign to tell employees about ethical practices. Then, along came the vitamin conspiracy. It does make one wonder about the corporate culture. Even if Mr. Gerber and Mr. Humer didn't know what was going on, then the alternative is they were woefully uninformed, which doesn't say much for them either. As the company's top officers, they are still ultimately responsible. The same goes for Cendant's CEO and CFO.

- **"It's not our fault" does not work as a defense.**

Do as I Do

In the past examples, employees understood there were expectations from the top, which had to be met. It brings to mind a CEO who was told the quarterly earnings he proposed to announce weren't accurate. The CEO yelled, "Stop fooling around with my numbers. The number one job of management is to smooth out earnings." There is another story about a CEO telling his CFO to hold back some of the earnings, which were well beyond analysts' expectations. The CFO objected, saying, "Don't even go there. Don't you know what the SEC is doing to people?" The boss turned to him and told him he was in "career-limiting territory." Luckily for the company, the CFO, the auditors, and the audit committee got together and were able to stop him.

Bankers Trust wasn't so lucky. It pleaded guilty to a $6.3 million scheme of misappropriating money that belonged to security holders but hadn't been claimed. Prosecutors say employees working in the securities-processing business misappropriated the money to meet top management's call for good results. The SEC, out to curb fraud, emphasized the "tone at the top." Prosecutors said they were beginning to believe Bankers Trust's management was tone-deaf. A couple of years earlier, the company got into trouble for unprincipled selling of derivatives. The SEC had also been investigating possible problems with loan-loss reserves.

Needless to say, those further down the ladder are often troubled and worried by what they are asked to do, but do it anyway. One lawyer investigating the Cendant case talked to a woman implicated in the fraud. She suddenly burst into tears and said, "I'm so glad to have someone to talk to about this."

So, while employees are likely scapegoats, the environment is created by top management, and the chief executives are still culpable. Not only are top executives losing their jobs, they are paying hefty fines. Some are even going to jail.

The moral of these stories can be summed up by Peter Drucker's creed:

- **"Value and service first, profit later. Maximizing profit, perhaps never."**

Sharpen Your Pencils

How committed are you to taking moral responsibility in a crisis? Judge for yourself.

Rate your company's values, on a scale of 1 to 10 with 10 being the highest:

_____ We believe people come before dollar signs.
_____ We have stated core values, which we take seriously.
_____ We practice what we preach.

_____ We honor our commitments.

_____ Honesty is our best policy.

_____ We get bad news out fast.

_____ We are committed to finding the cause and fixing a problem.

_____ We keep our audiences informed, beginning with employees.

_____ Employees, shareholders, and customers believe we practice what we preach.

_____ We consider our employees people, not figures on a balance sheet.

_____ We have developed a crisis plan, which incorporates the above.

_____ We love our crisis-management consultant.

How did you do? If you rated each one 8 or higher, you're in good shape. You're okay if your answers fell in the 5 to 7 range, but still aim higher. If any ranked below 5—you've got problems. I'm going to assume, even though I know "assume" is a dangerous word, that none of you fell into the murky 1 to 4 waters.

The Last Word

It's a shame we're living in a world where people are surprised when a company acts responsibly when there's a problem. The ones that do turn out to be big winners. Think of Ashland Oil, Luby's, Home Depot, and the coffeepot company. So it is really in one's own best interest to do the right thing.

In the immortal words of Mark Twain, "Always do right. This will gratify some and astonish the rest."

Just Say, "No Comment"

A CEO was walking back to his office one day when he heard someone behind him say, "Excuse me." He turned to find a well-known business reporter who said, "I just have one question."

Turning pale, the CEO gruffly muttered, "No comment," and hightailed it back to his office. The reporter, watching the executive flee, wondered what he was hiding. Something was wrong, or he wouldn't have run away. He began investigating. He talked to a disgruntled employee and competitors and checked out chat rooms on the Internet. His story began, "Anonymous sources say an internal problem is brewing at XYZ Company. CEO Smith fueled suspicions when he literally ran away from this reporter."

It was as if the reporter had yelled, "Eureka!" Other reporters raced to be the first to discover the mystery problem. Investors got nervous, and the company's stock took a dive.

Actually, the reporter had been on his way to another interview when he got lost and stopped the CEO to ask for directions.

Did this CEO have something to hide, or was he just afraid of the media? Either way, he would have been better off finding out what the reporter wanted. It's time to address the very hazardous Fifth Deadly Sin: Just Say "No Comment." This is where corporate responsibility, public perception, emotion, and crisis readiness meet. It's how these elements are used that counts.

There's one certainty in this uncertain world: "no comment" is the best way to compound a problem. As one reporter explained, "The press is like Dr. Kevorkian. It won't kill you, but it will help you if you volunteer to commit suicide."

First, recognize a company cannot stay mum during a crisis. In fact, communication is a necessity. Successful CEOs have to understand how the news business works and how speed is changing the dynamics of a crisis response.

Crisis management is not an exact science, but there is one golden rule. If a crisis erupts and your company is clearly at fault, get the bad news out fast, tell the truth, and apologize. It's a rule because it works.

• **When a company doesn't talk to the press, it is giving up control of the story.**

Basically a company is saying, "Our competitors and disgruntled employees will speak on our behalf."

Reporters need information fast. If they don't get it from you, they'll get it from other sources who have their own agendas, which do not include helping you. Former *Washington Post* executive editor Ben Bradlee put it this way: "Reporters don't write 'the truth,' they interpret what we know and what people tell us."

For Your Own Good

Public perception is determined by a company's external performance. As a great deal of the public's view is provided courtesy of the media, a company has to be out-front in good and bad times. Notice how:

- **Nobody runs away from reporters when things are going well.**

Whatever happens:

- **Never say the two words "no comment."**

In public-speak, those two words mean "guilty." A survey by the Opinion Research Corporation shows 58 percent of the public believes a company is guilty when its spokesperson responds "no comment." That means more than half of public support will be lost right off the bat.

The public reacts to an appropriate human response whether it comes from an organization or a person. Sometimes the right reply can let you get away with murder.

There's a story about a man who had just been arrested for killing his wife. The media were all over him. When he was taken out of his house and into the waiting squad car, a reporter asked, "Sir, did you kill your wife?" He responded, "I love and cherish my wife." For days, people talked about his innocence or guilt based on that quick statement. They remembered his statement more than any of the mounting evidence given in the prior news reports. This shows how the public tends to be less judgmental and more empathetic when the right emotional buttons are pushed. With a few words, that man evoked public sympathy based on perception.

Stage Fright

When opossums are playing "possum," they aren't "playing." They are actually passing out from sheer terror.

This can happen to top executives, too. Many first-rate chiefs are able to leap tall buildings in a single bound but turn to stone at the thought of talking to the press. Part of this "possuming" comes from a fear of losing control. Plus, there's the fear of legal ramifications, the fear of being found out, the fear of making glaring mistakes in public. All of these reasons are very understandable and valid. Yet, with careful training and planning, a CEO can gain control of the story and avoid negative consequences.

It's a harder challenge for those suffering from "the Ivory Tower Syndrome" (ITS). When people hang on someone's every word, agree with everything he says, and does what he tells them to do, it's hard for that person to realize he doesn't have that kind of clout in the real world. Many executives are caught by surprise when reporters dare ask particularly sensitive questions.

The first thing to do is let go of unreasonable expectations. Do not order subordinates to keep a problem out of the news. If companies had the power to keep a story quiet, you'd never read any bad press. Contain, yes. Keep out, no. One billionaire who spent tons of money to keep things out of the press wound up on the front pages of major tabloids because of his ugly divorce battle. His company's woes became part of the stories. In fact, the divorce story was so juicy, the mainstream press covered it.

Also, don't think a story will just go away if a company doesn't respond to media inquiries. The only guarantee in the news business is if there's a problem, reporters will be there. As one *Time* magazine reporter told a group of public relations people, "If we're doing a story on your company, chances are good that you're in big trouble."

There are times, if one is very, very lucky, a problem may pass unnoticed. However, those miracles are few and far between, so don't count on it.

The Sooner, the Better

One of the main reasons bad news has to get out fast is because the longer it's out there, the longer the story stays in the limelight.

Just ask President Clinton. He ignited a scandal with one public denial. With his index finger stabbing the air, the president said he didn't have sexual relations with Monica Lewinsky. Besides the unfortunate denial, finger-stabbing didn't help. All of this happened in January 1998. On camera before a global audience. His blatant televised statement was manna from heaven for reporters. He had just issued a challenge to call his bluff.

If he had fessed up then, the story would have blown over. Instead, because he failed to take responsibility for his actions, everyone was subjected to seven months of scandal coverage and Clinton jokes ad nauseam until he admitted he'd lied.

This is the quintessential example of a story that was exacerbated when it could have been contained.

Coke Classic

When a crisis breaks, there is often little information and a lot of chaos. However, to avoid major mistakes, there are basic principles that can help a company's performance. One is:

• **During a crisis, customers come first. Never minimize their concerns.**

Here's an example of what not to do. During Coca-Cola's contamination crisis, a company spokeswoman said, "There are no health risks at all. We withdrew the product not because of health concerns, but because it did not meet our high-quality standards."

No health concerns? Meeting their standards of quality doesn't translate into caring about customers' welfare. Asked how people became sick if the soft drinks were safe, one spokesperson said, "It may make you feel sick, but it's not harmful." Safely sick has a "let-them-eat-cake" ring to it.

The company's perceived lack of concern for customer safety—especially after children were the first to become ill—is one reason the problem exploded into an international story.

The longer a story hangs around, the more rumors and inaccuracies get added on to it. In Coke's case, doctors think numerous reports of illness may have been caused by mass hysteria rather than by the tainted drink. Then, there were reports of rat poisoning at Coke's Dunkirk plant. In a further twist, it was suggested the contamination was associated with an extortion attempt the previous May in Germany. If a company is not communicating, all sorts of reports take on credibility.

The story was covered globally *every day* for more than a month and never went away. On the other hand, there's the Belgium KFC crisis, discussed in the fourth chapter (Sin #4). When the restaurant discovered its chickens were contaminated, it quickly withdrew the guilty chickens and warned the public. The story only lasted for a couple of days, and KFC was lauded for its actions. Managed properly, the Coke problem probably would have gone the same way.

On the good news/bad news front, a company's widespread name-recognition factor has a downside as well as a beneficial one. A well-known company stuck in a jam tends to attract more media attention because the public recognizes it. It goes back to what the comedian explained about the effectiveness of a joke: people have to be familiar with the subject. Coca-Cola's name recognition amplified the magnitude of the outbreak. Due to mismanagement, coupled with name recognition, every time somebody drinks Coke and gets sick, it's reported even if the illness is not related to the beverage.

Show-and-Tell

As one continues to learn lessons from bungled crises, it helps to get a bird's-eye view from reporters' perspectives. The following press reaction illustrates what happens when a company makes a bad situation worse. After the 1996 crash of TWA Flight 800 in New York, several reporters who spent time at the crash site immediately following the disaster had the following to say about the airline's response. Although the subject is TWA, the opinions provide insight into media coverage in general.

According to a study conducted by *Ragan's Media Relations Report,* the reporters' big beef was the dearth of return phone calls from the airline's communications people during the first twenty-four hours after the crash.

- The journalists said the absence of a return phone call forced them to look elsewhere for quotes when they were on deadline—thereby taking control of the story out of the hands of the company.

Here's what individual reporters had to say:

- CNN's Keith McAllister said companies in the midst of a crisis must grant TV reporters access to the head honchos. "They have to have a system set up that makes it possible for them to answer our questions."
- *Newsday*'s Tom Incantalupo knew the TWA's small communications staff was being besieged by media calls. Nevertheless, he needed a comment the day after the crash for his sidebar on the airline's financial position. "They never did call that day—I had to write the story around them."
- Reporter from a major daily—name withheld: "I don't think it looks very good in print to say 'TWA did not return phone calls.' It made us look at them with a much more skeptical eye. We were able to speculate wildly, which is easier to do when they're not calling you back."
- Associated Press, Sam Boyle: "Rumor always comes in to fill the void."
- New York 1, Karim Hajee said at one of the early press conferences that TWA CEO Jeffrey Erickson simply read a short statement and "walked away without answering any questions. That really annoyed me." Hajee said Erickson made scant appearances before the media in the first few days after the crash, leaving him without a much-needed video of an authoritative corporate executive.

Another major complaint about TWA was the airline didn't immediately set up a media center where reporters could get information on the latest press conferences or find out when the CEO would be available:

- *St. Louis Post-Dispatch,* Charlotte Grimes: "There were a lot of reporters staked out at the Ramada Plaza because they didn't have any other place to go," referring to the hotel where family members of victims waited out the search for bodies. "That's probably the last place where the airline wanted reporters to congregate."

A reporter's job is covered further in this chapter, but those remarks show the vital need for information whether it comes from a company or other sources. It also brings out how reporters will run with rumors if there's no information. And, CEOs note, it points out top officials have to be accessible during the early stages of a crisis.

In a survey, journalists were asked to rate the best and worst CEOs in terms of visibility. The CEOs viewed as the worst were "ineffective either because they weren't visible, they weren't available, or were difficult to deal with." Think how that affects the attitude of reporters covering their companies.

Losing the Battle and the War

Although it can be done inadvertently, don't antagonize the media on purpose. It only alienates the very people who are writing about the company. Aspects of "no commenting" can have serious consequences. Such was the case when a CEO didn't understand them.

"All I said was, "No comment.'"

A venture capitalist bought a controlling interest in a financially troubled company. He convinced the board of directors to kick out the CEO and took over.

Until that time, the company had been accessible to the media and communicated with employees, thus keeping good relationships with both. As long as the company kept supplying information, the reporters weren't digging for dirt. They knew the company was having financial problems but weren't aware of the extent. Therefore, the coverage didn't scare away business. The company continued to maintain its popular image, thanks, in part, to its enthusiastic employees and its high level of customer service. At that point, the company had a good chance of surviving.

Then, along came the venture capitalist, who had never run a company. At his first and only press conference, he arrogantly derided the media and told them the company would have nothing further to say to the press in the future.

The company, once the good guy, suddenly turned into evil incarnate. In fact, it became the company reporters loved to hate. The media began predicting the company's demise. The CEO refused to speak to the press or allow a spokesperson to refute the allegations or correct inaccuracies. As far as he was concerned, reporters were all a bunch of idiots, and he wasn't out to win a popularity contest anyway. He didn't understand there was more at stake than what people thought of him.

Due to the bad press, customers became alarmed and shied away. Vendors panicked, refusing to fill orders without advance payment. By that point there was no cash flow, so checks bounced like basketballs. Shareholders began dumping stock. Employee morale sank like a rock, and service suffered. The company went out of business four months after the venture capitalist took over.

It's hard to say if the company would have gone under anyway. One thing's certain: The communication breakdown hastened its demise.

The Last Word

Another cautionary tale takes place at a $500-a-ticket gala held to celebrate the reopening of the Ohio statehouse. The event seems innocuous enough. However, before the gala, a reporter from the *Akron Beacon Journal* asked the woman in charge of the shindig for a list of those attending the party. First, the woman denied there was a guest list.

Upon refusing to provide the list, she said, "I can't think of anything that would be of interest to your sneaky, journalistic minds." The paper sued for the list. It finally got hold of the names on the day of the event.

Here's a problem that could have been easily avoided. Instead of a positive story about the celebratory dinner, the coverage focused on the planner's refusal to release a guest list and the resulting lawsuit.

In another case, a spokesman was extremely rude to an influential columnist who called about a rumor she had heard. The next day, there was a negative story about the company, running under a banner headline. Ironically, the columnist said, "It was just a mediocre item until he gave me all those snarky comments."

Say Cheese

Probably the most memorable part of the Clinton-Lewinsky scandal grand jury proceedings was the scenes of witnesses being swallowed up by cameras, microphones, and reporters after they left the jury room.

Why were these poor witnesses having to race down the street? They declined to make statements to hordes of media waiting for them when they left the building. Now, enter Leon Panetta, the president's former chief of staff.

- **Following Mr. Panetta's testimony, he calmly walked to the microphones and delivered a short statement. He didn't take any questions, but his appearance was enough to fend off further attention. He left the scene unhindered.**
- **Mr. Panetta demonstrated how to maintain control amidst media chaos.**

The Role of the Media:
How to Work with the Press

There happens to be reasons why news is covered the way it is. It all revolves around ratings and time.

It's a Jungle Out There

Back in the days of the O.J. Simpson murder trial, reporters would plead, "Do we really have to do another O.J. story tonight?" The answer from the higher ups: "The other guys have been leading with O.J. six straight days, so why shouldn't we?" So the world was treated to another evening of O.J.

Why? News is a business; the story is the product. Welcome to the race for ratings. Advertising rates are based on the number of viewers a news program attracts. Big bucks are at stake. In New York City alone, the difference in cash flow between the most profitable network affiliate and the one in third place is more than $100 million.

When President Clinton's videotaped testimony at Monica's grand jury was released, ABC and CBS preempted all of their regular morning programming in favor of joining CNN, MSNBC, Fox News Channel, Court TV, and C-SPAN. NBC ran it as well. An ABC producer and two senior CBS executives said they decided they had to carry the testimony only after they heard NBC's sister cable channel, MSNBC, was going to carry it. No way were they going to allow NBC to be a player via its cable channel in a major news story while they weren't. Then, it was only when CBS and ABC decided to carry it that NBC (the network) decided it had to match them.

CBS anchor Dan Rather explained his network's wall-to-wall coverage of the event this way: "We have to tell our viewers and our affiliates that we are a player in any big news story. Before NBC got into the twenty-four-hour news business (MSNBC), we might have just let CNN have it, but now we can't let NBC give something to their viewers and affiliates without us answering. We lost a lot of money doing it."

Today's competitive attitude has taken over news in a big way. A veteran New York reporter, speaking anonymously, said, "It's extremely competitive in this town, and being able to claim that you're first to a story is a very big thing. But too often what they're competing for is who can be first to a fire. It's meaningless garbage."

During the Atlanta shootings at two day-trading firms, CNN was gleefully ripped by the press for being among the last cable news channels to report it—especially as it occurred in its headquarters' backyard.

The race to be first has put Web reporters under tremendous pressure, leading some to go with a hint of a story that doesn't pan out. For example, one on-line journalist broke the news of a merger that wasn't even in the works, sending one of the companies' shares on a short-lived rally.

They Started It

The intense competition applies to print media as well as television. Look what happened to Richard Jewell, the security guard wrongly accused of bombing the Centennial Olympic Park during the Atlanta Olympics. The press tried and convicted him before learning he was innocent.

This stirred up a debate about ethics and the media. Explaining why they ran with the name of then-suspect Jewell, several editors and producers said that without competitive pressure, they would not have named Mr. Jewell or written so extensively about him.

"If this were a local story that wasn't available everywhere in the nation immediately, we would have handled it differently," said the national editor of the *Boston Globe,* which printed its report on the top half of the front page.

He also added his readers would have heard of the news on the radio, on television, and on the Internet anyway.

Here's an interesting take on the competitiveness of news. It's our fault. According to the president of the Chicago Tribune Publishing Company, part of the emphasis on speed is due to "the nature of human curiosity."

"It's very relentless," he explained. "It [meaning us] wants to know things now. It likes to know things first."

The executive editor of the *Washington Post* also blames us. "There's abroad in the air a lot more . . . gossip. . . . What it means is that we have to decide more and more often that our readers have heard so much about this from other places that if we remain silent on it, we are failing in our obligation to help them understand the world around them."

The Good Old Days?

Before we get carried away here, the need to break a story first is nothing new. In New York in 1900, there were at least sixty-five daily newspapers. Those were the days when they bought ink by the barrel. Reporters had to scramble to beat the competition. At that time, the telephone was the equivalent of the Internet.

And ethics? The newspaper god H. L. Mencken wrote in his memoirs of how he and a reporter for a competing Baltimore paper made up stories. Their target was a reporter who covered their beat for the city's third leading daily and refused to pool his reporting. The poor reporter finally joined the pool because his editors yelled at him for missing the stories Mencken and his buddy were reporting. In 1892, muckraker Lincoln Steffens complained how the *New York Evening Post* forced him to report the news "without prejudice, color, and without style."

And, to show the more things change, the more they stay the same, in 1872, Mark Twain said in a speech: "A Detroit paper once said I was in the constant habit of beating my wife and that I still kept this recreation up although I had crippled her for life and she was no longer able to keep out of my way when I came home in my usual frantic frame of mind. Now scarcely the half of that was true."

ThisFast

The major difference between news in the olden days and now is the way it's delivered. Today's "instant atmosphere" has changed the way CEOs and the media have to operate.

Companies have to act faster than ever before, and they now have the means to do it, thanks to cyberspace. If utilized, company Web pages can provide information directly to hundreds of thousands of people instantly. The Internet gives a new meaning to the term *mass media*. When President Clinton's grand jury testimony was released, CNN Interactive averaged close to 250,000 hits per *minute*. MSNBC's Web site was so busy people had trouble logging on.

This is the first time companies have control of disseminating accurate information. It can go straight to a broad audience without media filters and can be accessed at any time, any place in the world.

This also means companies have to have people (internal or external) who know how to create crisis Web sites.

* **Web pages should be a part of a crisis plan.**

People have to be designated to be responsible for getting a crisis Web site up and running ASAP.

The Internet has become an integral part of news delivery. For example, after the shooting rampage at the day-trading firms in Atlanta, one man interviewed had been in the same building where the shooting occurred. He and his coworkers barricaded themselves in their office for four hours. During the four hours, he said they followed the news via the Internet and radio.

People tend to forget radio's vital role in news dissemination. All of us listen to all-news stations or the snippets of news at the top of the hour or turn to all-news stations.

Don't underestimate the power of newspapers, either. They are still the largest source for news, off-line and on. In fact, the electronic media get most of their news from the print media.

Reporting on Reporters

It's time to look at the folks supplying all this news. It helps to understand a reporter's job. Actually, before we take a look at reporters, let's get back to CEOs for a minute. Think back to the days when you had a *very important* report due at 4:00 P.M. To complete the report, you needed some information from a colleague. So, at 10:00 A.M., you called asking for information. Then it was 1:00 P.M., and still no info; 2:00 P.M., nothing. At 3:00 P.M., you were scrambling to get the information elsewhere. How did you feel about that colleague? You probably hated that person. Plus, you'd always remember the incident.

Welcome to the world of deadlines. Reporters live by them. For a television reporter, going live at 6:00 P.M. on the evening news means having the story ready at 6:00 P.M., not 6:15 or 6:25. (Can you imagine at the top of the 6:00 news the anchor saying, "Reporter John Smith is at the scene live. What can you tell us?" The reporter replies, "Nothing. Back to you.")

Television reporters aren't the only ones playing beat-the-clock with deadlines. All reporters are under a tremendous amount of pressure to meet deadlines.

Reporting is a time-consuming, nerve-racking business of making phone calls, leaving messages, waiting for callbacks, and juggling simultaneous calls and callbacks while writing a story on deadline. On average, reporters wind up with thirty to fifty minutes of actual interviews with four or five sources.

It's best to help reporters do their jobs. CEOs need to insure their companies are available and will provide as much information as possible. If answers aren't available, reporters have to be called back. A promise to call back means just that—and the information has to be accurate. Also, remember:

- **Deadlines are ironclad and must be respected.**

Warning: a burned reporter typically stays burned.

Top Guns

Reporters aren't the only ones involved in delivering a story. News begins and ends with editors and executive producers and their immediate deputies, who give reporters their marching orders. They assign stories and have the right to run, kill, edit, package, and even rewrite them.

Their total authority lets them decide which events are news and which are not. That's not to say reporters don't pitch their own story ideas. However, news is usually whatever the boss thinks it is. The subject and content of a story are decided by an editor when a reporter is assigned to cover it. Reporters then have the job of filling in the details. Ironically, reporters are finding themselves in competition with technology. In this era of instant and live news feeds, editors often run with these accounts before reporters can do enough digging to find out if they are accurate.

In one respect, the reporter's role is often misunderstood. Reporters do not write headlines or choose pictures. A story headline can be a killer, but don't blame the reporter. It's written by a copy editor. Arguing about it after the fact doesn't accomplish anything except alienating the editor into writing more bad headlines.

Once producers and editors know the lead story, they will often use sidebars to increase the impact. The sidebars are separate-but-related stories providing more information and showing the impact on people.

When there's a national story, local news will find tie-ins. For example, if a bomb is found at an airport in Chicago, every local newscast and newspaper across the country will run stories on the safety of the closest airport.

The same kind of news packaging is used on the Internet, where the need to highlight breaking reports is critical. As soon as a story hits, news sites throughout cyberspace will run with it. The key information is reported utilizing links to related stories as a cyberversion of sidebars.

Up Close

Taking a behind-the-scenes look at how a crisis is covered, the following is an account of how the tragic search for the late John F. Kennedy Jr. was covered the first day by Allen Salkin, a reporter for the *New York Post*. This echoed the activity in newsrooms around the country.

The *Post*'s police reporter got the first tip about the missing plane at 5:40 A.M. He called the Saturday city editor, who called the managing editor of news. Fourteen hours later, twenty-six pages on the presumed death of Mr. Kennedy rolled off the *Post*'s presses.

Saturday newsrooms are usually staffed with a "skeleton crew," and most of the Sunday paper is already laid out. That Saturday, the editor, deputy editor, managing editors, and photo editor decided to forget the preplanned layout and increased the Sunday paper from 112 to 128 pages. By 9:30 A.M., the paper's assignment editor was watching six televisions, and a managing editor was determining a framework of stories needed for the new edition. Reporters were sent to Martha's Vineyard and Hyannisport. General assignment reporters were sent to the Essex County airport, JFK Jr.'s apartment, *George* headquarters, and the Bissette-Freeman house in Greenwich. They were looking for anyone who knew about the flight or the passengers.

Someone on television said JFK Jr. had flight-trained in Florida. The *Post*'s Florida correspondent was ordered to track down anyone who had trained, flown with, or seen Kennedy down there. A Washington, D.C., reporter went for official reactions. The newspaper's television reporter tuned in to critique television coverage.

At 10:30 A.M., the reporter, Allen Salkin, was instructed to write the main story and a "curse of the Kennedys or a list-of-tragedies thing" as well as a separate piece on air disasters involving the Kennedys. He called for clips from the library. Photos were pulled, and the librarian searched databases.

Columnists who had known JFK Jr. wrote pieces, and gossip columnists wrote about the Kennedys' social life.

All of this was completed by the 3:00 P.M. deadline for Sunday's paper.

Who Said That?

Having been dispatched (via the phone or in person), reporters already have an idea on how they'll cover the story. It's beneficial for all involved if correct information is provided on time with documentation. An editor's definition of a story can be changed. If a reporter understands the situation and has proof to justify a company's side of the story, it may be adjusted. This doesn't always happen. However, a company can't afford the alternative of playing possum.

Akira Kurasawa's movie classic *Rashamon* showed there are many versions of the same event. The same thing happens when reporters rely solely on sources. In the olden days, news organizations had to verify information received from a source. That doesn't happen much anymore.

When the topic of sources came up at an American Society of Newspaper Editors annual meeting, the *Washington Post's* executive editor said his paper didn't like to rely on anonymous sources, but did anyway when it had no way of publishing reliable information.

This is how one-sided a story gets when companies take the "no comment" route. With a quick response, at least a company's side of the story goes on the record. Also, it gives reporters more time to get the information and less time to go elsewhere. It also helps develop trust.

Think back to your uncooperative colleague you envisioned earlier who wouldn't give you information when you needed it. Then, think how you would have felt about the same colleague if he or she had promptly supplied the information.

FACE-ing a Story

Reporters work within a FACE formula, shared by veteran television ace reporter Clarence Jones. This is a television formula, but it works for all media. It defines all the elements needed for a story.

F—feelings
A—analysis/quick summary
C—catastrophe, crime, corruption, and color
E—energy

Knowing this can be quite helpful. It lets someone give reporters what they need while providing a quick analysis of the problem (A) and (C), showing concern and compassion (F) while speaking with energy to show conviction (E).

Chances are C for "color" won't be encountered. It stands for the cute little stories shown at the end of the news after being bombarded by the other Cs.

Back to perception and ratings. Audiences don't go to the theater to be bored. That's why the reality of a crisis may give way to "sexier" angles of the story. What makes a story sexy? We're back to the human element. There has to be one.

- **Never forget the FACE formula's F for feelings. Today, it's the emotional side of a story that counts.**

Over the past twenty years, there's been a shift in news content. News was more straightforward and downright boring by today's standards. Reporting focused more on hard news (without editorial comment or raised eyebrows), national policies, and foreign affairs. Today, the emphasis has turned to human interest, health, crime, entertainment, scandal, and celebrities. Ironically, the "Me Decade" of the 1970s did not put a human face on the news.

There was a lot less razzle-dazzle. The news was delivered with less theatrics. The legendary Walter Cronkite, anchor of *CBS Evening News,* did just fine sitting behind a plain wooden desk with nothing behind him but a blank dove-gray backdrop. Today, his replacement sits behind a huge semicircular mahogany desk, while behind him, CBS producers busily work the phones; the backdrop is a flashing wall of television monitors.

What Attention Span?

News content isn't the only thing that has changed. Television has altered the way we receive and retain information. Before the MTV generation, first-graders had an average attention span of twenty to thirty seconds. Today, that's the average limit for adults; it's even less for some. As a result, visuals have to change frequently in order to keep the viewer's attention. The public has become used to instant gratification. We expect it. People watch news with a remote control in their hand, poised to change the channel. These viewers actually have a name: "zappers."

The people who bring us our news are very aware of this. A lead story has fifteen seconds to hook a viewer. Otherwise, that viewer could "zap" over to a competitor's newscast. Therefore, producers look for the toughest angle of the story to grab attention. However, the other stories still have to have punch. After all, viewers may "zap" over from the competition.

Once upon a not-so-distant time, consultants came in and proclaimed a story can't be longer than 90 seconds and preferably should be shorter. They also issued the rule that nobody should talk on camera for more than 20 seconds. (Actually, today, that's long.)

To show how things have changed, in the 1960s, election coverage was given 42 seconds; today, it's down to 8.2 seconds.

Get Out Your Handkerchiefs

To be news, a story has to be unusual or different. It has to answer a viewer's question of "so what?" A banker married to a beautiful woman isn't news. A banker married to a beautiful woman who is indicted for fraud and flees the country is. On an average day, more than one hundred people die in car accidents around the nation, but you'll never hear about it. You would if those one hundred people were to die in one colossal car crash.

- **Today's news has to have a human slant.**

    Thanks to the human element as well as time limitations:

- **Complex issues are reduced into simple and familiar stories with villains, victims, and heroes.**

The villains are the usual stock characters: greedy businesspeople, heartless corporations, catchall "special interests," and insensitive politicians.

The victims, on the other hand, are real: regular people crushed by forces beyond their control. These folks are blameless, anguished, and crying out for help.

When the North American Free Trade Agreement was covered, the issue was expanded trade, but the story mainly focused on workers losing their jobs to foreign competition. It turned into a classic "Suits" versus "T-shirts."

Back when IBM was in big economic trouble and announced major layoffs, there wasn't better drama. A CBS correspondent interpreted IBM's actions as "torture for IBM's workforce." One ex-employee said the company had kept on making large computers when workers knew consumers wanted small personal computers. "Nobody listened to us. We were the peons of the company."

A problem is made up of a collision of elements. Nothing is cut-and-dried. The story failed to mention an important aspect: the economics of the computer-hardware industry.

If It Bleeds, It Leads

When watching news, notice it usually begins with some sort of crime story or accident. (Three out of the four Cs in the FACE formula.)

Who wants to watch this kind of stuff? Lots of people. A Roper Poll showed 68 percent of viewers are interested in crime. Another survey of one hundred stations found seventy-two news shows led with a crime story, and about one-third of all news stories were about crime.

One general manager of a television station found that out the hard way. When he became general manager of a local Orlando station, he said crime would be put in perspective and the news would cover more local issues like education and zoning. Community officials and citizens called to thank him.

Surely that would mean a large, grateful audience. Well, here's a comparison of the news that ran one evening on Orlando television: The general manager's station led with a breaking story about a local elementary school making the state's list of failing schools. Meanwhile, one competitor began with a story about a dog stabbed in the eyes. The other had an exclusive story about a four-hundred-pound man accused of intentionally sitting on a twenty-two-month-old child.

More than 80 percent of Orlando viewers were glued to the last two stories. Whereas the top-rated station collected $22,400 in advertising revenues for one night, the general manager's third-ranked station made $14,400.

Sad but true. People may claim that they don't like the violence on local news, but a study by the Pew Research Center found crime outranks sports, local government, religion, and politics in popularity.

More-sensational pictures of tragedies are drifting into mainstream news magazines as well. *Time* and *Newsweek* have been slugging it out to the tune of more than $100,000 for photos of victims, crime scenes, and other images of disasters. The gorier the better.

Huh?

There are some subjects that are clearly television-unfriendly. They flunk the FACE formula. When it comes to being dull, anything having to do with math or science leads the list. News stories have to be brief and relatively simple. Economic or scientific problems are usually complex and abstract. Plus, for television, the story has to be visual. For example:

- **The savings and loan crisis in the 1980s was not a story until greedy bank presidents and devastated victims came into the picture.**

A few years ago, the word *derivative* would have made most reporters run for the hills. Then, it began to bear victims. It started with the "Big One." The Orange County story. The county treasurer's high-yield, high-risk investment strategy ran amok, causing the county to lose millions and declare bankruptcy. Victims. A story! In this case, there were two bad guys: the county treasurer and "derivatives."

When in the midst of a financial crisis, it's important to know that some reporters aren't financial wizards. A newspaper "business" reporter once asked me what was the difference between a net profit and an operating one. A senior editor at *Forbes* magazine had a television reporter ask her how to figure how much a taxpayer making $50,000 a year would pay under Steve Forbes' flat-tax plan. Another newspaper reporter covering Mr. Forbes' plan admitted, "I don't want to understand the economics of it. I just want to understand the politics of it."

It's important to realize reporters won't necessarily understand what an executive is talking about. Therefore, interpret information for those who have never had to add without a calculator.

In addition to math, woe to those who have to explain a problem involving scientific matters. An executive from a utility company told how they were getting beaten up over an environmental issue. He said the problem was scientific, complicated, and hard to explain. He added that the local reporters didn't understand the problem and they were using information supplied by their opponents' scientists, who were blowing the issue out of proportion. The reporters went with the opponents because the scientist found an understandable way to talk about their side of the issue.

Another client dealing with a problem involving a scientific explanation required spending half a day translating the information into understandable English. All of a sudden, bingo! The chief scientist came up with an analogy that easily explained the issue. I don't know who was happier. (It's always helpful to use analogies, regardless of the topic. It makes the subject easier to understand.)

Sometimes, when it's just too hard to find a human face to a complex story, you won't see it on television. Take the broadcast spectrum nonstory, one that had a direct impact on the broadcast industry. A multibillion-dollar battle raged in Congress in 1996 over whether TV broadcasters should pay the government for high-technology digital slices of the broadcast spectrum, or receive them free, the way they got access to other airways. The networks said the spectrum debate was too complicated and boring for the viewing public. An ABC senior vice president of news called the topic "a relatively abstract question." A CBS news vice president explained the story "had not caught fire with people out in the country." Maybe because nobody explained it.

Newspapers, by the way, which don't have to be as snappy as television, did cover the story. Whether anyone read it is another matter.

The Joys of Being Boring

Sometimes, boring is good.

A client settled with the Federal Trade Commission (FTC) to resolve a product-ingredient claim dispute. The company decided to comply with the terms of the settlement in order to avoid a costly and lengthy legal process.

As part of the settlement, the company had to stop using claims about a key product ingredient. This could have seriously damaged sales as well as the company's relationships with distributors and shareholders.

In fact, a competitor had faced the same problem a few years earlier and wound up filing Chapter 11. The perception was that the company was selling snake oil, and sales plummeted, distributors stopped distributing, and shareholders bailed out. The client was facing a dismal prospect. Yet, instead of hiding, the CEO decided to take a proactive stance.

Understandably, the management team was upset. Their draft of the initial press release was emotional and attacked the FTC. That's hardly the way to minimize attention. The release was rewritten, simply stating all of the facts. No emotion. No unanswered questions. Versions were also written for all of the company's audiences, including employees, distributors, and shareholders. They determined what the responses would be and practiced answering negative questions.

It was important for the company's press release to come out a day before the FTC's. The release went out to all of the client's audiences at the same time. By the time the FTC released the settlement the next day, it was already old news.

The total result was two phone calls from the local media. That's it.

Another client was saved by being boring. He was testifying before a Congressional subcommittee. Reporters were out in droves. His testimony began and worked better than a sleeping pill. The client's initial statement and answers to questions were technical and complex. Plus, he had been coached to keep his temper and stay calm. The next witness was far more interesting because he got angry and combative. The client was not even mentioned in the news coverage of the issue.

There's an anecdote to this story. The evening before the testimony, everyone was still in the lawyers' office prepping the CEO. For some reason, one of the lawyers panicked, insisting a press release be issued that evening because the client was going to get slaughtered. Yet, he didn't know which issue would land the client in trouble. A release stating "whatever it is, we didn't do it" doesn't help the cause.

- **Do not try defending a position if you don't know what it is.**

Thankfully, the client stayed mum. Putting something out would have focused attention on the company.

Unfortunately, boring crises are few and far between. Boring applies to the content, not the person delivering it. In other words, a perpetually dull CEO can't rely on his dullness to keep the media away from a story. It just drives reporters to go to others who are more interesting.

Actually, a *New York Times* article ran about how one of Microsoft's most important witnesses in the government's antitrust trial was so boring the judge asked Microsoft lawyers to hurry up and finish.

A boring witness isn't news. A judge wanting the boring person to go away is news.

Practice Makes Perfect

The first time an Air Florida flight was hijacked, reporters descended on the ticket counter and ran around the gates filming the empty space where the plane was supposed to be. Press briefings were conducted, but there wasn't much information: the plane was still in Havana. As the night wore on, reporters were draped over chairs like fallen leaves.

Meanwhile, plans were being made to try to prevent media chaos when the flight returned. Reporters would want to interview everyone, but it was important to protect passengers and crew members who didn't want to talk to the press. At the same time, it was necessary to provide the opportunity for those who did. The plan didn't work as well as anticipated. When the plane finally arrived, the passengers were greeted with modified confusion.

Then came a run of hijackings. By Air Florida's fifth and last one, things went quite smoothly. Passengers who wanted to talk to the press were led one way, those who didn't, another. No confusion. Everything was orderly, and reporters had what they needed.

There's a lot to be said for repeating drills over and over. In this case, the incidents were real, but it goes to show the more it was done, the better it got.

The Anatomy of Coverage

Regardless of the style, the common denominator for media outlets is an audience with a voracious appetite. Remember the spectator interest in crises. When an incident occurs, the news race turns into a marathon. The problem is information doesn't always move as fast as reporters have to. After all, television news outlets have hours of airtime to fill. They can't show blank screens. Thus, the media are ravenous when a story continues but hard news doesn't. One would like to think the media could cover other stories in the meantime, but it doesn't work that way. A crisis stays a story until there is a conclusion—unless a major crisis erupts somewhere else. The period between start and finish is limbo-from-hell time. With no hard news, anyone "almost," as in "almost" friend or "almost" expert, starts looking good to harried producers and editors scrambling to fill space and airtime. Any scrap of information, any rumor, any speculation is fair game.

A company can generally expect four phases of crisis coverage:

Phase I

The problem occurs, and the press is knocking at the door. Or, the press is knocking at the door before anyone in the company knows there's a problem.

- When the company is facing a crisis, this period is pure madness. The company is trying to determine what happened while reporters are screaming for information *now*. Chances are, they know more than the company. This period roughly lasts four to six hours, though it could be longer, depending on the circumstances.

- If it's more of a corporate-related problem, such as an SEC investigation or sexual-harassment suit, a company may have a longer lead time to prepare before the news breaks.

Phase II

The company begins getting information to disseminate.

Phase III

The story may be a story, but all the news has been released. This is the most dangerous phase because it's a time when speculation runs rampant. Stick to facts and be sure to correct inaccurate information.

Phase IV

End of story and on to the aftermath.

- It's clean-up time. The company may have a bruised reputation and has to develop a long-term strategy to mend it.
- There may be lawsuits to address. Depending on the severity, this could turn into a new crisis episode.
- This is also the time a company is held under magnified media scrutiny. For example, after a Korean Airlines jet crashed in Guam, a Korean Airline jet that was making an emergency landing in Japan because an engine warning light flashed became big news. This is not an uncommon problem in the industry. These episodes aren't reported unless an airline has already been the focus of scary news.

In terms of control, sometimes there's not much that can be done during an unfolding incident because not much is known. However, it's important to make sure the media know the company will be accessible and provide information as it becomes available. This message should be part of the company's initial statement acknowledging the crisis.

In other cases, a company has control over the duration of a story if it can take action and provide facts before other sources do. If a company doesn't take charge of a problem quickly, coverage of mismanagement incubates and hatches during the limbo period, and becomes part of the story. Think of Coca-Cola's and TWA's misfortunes.

With the competition among news organizations and the number of news outlets so intense:

- **Recognize the "if-it-bleeds-it-leads" factor.**

It is here to stay. What really counts is how well CEOs operate within those parameters.

The Crisis Response:
How to Maintain a Reputation

Standing in the Spotlight

One of the greatest challenges of leadership is the ability to communicate effectively. This is where "it's not only what you say, but how you say it" comes in.

Top executives have more control than one would think. A CEO has the choice of letting the public see him or her as a warm, caring, and personable executive rather than an icy-cold one who fits into the villain category.

By communicating, a company is showing the public it is in control of the situation. Here's what to do:

- To combat negative coverage, provide a consistent message and constant updates.
- Never, ever attempt to cover up or purposely mislead the press.

Also, utilize a good, experienced spokesperson who has established credibility with the media. That person needs direct access to upper management. He or she has to know what the CEO is saying, not what someone else down the line is interpreting. (Which is why he or she needs to report to the top company officials.)

The company spokesperson is often the first to get word of bad news because reporters call asking for a response. This was the case when Air Florida Flight 90 crashed in a snowstorm. An NBC news crew knew about the accident before the airport control tower did because they were nearby and saw the plane go down. However, they couldn't recognize the airline. They called airline public-relations departments to find out. Air Florida learned about the accident via the news.

Did I Say That?

Lots of people act well but few people talk well, which shows that talking is the more difficult of the two.

—Oscar Wilde

When it comes to conducting interviews, the best advice: *get to a media trainer and take top executives with you.* Then, practice, practice, practice. No one becomes an adroit communicator overnight. In fact, most effective speakers are also the ones who rehearse the most. It takes a lot of effort to appear to be talking effortlessly.

Media training does not mean learning how to become artificial. Saints preserve us from overtrained executives on television interviews saying, "Dan." {Smile.} "I'm glad you asked me that." {Smile.}

- **Learn how to develop a message and cut to the chase.**
- **Understand the editing process in order to control your message.**
- **Know how to answer tough questions, e.g., "If the economy declines, will you cut customer services, or will you raise prices?"**

(The answer to the foregoing should run along the lines of, "I never speculate.")

There are different techniques for television and newspaper interviews, as well as for talking to someone face-to-face versus on the telephone. Learn to know what to do in all situations.

It's a Dirty Job but . . .

There is no "one-size-fits-all" crisis response. However, there are basic guidelines.

First, a response depends on the problem:

- If the company is responsible: Get the bad news out fast and apologize.
- In an uncertain situation: Say you'll get to the bottom of it and follow up.
- If allegations are false: Be indignant and provide facts to prove that the allegations are wrong. Warning: Don't try to bluff your way out of this kind of situation. Make sure you actually have facts to back you up.

Also, be aware of the basic steps a company should incorporate into its response:

- Communicate with the public ASAP via a media statement acknowledging the problem.
- Provide candid, accurate information.
- Show compassion.
- When you don't know an answer, say so and why.
- Clarify questions.
- Let the media know the company will provide updates and who will be giving them.
- Don't speculate or assume.
- Beware of making promises you can't keep.
- Don't interfere with a reporter's legitimate duties.

That being said, there are general elements in a response:

- Focus on victims as well as the cause (e.g., "Our first priority is to take care of family members or the victims" or, "Our first priority is the health and safety of our employees and neighbors"). *Show the public the company believes people come before dollars.*
- Take responsible action. Say what went wrong and how the company intends to fix it.
- Do not blame, finger-point, or complain.
- Reemphasize concern for those involved.

The need for compassion can't be stressed enough. Besides personal feelings, also think of perception. Don't forget to provide a response on the Internet. There's nothing as tacky as going to a company's Web site and finding that it doesn't acknowledge the problem but provides instructions on how to win a dream vacation instead, as one company did.

Actually, that brings to mind a woman who lost her husband in the December 1988 Pan Am Lockerbie crash. After hearing the news, she called Pan Am frantically trying to get information. She was put on hold and had to listen to cheery Christmas music. A crisis has to be treated with sensitivity. This holds true for a Web page, a press release, or toll-free help lines.

That woman's story is haunting because many companies tend to overlook certain unintentional, but hurtful, actions to the detriment of those suffering.

To Speak or Not to Speak

When does a CEO step in as spokesperson? It depends. Although a company has to be able to respond to any problem, it does not mean CEOs have to be out-front all the time. They have to take center stage when a crisis is serious enough to adversely affect the welfare and safety of their employees, the public, the community, and the environment. The crises discussed in this book—Bhopal, TWA Flight 800, Exxon Valdez—all required initial statements by the top official.

In tragic circumstances like those, solely using someone from middle management or a public relations spokesperson makes the company appear as if it is not taking the problem seriously, is insensitive, or is hiding. There may be times when other executives or middle managers are the only ones at the scene. In those cases, it's important to let the media know a top executive will be available as soon as possible.

Lesser, though still serious, problems like a computer system crashing (unless it shuts down the whole Northeast), or a product glitch, should be handled by a company spokesperson. If a CEO were to respond, it would make a problem seem more serious than it actually is.

Put it this way—a near miss between airplanes should be handled by a spokesperson. If they collide, it should be handled by the CEO. A single discrimination suit goes to the spokesperson. A mass discrimination problem à la Texaco goes to the CEO. There is no cookie-cutter approach to a crisis response; it depends on the problem at hand.

• **Although I have said a company should act, there are times when it shouldn't.**

If a problem doesn't point directly to the company or the CEO, be prepared to respond, but wait. If attention can be avoided, by all means do so. As in the case of the client's boring testimony before a Congressional committee, have a basic statement available, but wait to know what problem to address—if any. In Sin #7, there's a story about a company that unnecessarily released damaging information because it thought it would come out in a magazine article. The story never ran.

Here's a basic rule of thumb on the order of communication in the early stages of a crisis requiring companies to respond in public:

• A media statement is needed to rapidly acknowledge the crisis and express concern for those affected.
• The CEO/top-ranking official publicly expresses the company's feelings for those affected and provides information.
• A designated spokesperson takes over disseminating information throughout the crisis.

The severity of the crisis will determine the number of CEO/high-level briefings. Experts can be utilized as well, provided they are able to conduct professional interviews. Keep anyone who is obviously nervous, shaky, or hysterical away from the media.

Designated substitutes are also needed. The first-choice representative may be fishing in Iceland when something happens. Another top executive has to be ready to step in. For example, TWA's CEO was out of the country when Flight 800 crashed, and there didn't appear to be anyone else in control. The same thing happened during Union Carbide's Bhopal disaster when CEO Warren M. Anderson's trip to India kept him away from command for nearly a week. Now it's possible the designated backup won't be available. Have a backup for the backup. That's why, along with the CEO, all top executives have to be media-trained.

If a CEO truly does not believe he can be effective, another top executive should be designated to assume the role. However, in a very serious incident, the top official still has to appear, make a statement—even read it—then introduce the designee to take questions. The point is to utilize the executive who can best represent the company.

In addition, have a band of defenders talk to the press, such as friendly experts, analysts, and other positive third parties, to put the problem in perspective.

A word about experts. It's smart to form relationships with experts in your industry/services. However, do not pay them. Both the company and expert will lose credibility. The exception to this rule is if an expert is brought on board. It's also wise to form relationships with local, state, and government officials. They should be familiar with a company's good side if the bad side appears. Balance is the operative word here.

On the Scene?

One of the thorniest questions is where a CEO should be when a crisis occurs. Although there are various opinions on this—and depending on the circumstances—it's far more practical for a CEO to be at the company's crisis command center and close to a designated press room. Again, I stress it depends on the situation. There may be times when a story is focused on a specific location, as happened in the Xerox crisis in Hawaii in which six employees were shot. Xerox employees at other locations were not part of the story. In that case, it makes sense to operate from that site.

Based on experience, when a crisis hits a company, all hell is breaking loose, and CEOs are under tremendous pressure to manage the situation. Time goes *thisfast*. It's often hard to tear them away from the crisis control center for press briefings. Therefore, it's easier for a CEO if the press center is nearby. Also, as all information flows into the crisis center, a CEO is positioned to have the latest information.

A predesignated crisis "go" team should be dispatched to the scene as soon as possible. One team member should serve as a trained, designated spokesperson to provide basic information to the media on site. Or, there may be an executive (media-trained) already on site. Coordinate the release of information. It's crucial that everyone sings out of the same hymn book.

Again, depending on the circumstances, the CEO should get to the scene by the second or third day, first meeting with those affected before talking to the press. On the other hand, there are times a story moves quickly from a site—or there isn't a site—and the story focuses on headquarters. The CEO can stay put.

A Xerox Copier

Sin #3 described how Xerox provided an excellent crisis response when an employee shot six coworkers at the company's facility in Hawaii. In this case, Glenn Sexton, vice president and general manager of Xerox Hawaii, became the initial spokesperson on the scene in Hawaii while information was released from headquarters in Rochester, New York. CEO Rick Thomas was informed of the news while flying back to the United States from Germany and asked that the flight continue to Hawaii.

The following shows how quickly Xerox responded and how it provided an ongoing flow of information. Also note the visibility of top-ranking officials. (All times are in EST.)

The tragedy occurred on November 2, 1999, at 1:00 P.M. EST.

November 2, 1999

- 3:20 P.M.—Statement acknowledging tragedy
- 8:00 P.M.—Press conference conducted by Xerox vice president Glenn Sexton

November 3, 1999

- 2:00 P.M.—Background/fact sheet press release
- 2:47 P.M.—Press release on the CEO's actions in Hawaii
- 3:00 P.M.—CEO press conference advisory
- 4:00 P.M.—CEO press conference
- 6:30 P.M.—Press release of the CEO's statement
- 9:00 P.M.—Press release announcing fund to help families of victims of violent crimes

A few points. All communication expressed compassion for the families and Xerox employees. During the first press conference, Glenn Sexton announced the CEO would be arriving the next day. A background sheet refuted inaccurate media accounts and provided information on the victims, the shooter, and the company's facility in Hawaii, thus providing reporters with the facts needed for their stories. With all the information disseminated, the basic story was contained.

Good News for Bad News

The next story also provides a model press response in a crisis. The *New York Times* ran a story on how well Atlanta major Bill Campbell performed when a deranged Mark Barton went on a shooting rampage, killing nine people. The mayor appeared on the scene quickly and provided regular press briefings. (Like the Xerox tragedy, this story was confined to the geographic area of the shootings.)

Atlanta journalists gave him high marks for preventing rumors from overtaking the coverage.

"I have to commend him for being accessible and for being in command of the situation," said David Roberts, vice president and news director of Atlanta's NBC affiliate WXIA. "The leadership role he took in disseminating information made it easier to prevent the report of speculation, rumor, and potential misinformation to viewers."

The news director of ABC affiliate Ray Carter agreed with Mr. Roberts. "There certainly was an ease of information, which we are not accustomed to . . . not that it was fast and furious, but it was forthright and full of detail."

The mayor's performance provides a great example of effective crisis communications.

- He quickly established a leadership role and kept reporters briefed.
- The accessibility of information kept the media from reporting rumors and speculation.

In short, the mayor helped reporters do their jobs, and by his doing so, the media reported accurate information. That's a win/ win situation.

Focus on providing accurate information while being accessible and let reporters know the company will release accurate facts as soon as they become available.

Much information comes from communication, and much communication comes from misinformation. In a crisis, especially during the initial hours, with so much "information" floating around, it's hard to determine whether it is fact or fiction. It could even be that the press knows more than you because they have other sources.

Make sure that whatever is said is correct. If there's no confirmation of the information, say so. It can be very exasperating to be badgered about information that may seem correct but hasn't been confirmed. Hold tight. It's unlikely a reporter is going to say, "Go ahead and give us something wrong."

- **Maintain credibility. Once it is lost, it is hard to get it back.**

Don't Shoot the Lawyer—Unless You Have To

Alan Fein, a partner in the Miami law firm Stearns Weaver Miller, was asked about the balancing act of protecting a company and making public statements. He noted a company often faces insurance concerns as well as legal ones, which have to be taken into consideration. As a result, he said there has to be some wiggle room when responding. Fair enough.

However—he says he feels *a company should not be driven by litigation. Rather, litigation should be driven by what's best for the company.* He advises his clients to take responsible action, and he'll pick up the ball from there.

He pointed out the real determining factor is the jury. As we've seen in the earlier examples of CSX, Philip Morris, and Miller Brewing, jurors are regular folks who are going to root for the good guy—and sock it to the bad guy. So it all goes back to doing the right thing. Think how it would look if a lawyer representing an injured party told the jury the XYZ company has not even apologized for the damage it caused.

There's that human factor again. When it comes to media coverage, it becomes the strongest element in determining public/juror perception. Points won't be won if the only thing the public sees is the front of a headquarters building. Avoiding comment for legal reasons rarely satisfies a company's stakeholders and usually provokes more scrutiny.

The point is:

- **A reputation can be ruined in forty-eight hours or less, which is substantially less time than it takes for a lawsuit to get to court.**

It Ain't Over Till It's Over

In terms of conducting interviews, remember these pointers:

- **You are on the record from the minute you say hello to a reporter to the time good-bye ends the conversation. This** includes waving at the door or hanging up the phone after an interview.

- No chitchat is idle. Reporters can make mental notes. And, just because a television camera has been turned off, it doesn't mean the audio isn't running.
- Be familiar with the editing process. Most interviewees have probably had their quotes taken out of context due to editing.

Time restrictions of television news have led to condensed information. Like a skillful surgeon, editors cut and restitch bits of interviews and information into ninety seconds, and a viewer can't tell. A twenty-minute interview is sliced until a fraction of that ends up on the air. It's hard to know what fraction will air. Or, the entire interview could wind up on the editing-room floor.

This means an interview is not a conversation, but a series of potential sound bites about twelve to fifteen seconds long.

Editing isn't new. Newspapers have been doing it forever. The only difference is a newspaper story is covered more thoroughly because it doesn't have to be condensed into seconds. However, the story will be edited, taking a phrase here, a phrase there, often out of sequence. Unlike television news, newspapers have to put in three dots (. . .) to tell readers where the editing has been done on a direct quote.

There is a television version of dots. When reporters are shown listening intently and nodding their heads during an interview, or any other visuals are used, it means the speaker has been edited. Without the visuals, it would be pretty obvious the bites were taken out of context.

In order to control a message, stick to it throughout the entire interview. This applies to both electronic and print media. What was said at the end is as important as whatever is said in the beginning. This sometimes causes the speaker to feel ridiculous repeating a message over and over. But it feels even worse to be quoted out of context. So, stick to the points that are essential, even if reporters seem exasperated. They only have so much time, so they have to go with whatever they have.

Are We Off the Record?

The subject of on the record/off the record puts us in dangerous territory.

- **Stay on the record.**

Not to cast aspersions on the entire media world, but there are times reporters are going to use off-the-record information anyway. In a past situation, information was given off the record to a trusted reporter. He called later that day to say his editor was making him use it. He was truly appalled. He even bought lunch later to apologize. The editor had found a verifying source and therefore ran with the information

A managing editor of a newspaper who requested anonymity admitted it was better to stay on the record. She told of a time her paper was doing a major follow-up story and was using a reporter's old notes. They didn't know he used a certain code to indicate off the record, so they used the information.

The Proverbial Banana Peel

Beware of promises. There's the Chiquita Brands International affair, where a reporter gave up his source for a lighter criminal sentence. It so happened that his source was a former lawyer for Chiquita who had helped the reporter gain access to Chiquita's voice-mail system. The source wound up being charged with unauthorized access to a computer and violations of Ohio's electronic-communication privacy law. The reporter, by the way, had promised the ex-lawyer he'd go to jail rather than reveal his source.

In a case of victims being victimized, *Time* magazine ran a story about videotapes made by two teenage gunmen as they planned a massacre at Columbine High School. When the story broke, the Jefferson County Sheriff's Office in Denver showed the tapes to reporters—before families of the victims saw them. Understandably, the families were angry and upset.

The spokesperson for the sheriff's office said the tapes were released to reporters because *Time* had violated its agreement with investigators by using direct quotes from them. He said he had shown the tapes to *Time* for "background purposes only." *Time* said it had made no such agreement. There are two lessons here:

- **Do not release information if you don't want it to get out.**
- **Always provide information to victims or victims' families before releasing it to the media.**

While I've provided cautionary tales of what can happen off the record, to be fair, terms are bandied about, and it's important to know what reporters are talking about. The following are options reporters may suggest when they are trying to get sensitive information.

On the Record:
Anything you say can be quoted directly and attributed to you by name. Unless you have clearly established otherwise, you are always on the record.

Off the Record:

You are giving the reporter information that he can't use in the story. Off the record does not apply retroactively, so be sure to establish this ground rule before you reveal sensitive information. (In other words, you can't provide information then say, "By the way, that's off the record." Too late.)

Warning: Anything you say off the record can still be used against you in a court of law. Many news organizations, facing legal action, will turn over their reporters' unabridged notes, which may include off-the-record remarks made by sources, according to the TJFR Business Reporter.

Not for Attribution

The reporter can directly quote the information, but he can't ascribe it to you by name. If you're worried about being identified, be sure to negotiate with the reporter about the exact wording of the attribution—"a knowledgeable insider," "an observer," a "Wall Street analyst."

Background

The reporter can use the information but not quote it, and the attribution must remain general, as in "according to a company official."

Deep Background

The reporter can use the information but not quote it, and he may not attribute it to anybody. If you provide background information, still be careful what you say and agree to the term of attribution beforehand.

Then, remember Chiquita. Also one more warning:

- **Don't assume friendship with a reporter will insure positive coverage and don't assume what is said is automatically off the record.**

Loud and Clear

When conducting interviews, be prepared. Don't count on winging it, or some humdinger questions will bring the same reaction as a deer caught in the headlights.

Now that reporters can pull up files in a flash instead of having to literally go through newspaper clippings, many will have researched the company. In a crisis, a company's past problems often become part of the current story, so be prepared. Do not assume they do not know about a company's past trangressions. It's a good idea to have a thorough company history available for the media. Better they get it from the company, even if they already have information.

Prepare a message that contains three key points and stick to them. Think of it as utilizing verbal bullet points. Make sure the message is clear and understandable, leaving no room for misinterpretation. Many executives have complained, "That's what I said, but I didn't mean it that way."

"Gotcha"

Reporters want to get a CEO at his best. Meaning best for them, not so good for the CEO. A bad-tempered executive is far more interesting than a calm one. That means reporters use intimidating techniques that are calculated to hit hot buttons. That's their job. A CEO's is not taking the bait. CEOs must be asked nasty questions when prepping for a press conference. When I am working with CEOs, invariably many instinctively sit back and say, "They'll never ask me that." They still have to determine an answer. Without fail, it's usually the first or second question that comes up.

- **Under tense circumstances, it's very easy to get provoked, again proving the importance of media training.**

Think how many times we've seen the back of an executive running away from reporters or an executive keeping his or her face down or covering his or her head. Whichever way, it's not great for someone's stature. Think of the impression people get of an executive running from reporters or saying, "No comment." Reporters need *something* for their stories. Reporters and cameras will insist on following their target, and they are not going away.

Let "Remember Leon Panetta" become a rallying cry. Remember, he left his grand jury testimony with his dignity intact by stopping and giving a statement to reporters. Think of watching stories involving legal trials; usually there's a lot of action in front of a courthouse. The smart people stop in front of hordes of reporters and make a statement, then continue on their way. On the other hand, some try to run down the steps, heads down in tackle position, saying those two bad words "no comment." Who looks better?

When CEOs are in the midst of trouble, reporters aren't expecting them to be cooperative. They almost faint when they are. If it's not possible to talk about the situation or if one is unsure of what to say, it's still good to stop and acknowledge reporters and tell them information can't be provided at the moment (e.g., "We're in the midst of negotiations, and nothing has been finalized. We'll release information as soon as it is available"). Ignoring reporters or running away makes an executive look like the bad guy. So as a precaution, during difficult times, have a statement—verbal and written—ready to go.

What if a reporter and camera crew sneak up for a surprise interview as a CEO is walking to the office? Suggest talking off-camera first, or, set up an interview appointment. This buys some time to get prepared. Let them ask their questions. One way or another, the reporter and camera are going to follow a subject and probably show that person in some unflattering way. A CEO doesn't have to provide information he doesn't want released, but something has to be said. Don't lie. Remember, it's on tape, so it can come back to haunt the speaker. It's hard to fool a camera. It's better to explain why a question can't be answered. Otherwise, it appears the question is being evaded, which translates into "guilty." Tell reporters it has to be checked, and an answer will be provided.

Talking to reporters can be helpful in finding out where they're going with a story. Perhaps they're off-base, and the correct version can be proved.

In the book *How to Speak TV,* Clarence Jones shows it can happen:

An anonymous caller told a reporter he should investigate why the Urban Renewal Agency paid the city attorney twice as much for his house as it paid the owners of other identical houses on the same block. The reporter went to the property records at the courthouse and discovered the tip was accurate. The lots on the block were all the same size. They were similar, built at the same time, and were carried on the tax assessor's rolls at the same value. Yet when the Urban Renewal

Agency bought the entire block, it paid the city attorney, with good political connections, twice as much as anybody else.

The reporter went to the city attorney, his last stop before broadcasting the story.

Yeah, they paid me twice as much, said the city attorney. But I didn't keep the money. You see, I had leased the house to a color photo-processing company. The lease said if they ever had to move for any reason during the term of lease, I would have to pay for their relocations and build them another processing plant. I've got a copy of the lease in my file if you'd like to read it.

- **Three days of research down the drain. No story.**

Just think how the story would have played if the attorney hadn't consented to do the interview.

Of course, this kind of miracle doesn't happen all the time. But it goes to illustrate the value of finding out what a reporter wants, especially when there's nothing to hide.

He could just be asking for directions.

Live on the Scene

A company has to speak with one voice providing consistent information to all of its audiences. That being said, allow for the reality that sometimes the media are in one place while the press center is in another.

For example, pretend there's a fire at a plant in Mississippi. The company headquarters are in Chicago. In any accident situation, reporters will go straight to the scene. In this case, they find the general manager of the Mississippi plant.

First, let's look at three doomed scenarios:

Scenario 1

Reporter:	When did the fire start?
Manager:	You'll have to ask headquarters.
Reporter:	Have there been any injuries?
Manager:	You'll have to ask headquarters.
Reporter:	Why can't you tell us?
Manager:	I'm not allowed to talk to the press.
Reporter:	Who's in charge here?
Manager:	I am.
Reporter:	But you can't tell us what's going on?
Manager:	No.

Scenario 2

Reporter #1:	I couldn't get through to your headquarters.
Reporter #2:	I got through, but your press department says it doesn't have any information.
Manager:	Keep trying.

Scenario 3

The manager gets a bit out of control and begins cursing at reporters. Good stuff—for the media, that is.

None of those scenarios are appealing. Let's try this one:

Scenario 4

Reporter:	What can you tell us?
Manager:	The fire started at 3:00 A.M. this morning in Building A. One of our guards discovered it and called the Fire Department. Luckily, as

the plant was closed, no one was injured. At this point, it's too early to tell how the fire started or the extent of the damage.

Notice the difference. The manager provided all the pertinent information in no time without giving away state secrets. For planning purposes, the basic questions asked in a crisis are:

- What happened?
- Why did it happen?
- What are you doing to fix it?
- What is the extent of the damage or injuries?

Some or all of these can be answered on site—provided the answers have been coordinated first with the crisis command center at headquarters.

As I said earlier, it's not smart to antagonize reporters. It only turns a bad situation worse. Remember, they always get the last word. Therefore, utilize top local management, making sure they are media-trained. As a Public Relations Society of America survey found, local figures have a high credibility level to the general public.

The reality is a company has to be practical and determine a way to coordinate and release information. Virgin Atlantic Airways North America did and changed its "no comment" policy at airports. If there was an accident, it's pretty obvious a station manager knows basic information. If reporters are told to call headquarters while they are staring at the information source, the lack of cooperation will become part of the story—and it will not be good.

Virgin Atlantic determined that if a crisis were to occur, affected airports would hold press briefings providing basic information during the early stages while the press is on the scene. A plan was developed to coordinate the information with the crisis center at headquarters to insure the same information was released at the same time.

• **To ensure a new policy is effective, employees have to be trained so they can follow the new procedures.**

The airline wound up conducting a major crisis training program for all airport management, staff, and district sales representatives. If a problem occurred in Orlando, for example, it's a safe bet reporters would show up at other ticket counters to get a local angle on the story. Managers received crisis media training. To avoid the specter of ticket agents covering their faces, running away, or hiding behind counters, they were trained to refer reporters to designated press centers, thus becoming an information source instead of news. Many agents were familiar with an incident where, after an airline accident, the airline's staff ran away from reporters. The dash to escape wound up on the evening news, along with complaints that the airline wouldn't provide information.

You Figure It Out

Many companies tell employees not to talk to reporters, but they don't tell them *how* to not do it. The result is a response showing either visual or verbal fear with hands covering faces à la *60 Minutes*, and yes, fear does comes across on the phone.

A particular client was facing a potential problem with a new product. When I called several departments pretending to be a reporter, the phone was answered by a perky person who suddenly said, "Oh," and unperked as soon as I identified myself as a reporter. They said they weren't allowed to talk to the media.

A reporter's dream. The poor people were badgered and gave all sorts of interesting responses: "They won't let us talk to you," "They want to keep all the power," and "I'd talk to you if I could, but I'm afraid I'd be fired." Later, a session was conducted on how to refer press calls professionally to the designated spokesperson. Afterward, the participants confessed they felt relieved to know what to do should they ever come up against someone equally as obnoxious.

Several clients now include "how-not-to-talk" sessions in their employee orientation programs. It's interesting that most employees don't want to talk to reporters. There are some who are flattered by the attention and disgruntled employees who have scores to settle, but many just don't want to have to deal with taking to the media. Neither do a lot of executives, but that's another matter.

Letting Your Right Hand Know

It's not possible to depend on the media to deliver a message. A company has to convey the correct story to all audiences, beginning with employees. In numerous cases, employees get company information via the news.

- **One of the biggest mistakes companies make is not telling their workforce what's going on when there's a problem.**

Employees are a company's main news disseminators, the people on the front lines talking to customers, friends, neighbors, and loved ones. They are put in an awkward and embarrassing position when they can't answer questions about their own company. The result is anger, which leads to rumors and leaks. Providing employees with information they can use is a great opportunity to get your story told, and they are relieved when they know what to say. Internal communication has a major impact on a company's external response.

Irking Allies

There are other members of a company's audience. Shareholders, analysts, customers, government and community officials, vendors, and any others who have a stake in the company need to hear from it. They don't like being the last to know. All of them should get the same information at the same time it is released to the media. This keeps a company in control of its message and avoids the appearance of playing favorites, as happened when Jack in the Box talked to financial analysts before the general public during the killer-hamburger episode. An organization needs a liaison, thoroughly briefed for each audience, to address questions and concerns. Don't forget about the cyberspace audience.

In the story of the company that settled with the FDC on a product-ingredient dispute, the company's liaisons were trained in preparation of the news going public. They said providing information and answering questions had a calming effect on anxious callers and employees.

Investors get riled up when a company is late announcing bad news. Yet, it happens. Take Maytag. In September 1999 it touched off an uproar on Wall Street because it failed to get its disappointing financial information out fast enough. As a result, Maytag's stock and image took a beating.

The saga began with heavy trading on a Wednesday and Thursday. Tuesday's trading volume of 282,000 shares climbed to 1.6 million shares on Wednesday and 3.9 million on Thursday. Word was big institutions were dumping their stock. On Thursday, as a result of this activity, the New York Stock Exchange asked Maytag to release information that could explain the volume. The company said it didn't comment on rumors or market activity. Too bad it didn't go public at that time. It's now apparent the information was available.

On Friday, before the market opened, Maytag issued a press release saying third- and fourth-quarter earnings would be lower than expected.

This caused greater anger because some analysts said they had talked to company officials the evening before the announcement and were told there weren't going to be any major changes to the company's earnings forecast.

Wall Street analysts were mad as hell. The stock took a dive, falling almost 44 percent from July's high of $74 a share. Some wondered if large investors received advance information about Maytag's falling profits before it went public. Others wanted to know when Maytag management knew its earnings were disappointing and why they didn't say anything.

All of this furor was accompanied by major headlines in the business press. Although investors would not have been happy with Maytag's financial performance, the company made matters worse with its slow response.

Maytag's chairman defended the company by explaining it hadn't been able to release details until the information was made public Friday morning. However, as the volume indicated, information got out. The CEO admitted, "I've got to figure out how to improve the communication process."

The chairman talked to analysts on a conference call; he discussed the company's flat profits and explained how he intended to cut costs.

Maytag is not alone when it comes to some companies not providing enough information. Web-based TheStreet.com published a dicey story about companies providing professional investors more information than the average investor would receive. A TheStreet.com reporter eavesdropped on a conference call between on-line grocer Webvan Group, Inc., and a group of institutional investors to discuss its upcoming Initial Public Offering (IPO). Neither journalists nor individual investors were invited. Not only did the article stir up what has become a major controversy, it also showed how the uninvited can still get into the private loop.

The lack of disclosure can hurt relationships as well as stocks. There was the case of the senior Disney executives who were not pleased to read in the *Wall Street Journal* that Coca-Cola had joined a marketing partnership with Disney's arch rival Universal. This strained the relationship between Coca-Cola and a major Disney customer. It also opened the door to Coca-Cola's nemesis Pepsi.

When New York's transit union threatened to strike during the Christmas season, many workers were disgruntled as management. Others were not enthused about taking action. They said most of what they knew came from reading the newspapers. In fact, some said they didn't trust the union any more than they trusted the transit authority. One train operator said, "We hear more rumors than anything else. We never hear from the union. You don't see representatives in here telling us what is going on."

This lack of communication left a number of workers noncommittal instead of rallying to the cause during negotiations.

The Joys of Cyberspace:
Protecting Your Company on the Internet

Faster than a Speeding Bullet

People who don't scuba dive only see the ocean; they are not aware of the undersea world below. The same is true for those not paying attention to the Internet. They can't see the instantaneous flow of information, which needs to be both utilized and monitored.

While many executives may be cyberactive, there are many who aren't. According to *Brill's Content,* only 18 percent of all CEOs use the Net compared to 83 percent of teenagers.

Along with its benefits, cyberspace is an amorphous world where faceless beings spit out all sorts of things about unsuspecting beings. As a result, companies have to be vigilant. They also have to realize the dangers of "no comment" in cyberspace.

Information spreads around the Internet with the snap of fingers. Let's take a closer look at some of the dubious consequences. The next tale is hardly earth-shaking news but shows how fast information moves. When the singer Madonna was once a guest on the *David Letterman Show,* her crude behavior surprised both Letterman and the audience. A sound engineer on the show had to bleep twelve of her remarks. When he got home, he went on the Net and found people in chat rooms already talking about Madonna's performance. This had begun before he had returned home from the taping and before the program aired. How did the news move so fast? Members of the audience went on-line spreading the word. Why is another story.

Alt. Conspiracy

No one has total control over what information is running around in cyberspace. As the Madonna story illustrates, some is show-and-tell. Some is legitimate. However, a lot of it is false. Messages can spin out of control, turning into rumors, lies, and off-the-wall theories. All one has to do is distort mainstream media reports, make weird assumptions about evil governments, or just make things up, and they wind up having an air of legitimacy.

Take TWA's Flight 800. After the July crash, some Net theorists said the true target of the "attack" was Henry Kissinger. He was said to have been on board, although he wasn't. Over time, the theories included such ideas as the jet being zapped by a death ray possibly operated by a consortium of Russians, North Koreans, and the Japanese Aum Shinrikyo cult. Of course, the UFO theory weighed in.

However, one theory grew legs as time went on. Net theorists said the jet was downed by accidental "friendly fire" from a navy ship on a training cruise. They claimed the terrible blunder was covered up by a conspiracy involving federal investigators, the military, and President Clinton.

As time went on, and the Net rumor grew, it wound up being carried by mainstream news. A WCBS-TV reporter in New York reported investigators were examining whether a missile from a U.S. military plane might have torn through the jet without exploding.

By September 8, *Newsday, Newsweek,* the Associated Press, Reuters, and CNN decided to take a look at the friendly-fire theory. CNN had investigated the theory in July and found no evidence to support it. Why did it come up again? A CNN producer explained, "Because so many people were talking about it we felt it was the responsible thing to do, to revisit the question . . . the Internet was part of the reason."

By September 16, the FBI and National Transportation Safety Board officials found themselves under unfriendly fire from a fixated press corps grilling them on the friendly-fire theory. Then, in November, Pierre Salinger went public with the friendly-fire theory. He said his source was a document given to him by "someone in French intelligence in Paris" written by an American who was "tied to the U.S. Secret Service and has important contacts in the U.S. Navy."

Turns out the very reliable document was a copy of an E-mail written by a Net conspirator, dated August 22.

This goes to show how even off-the-wall theories can be taken seriously by mainstream media and the public. All in a very short time. The crash occurred in July. The conspiracy rumor gained legitimacy by September.

Just Fooling Around

There are all sorts of cyberpranksters creating lots of mischief. Ask Gerber. Contrary to a widely circulated Net rumor, the baby food company is *not* required to give every child born between 1985 and 1997 a $500 savings bond as a result of a class-action suit. A Nike rumor hurtling cyberspace caused thousands upon thousands of people to send their old odoriferous sneakers to the company's factory in Wilsonville, Oregon, expecting they'd be redeemed for spiffy new athletic shoes.

Forget about getting free cargo pants and Hawaiian-print T-shirts from the Gap. An E-mail was circulated around saying the retailer was conducting a "beta test" and would generously compensate test participants. It was incorrectly reported that

Gap would provide free clothing in return for sending the message to others.

Miller Brewing received thousands of E-mails asking if the offer for a free six-pack was real. A false chain letter said if two million people signed their names to an E-mail and sent it to the beer company by December 31, all senders would receive the six-pack.

True or False?

When Intel CEO Andy Grove was talking about the fundamental ways business is affected by change, he brought up the Internet. "What's unusual right now is that we're all being affected by the Internet at the same time. Corporate America looks like a flotilla of boats in a stormy sea." That storm is not going to calm down any time soon.

Here's the problem. Anything written tends to have more credibility than the spoken word. That leads to the scary task of distinguishing fact from fiction. Thanks to cyberspace gremlins, businesses are being hit by rumors, misinformation, leaks, smear campaigns, and rogue Web sites. With the public's mistrust of big corporations, urban legends are becoming fruitful and multiplying. Often, they are localized and modified in the retelling. This means any company is a possible target and can become part of a story zipping around.

Here's an example. The following E-mail message circulated, attacking certain consumer-product companies (whom I won't mention):

"Check the ingredients listed on your shampoo bottle and see if they have this substance by the name of Sodium Laureth Sulfate or simply SLS. This substance is found in most shampoos and the manufactures [sic] use it because it produces a lot of foam and it's cheap." It went on to provide statistics on getting cancer from the stuff. It was signed by the executive secretary of the University of Pennsylvania Health System Office. So is it a hoax or not? The University of Pennsylvania Health System was contacted and extended a quick reply:

The message in question was received by one of our employees as unsolicited E-mail. The employee then forwarded it to some of her acquaintances with her signature file attached. Eventually, the message was posted to various UseNet newsgroups and to sites on the World Wide Web. The employee had no intention of distributing this message to anyone other than the friends to whom she forwarded it.

The University of Pennsylvania Health System does not endorse this message and cannot address the accuracy of the information it contains.

If you know others who have received this message, please feel free to forward the entire text of this reply to them.

Look at the path and potential damage of one innocuous E-mail. After all, companies and their brands were named. It's daunting to think how many consumers took this warning seriously and stopped using the bad brands in favor of the one not containing SLS. Also notice how the University of Pennsylvania Health System had a ready response.

In another incident, the reputation of an upscale department store was under attack when a customer said she had been overcharged for a cookie recipe. The customer E-mailed her story and the overpriced recipe throughout cyberspace. It was widely received and believed. Turns out the story has been floating around for years, to the embarrassment of all who assumed it was true and passed it along. There are now Web sites dedicated to tracking hoaxes. For example, the Department of Energy is one of many that has a site that includes up-to-date warnings and sections on chain letters, hoaxes, and viruses. Yet, in the course of a day, there's rarely time to check the legitimacy of all the information flowing in.

Passing It Along

A lot of cyberspacers believed the following rumor, to the detriment of clothing designer Tommy Hilfiger. For two years, an Internet rumor circulated accusing Mr. Hilfiger of making racist remarks on the *Oprah Winfrey Show*. The rumor wound up being taken seriously and was picked up by the national media. Considering Hilfiger has ethnic customers, the rumor did a lot of harm.

Ignoring the rumor didn't work; it made it grow. Although Hilfiger's response was too slow, the PR folks finally wrote a press release explaining the designer had never been on the *Oprah Winfrey Show* nor had he made racist comments. Quite effectively, they posted the release on every site that mentioned the rumor.

Two years is too long a time to sit back and hope a dangerous rumor will disappear. It would be impossible to track down every rumor on the Net, but the ones that are having a negative impact on a company have to be addressed.

- **Whenever cyberspace consumers are posting blatantly inaccurate information that is hurting the company, respond openly and set the record straight.**

Cutting It Off at the Pass

An executive of an international company told a story that began with the introduction of a state-of-the-art product praised by the media. It's the only product of its kind.

One day, the company received a phone call from a customer saying he had read negative comments about the product in a chat room and wanted to know if they were true.

This was the first the company had heard about the problem and the chat rooms. They took a look, and sure enough, there were all these people on-line saying there was a problem with the product, and some remarks were pretty unfriendly.

He said the company knew most of the people didn't even own the product because the company had introduced a limited edition.

The company examined the product and found a small flaw, which had gone undetected. In fact, it was hard to tell where the flaw was until it was pointed out. Top management called a crisis meeting. They were confronting two problems: a product flaw and Internet rumors.

The tech people said the flaw could be fixed with a small adjustment. The company sent out notices to all who had purchased the product, explaining the minor flaw and asking customers to bring the product in to their dealers so it could be adjusted at no charge. They also put the announcement on their Web page and scripted their customer-service people with the same message.

Meanwhile, back in the chat rooms, the subject had spread to include the company's other products, participants were making negative claims, which weren't true.

With more investigation, it turned out the tech people knew the person who had announced the problem because he called them frequently. He hadn't talked to the company first because he was eager to be the first to post the discovery. The company decided to go into the chat room itself to discuss what they were doing to fix the flaw. Within a few days, interest died away. Luckily for the company, it discovered the chat room early on and took action. If that customer hadn't called with questions about the postings, they wouldn't have been aware of the serious problem developing in cyberspace. Also, the product flaw never became a story because the company jumped on the problem quickly and fixed it.

By the way, the company now monitors the Net.

Here's another way a company managed a Web crisis. A disgruntled customer had posted a Web page that was beginning to hurt a company's special promotion. The customer was relating his horror stories about dealing with the company, eliciting postings from consumers thanking him for the warning. Top management was going ballistic, yelling at their lawyers to do something. Lawyers were yelling at each other because no one knew exactly what to do.

The vice president of public relations took a different route. She called the customer. She agreed he had received terrible service, and she apologized. She made sure he received everything promised plus some extra goodies. He was floored. He said he never expected a huge company like hers would call and pay attention to "a little nobody." He was so impressed, he reported the experience on his Web page before he shut it down.

Mad as Hell

Some people venting on the Net are not as anonymous as they once thought. In this incident, a CEO not only exposed some on-line critics, he sued some of them. HealthSouth's Richard Scrushy found himself having to fend off rumors coming seemingly out of nowhere. At an investor conference, part of the mystery was solved. He discovered he had a very serious problem on his hands.

It turns out there was a bulletin board on the Internet devoted to his company. People were posting disparaging messages, including false claims about the company. One said the company was a house of cards; another said Mr. Scrushy was going to be probed for billing fraud. (Neither true.) When the stock price began to fall, posted warnings included "Get out and stay out. I can't believe anyone would invest long-term in this pyramid scheme calling itself a company." In reply, someone said, "You may not be far wrong. I have heard rumors of a federal lawsuit for several weeks now," according to the *Wall Street Journal*.

There never was a suit. That was just the problem. The rumors were false, but plausible. For example, another message claimed HealthSouth had been downgraded although it hadn't been. This venting attracted the interest of analysts and investors, who began calling.

The messages didn't just stick to business. They got personal. Somebody wrote he was having an affair with Mr. Scrushy's wife and claimed to have been in the Scrushys' home. This was taken seriously. In fact, Mr. Scrushy cancelled a deal to acquire a company because the company's president had the bad manners to bring the subject up during a dinner.

Anyway, the on-line rumors were damaging. He hired a computer detective to track down the offenders. The detective managed to flush out several, including a former employee who wrote some of the more inflammatory messages. The company sued her for defamation.

"Scrushy should resign" was the last message "Dirk Diggler" ever posted before he was caught. Mr. "Diggler" turned out to be a manager at Pennsylvania State University and a former HealthSouth employee. He was also the one claiming to have had the affair with Mrs. Scrushy. The Scrushys pressed criminal charges of harassment and stalking, which they dropped after he apologized.

Although some companies have tried to reason with rumor-mongering posters, others, like HealthSouth, are not taking false rumors lying down. When the E*Trade Group found a wayward poster on its Yahoo board, they discovered the board was using secrecy software. They hired a computer whiz to zap the shields.

Minding the Store

Net surfers have become a serious and important audience. The HealthSouth story points out how analysts and investors were reading the dubious bulletin board.

One investor said he scanned the HealthSouth board as an "early warning system" for public reports he might not know about otherwise.

An analyst said the postings wouldn't make him put a buy, sell, or hold recommendation. He did say, however, ". . . looking at and monitoring the boards is something a prudent analyst has to do."

Just as a company has to respond quickly to earthbound media accusations, it has to do the same with whatever is on the Net. Internet troublemakers have created a new cottage industry—Internet monitoring and intervention. There are companies who monitor on-line information sources such as newsrooms, public forum sessions, and Web sites for companies. Some companies have their own staff monitoring the Net.

One way or the other, do it.

Sometimes, it's best to sit back and watch what's happening; a negative remark may not develop into anything, and overreacting could turn it into a major issue. Other times, a company has to respond. Some go into a chat room as an anonymous individual and defend the company, addressing the issue. For example, outraged consumers were venting during an on-line discussion about an offending product. Then, someone asked if the product was so awful, how could the company have moved from number ten to number two in the last year? After that, the criticism faded.

This "Internet Outreach" has one caveat. Some Internet forum folks are getting suspicious of companies practicing what they call on-line deception. But, if this method is used to respond to blatantly inaccurate information or personal attacks on individuals, set the record straight. It is a quieter option than a lawsuit, which can attract public attention to the problem.

This is what Web monitors should be monitoring:

- A legitimate problem or a complaint.
- A readily identifiable individual or group trying to influence behavior.
- A stock manipulator.
- Revenge.
- Misinformation and disinformation.

There is an upside to monitoring. By checking out chat rooms and messages boards, it's possible to obtain valuable market and investor research information and to get a handle on perceptions. Also, it's important to know what is being said because it can bring up issues that were unapparent.

There are millions of people who could be watching a company, and it might not even know. In only four years, the number of AOL subscribers jumped from approximately 1.5 million in December 1994 to 15 million in December 1998. And that's just one Internet provider. We're talking about zillions of people.

Cyberspace alone is a crisis challenge.

Everyone in the Pool

Communicating in a crisis is not easy, yet, there is no choice. The battle lines have been drawn in perception. Those companies who say nothing are presumed guilty, whereas those who come forward are considered responsible.

The only thing more interesting than our own affairs is other people's affairs. Montaigne said, "Men are generally more anxious to find out why things are so than whether things are so."

That is why people through the ages have been addicted to news. It's ironic that curiosity seems to be the only thing that never changes in a rapidly changing world.

Therefore, if a company becomes the object of curiosity, it has to tell people its side of the story. Otherwise, they'll come up with their own versions.

6

Just Numbers on a Balance Sheet

After two companies merged, employee uncertainty and fear hung in the air, affecting productivity and customer service. The CEO called a meeting with his top deputies to discuss the situation. They decided to come up with a snappy campaign with a slogan to change the climate. "One for all, all for one" was chosen. The CEO decreed the slogan would be plastered everywhere and all employees would be given a free slogan-adorned mug.

His orders were carried out. The slogan was everywhere: internal newsletters, E-mail, Intranet, and bulletin boards. Letters were sent to every employee's home. And, employees got their mugs.

They, in turn, smirked and wondered why management had spent so much money on a stupid, meaningless campaign when it couldn't afford to save jobs.

The employees had such major concerns as their job status and severance packages. Plus, the corporate cultures weren't blending. None of this was addressed with a slogan. The slogan campaign became a joke shared by all employees, so at least the cultures finally had something in common. Fear and uncertainty turned into anger. It wasn't long before employees began calling the press. . . .

We've come to the Sixth Deadly Sin: "Just Numbers on a Balance Sheet," committed by those who don't understand the changing workplace and the resulting ramifications for employees and management. Internal forces are having an enormous impact on a company's performance.

Although it is essential for a CEO to be thinking about a company's future growth, stock, and profits:

• **Maintaining internal stability also requires serious attention.**

The internal aspects of a company tend to get overlooked in crisis management. Yet, this is where many external crises begin.

This chapter examines how problems develop and how they can be avoided or contained. This includes understanding how major decisions affect employee attitudes and how workers react—both positively and negatively. Thorny issues and incidents *can* be managed through communication.

It's important to remember employees are a reflection of a company—which means they are also a reflection of the CEO.

Brave New World?
How to Stay on Top of Change

Many grew up in a world very different from today's. Yes, technology has changed the way the business world operates, but there are other challenges as well. Executives now face greater threats from such issues as sexual harassment, violence in the workplace, wrongful-discharge suits, and discrimination. Add political correctness, and executives have to tread very carefully.

On top of everything else, internal issues have joined the realm of "sexy" news stories. With more focus on CEOs, such subjects as financial damage and executive dismissals have become delicious fodder for the media.

For those feeling the changes in the environment unsettling, they are not alone. In a *Fortune* magazine article, clinical psychologist Steven Berglas explained many people on all levels of the company are living in a new world and don't know the rules. ". . . New knowledge is scary, or you don't feel you need it, or you just delegate it to somebody and hope that will be enough. Doing things the old way gives rise, in many managers, to paranoia—because they are aware on some level that the old ways are no longer working but they don't know what to do about it."

Trust You?

In the olden days, people worked at one company until it was time to receive a gold watch and retire. Now, it's rare to be with the same company for more than five years.

- **The days of downsizing and reengineering did more than eliminate jobs: they changed the dynamics of company loyalty.**

A client overheard a young man telling a friend he had worked at IBM for a year and he really liked it. Then, the young man said he thought he'd wait another year before he started job hunting. There was a time, not so long ago, when job-hopping was a real liability on a resume. It was a sign of instability. Now, length of stay is not important. In addition to executive recruiters, the Internet has become a swashbuckler, pirating people away via the Web—on company time, no less. So, say good-bye to mutual trust. Companies aren't guaranteeing long-term employment; therefore, employees aren't sticking around. The new attitude is "I'll give you one year versus my life," notes Pam Banks, a human-resource expert specializing in systems and organizational change.

Taken for Granted

Comfortable as an old shoe may be for some relationships, it is not when it comes to management and employees.

- **Employees, one of a company's most important audiences, tend to be the most forgotten.**

These people are not simply figures on a balance sheet. If they are treated as such, there are consequences that have a direct impact on the bottom line.

- **Many external crises begin internally.**

Take Texaco. The disclosure of its discriminatory practices wound up being front-page news. Besides the bad press, the company had to pay record-breaking fines. Or, in another case, internal problems erupted in public at the Shoney's restaurant chain. African-American workers said the chain deliberately shunted them into low-paying and low-visibility jobs and clearly showed a preference for white servers, cashiers, and managers. Shoney's, without admitting wrongdoing, wound up paying $105 million to an estimated ten thousand African-Americans who either worked for or were denied employment by the company for a seven-year period. This story received a great deal of play in the media. None of it was good.

Get Mad and Even

Sin #3 focused on how anger motivated victims to take highly visible action against a company. The same is true internally, perhaps even more so.

- **Employees who feel valued and are treated with dignity are not going to turn on a company in bad times.**
- **Those who feel undervalued, will.**
- **The underlying factor in internal "act out-iveness" is anger.**

Resentment triggers direct and indirect damage. In terms of retaliation, violence in the workplace is certainly one result. In fact, most violent episodes are caused by a disgruntled employee who has been fired. However, there are also other forms of sabotage, including employees quitting and taking competitive data with them and leaking information to the press. Anger can be contagious, and the results aren't pretty.

Employees are also venting on Web sites. One site put up by several Union Bank employees was critical of a proposed merger. They resentfully talked about the prospect of dismissals. Sarcasm about the proposed merger between Union Bank of Switzerland and the Swiss Bank Corporation led to employees telling such jokes, including UBS stood for "Unemployed Before Summer."

Employee griping has turned corporate cybergossip into a lucrative business. Take VaultReports.com, a Manhattan-based on-line company that dishes out the latest dirt on big law firms, investment banks, and management consultants. In eight months, it grew from ten to sixty-five full-time employees and has quintupled its revenue.

VaultReports.com also sponsors a series of gossipy message boards on which employees are invited to anonymously "bitch about your boss." It should come as no surprise these boards have been a quick success, drawing more than 130,000 regular visitors to the free Web site. Morgan Stanley Dean Witter & Co., among other companies, wound up blocking its employees from posting messages on the VaultReports chat board. This attempt made news and brought a wealth of free publicity for the Web site.

Speaking with Forked Tongue

First, we have to look at why some employees seek retribution. Dr. Marilyn Puder-York, a psychologist and executive coach, says most of it boils down to communication, or lack thereof. This points right to top executives who fail to realize, or don't care, about the impact a decision has on people.

Meanwhile, today's workers have grown more sophisticated

"And here's our new director of human resources."

and can recognize transparent gestures. As a result, posturing can blow up in a company's face.

There was one company that ran a "slogan on a mug" kind of campaign along the lines of "we care about you." A year later, the company downsized, giving employees little warning. Worse, severance packages were downright stingy. It was bad enough for those who exited. Think about the job survivors. They saw how much the company "cared" for them. Workloads increased, but salaries didn't. Some employees sued for overtime pay. The company wound up agreeing to a $7 million settlement with the Labor Department to pay uncompensated workers.

At another company, a CEO told employees they were the company's greatest asset and he wanted everyone to grow and get ahead. That sentiment was always prominently mentioned in the annual report. Yet, the company never promoted minority white-collar or assembly-line workers. Fed up, some employees turned to the press. The problem was reported in a major newspaper. Suddenly, many minority workers were promoted. Some deserved the promotions, others did not. Internally, resentment grew over the obvious insincerity of the company's actions. The newspaper article attracted the EEOC's attention, prompting an investigation that led to a multimillion-dollar lawsuit.

In another instance, a company had to cut costs and contemplated downsizing. Rumors began circulating. Employees asked their managers what was happening. They didn't know. Work almost came to a halt as employes huddled together, wondering about their fate.

The human resources director told top management they needed to say something to their employees, but management said they were not ready. However, to "lift spirits," otherwise called trying to increase productivity, an executive vice president sent an E-mail to all employees telling them not to worry about their future at the company. Some were about to buy new homes, cars, and other big-ticket items. After the E-mail, everyone sighed with relief and spent their money instead of saving it and cutting expenses.

A month later, the company announced it was reorganizing and one-third of its workers would lose their jobs. Employees were outraged that they had been misled. In retaliation, they staged a massive protest. The public was angered by the company's actions, and many boycotted its products. Some employees downloaded sensitive financial information and gave it to the press. Reporters had a field day. Analysts didn't. They began dumping stock. The company wound up filing for bankruptcy protection.

Embittered employees can get a boss in big trouble. Disgruntled workers brought down a government-appointed prosecutor who had been a rising star. She improperly used drug forfeiture money to buy expensive office furnishings and used office personnel for personal chores. In addition, a group of office workers sued her for age and sex discrimination in promotions and assignments. Workers in the office began sending a series of anonymous letters to county and state officials, alleging improprieties. These letters were also sent to the press. The employee letters led to an investigation of the prosecutor. The upshot is the governor stripped her of her power.

As these cases show, internal problems lead to such grim consequences as bad press coverage and lawsuits.

• **What goes out comes from within.**

Danger Zones:
How to Avert Problems

Don't Even Think About It

In the past, employees went to work and did their jobs. They were evaluated solely on results, not on how they got along with others. With the advent of discrimination laws, companies had to evaluate employee interaction as well as performance.

Many didn't know they were acting badly.

• **The rules of the business world were changing.**

The Clarence Thomas Supreme Court hearings brought the issue right into our living rooms and offices. A chorus of "whoops" and "uh-ohs" circulated throughout the corporate world as sexual harassment was being socially defined.

As a result, the growth and expense of sexual harassment lawsuits are scary. It's so prevalent, there's now insurance for it. Ten years ago, a corporation might have tried to cover up inappropriate behavior or toss it off as horseplay. Those days belong to the dinosaurs. Today, a company confronted by a harassment suit has to take swift—and public—action.

- **Mishandled, an internal situation can turn into a high-profile lawsuit.**

Discrimination doesn't discriminate. Men can wind up in the same boat as women. There are also other forms of bias. A former Smith Barney broker with a congenital facial deformity accused a branch manager in an arbitration claim of a cruel campaign of insults before firing him in 1990.

Out You Go

Today, many top executives are being caught with their hands in the cookie jar, and they are getting more than a slap on the wrist.

The American subsidiary of Astra of Sweden, now a unit of London-based pharmaceutical giant AstraZeneca, got rid of its chief executive and the entire senior management team when allegations of sexual harassment arose. Astra officials and managers were allegedly making sexually offensive comments and requiring women sales representatives to socialize as a condition of employment. Other bad behavior included propositioning, grabbing, and kissing.

These accusations were reported in *Business Week* magazine. Shortly afterwards, the EEOC filed a suit against the company.

Astra USA wound up settling the suit for $9.9 million without admitting guilt. It's important to note:

- **In these situations, negative press coverage leads to many EEOC investigations.**

The sexual harassment suit against Astra opened a can of worms. Astra officials not only fired the CEO, they sued him for fraud, breach of fiduciary duty, waste of corporate assets, and of course, inappropriate conduct regarding sexual harassment. The CEO denied the allegations. However, he did plead guilty to criminal charges of filing false tax returns and wound up in prison.

There were also the goings-on at Lew Lieberbaum, a small brokerage firm that employed three hundred people in Manhattan and on Long Island. This is a doozie of a sexual-harassment story. It was so risqué, the media couldn't report some of the allegations. The problem went beyond catcalls and lewd comments. The EEOC filed suit. It was later settled for $1.8 million, and the firm is no longer in existence.

One of the cofounders said the allegations were "misrepresentative" but admitted some had a scintilla of truth. His rationalization was "We had 300 employees; 250 were under age thirty. When that happens, you're going to have intracompany relationships. It's unavoidable." Besides blaming some of the questionable behavior on a young workforce, he also pointed to a tense environment. Apparently, the young men did not know how to react to a bad market so they become stressed out. The only way they knew how to let off steam was to behave badly. The public wasn't amused.

At CNA Life Insurance Company, two women began complaining about offensive sexual remarks. One of the people making them happened to be the president. The two women went to the president's deputy, but no action was taken. Apparently, both executives had made extremely offensive remarks about the women's "body parts." The next thing you know, CNA announced the resignation of both the president and his deputy and faxed a statement to the media.

Notice how:

* **CNA made a point of going public with the resignations.**
* **The company was aware of the potential damage if it got pilloried in the press for not taking appropriate action.**

They were right to announce the information before the press did.

Be Careful

Ever notice there are no stories proclaiming the lack of sexual-harassment claims at a company? Good behavior rarely receives public kudos in the press. Employees who feel they are treated fairly don't call reporters to cooperatively point out internal problems.

That being the case, it makes business as well as moral sense to insure employees know sexual harassment or any other form of discrimination will not be tolerated.

This means establishing strong harassment policies and making sure they are repeatedly communicated to employees, verbally, in employee handbooks, during orientation programs, and on the Intranet. Insure the employees understand the complaint process. As one lawyer noted:

* **If a company doesn't have a written policy, it might as well paint a target on its back.**

Lawyers also note the importance of documenting questionable behavior. These are the best prevention tools.

Just Say No

To protect themselves from liability and bad press, many companies have gone so far as to adopt rules not only against gropers and lewd joke tellers, but also against a manager asking a subordinate for a date.

Romances between unequals are potential breeding grounds for harassment complaints, especially after the relationship sours. At one company, the president had to ask Human Resources if he could take out a young woman who worked at one of his stores. The HR dating police said no.

The president—make that the former president—of a major office-supply company was arrested at the home of a female subordinate and charged by police with assaulting her. He was subsequently terminated for violating the company's "fraternization" policy.

The CEO of a large computer-software company went to court when his steamy relationship with an executive assistant who was twenty years his junior went awry and his former paramour was convicted of sending false E-mail messages to bolster a sexual-harassment claim.

Notice that executive wrongdoing makes for titillating reading. Forget privacy when there's a spicy story.

Taking the Wrong Route

Speaking of media attention, Mitsubishi encountered more than its share of headlines when it mishandled a massive sexual-harassment suit. Its major missteps have provided many lessons, even though that probably was not the company's intention. In 1996, the American subsidiary of Mitsubishi Motor Corporation wound up facing the largest sexual-harassment suit by the federal government. The company was charged with sexually harassing hundreds of female workers at its automobile assembly plant in Normal, Illinois. The suit complained of routine groping, graffiti-writing, and degrading remarks directed at women who made up about a fifth of the four thousand plant employees. It was also asserted that Mitsubishi managers had created an atmosphere that condoned such behavior. These same charges were also made by women who filed private sexual-harassment suits.

In response, Mitsubishi played hardball. The company denied the charges and argued it had actively investigated accusations of harassment or discrimination brought to its attention since 1987, when the plant opened. According to a company spokesperson, there had been some limited, isolated incidents, but the spokesperson said they were managed effectively by the company's policies and procedures. He said the company had a "zero tolerance" policy against sexual harassment and discrimination and added company officials had "thoroughly investigated the allegations."

Internally, the company sent a letter to its employees saying it "cannot allow allegations of political and monetary motivation to dampen our morale or efforts."

Mitsubishi staged a rally intended to embarrass the EEOC and discredit the complainers. The protest was held outside the EEOC's Chicago offices. Employees who participated got a full day's pay, a free lunch, and a three-hour trip on one of fifty-nine buses equipped with video units so they could watch movies. The company kept a tally of who attended and who did not. No intimidation there. Mitsubishi also set up phone banks at the factory to call lawmakers and defend the company—all on company time. The rally idea was thought up by an employee and quickly endorsed by the company. Many attended because they were concerned the lawsuit would hurt sales and they would lose their jobs.

After the suit was announced, the spokesperson gathered employees in the cafeteria to "keep them fully informed." According to a taped transcript, "informed" meant promoting the rally in Chicago. "We've got to win the media by parading a thousand strong in Chicago," he said.

Meanwhile, Mitsubishi was taking no prisoners on the legal side either. In addition to refusing to cooperate with the EEOC, company lawyers asked for some of the womens' gynecological and psychological records.

The spokesman said he felt the company had nothing to lose with a high-profile campaign. Well, that's a matter of opinion. The Reverend Jesse Jackson and the National Organization for Women (NOW) organized demonstrations at company headquarters and dealerships around the country. Needless to say, the protests received national media attention. Thanks to all the public hoopla, nearly all the Mitsubishi companies in the United States received calls from worried customers, and some women tried to return newly purchased cars, citing the harassment suit. Sales began to decline.

Well, actually . . .

After the rally, Minoro Makihara, president of the parent Mitsubishi Corporation in Japan, offered conciliatory statements expressing condemnation of sexual harassment. Mitsubishi wound up settling the suit for $34 million. Kohei Ikuta, executive vice president of the American subsidiary said, "We want to reaffirm today what we have said previously: We have had problems involving sexual harassment, which required correction and we extend our sincere regret to any woman who has been harmed." The company said it would institute mandatory training programs for all employees and other changes to prevent future problems, including encouraging employees with complaints to come forward.

- **The company wound up doing what it should have done in the first place.**
- **Denial prolonged the story.**
- **The crisis could have been avoided by acting responsibly.**
- **The chairman and president of the U.S. division were fired.**

Expensive Blinders

The first sexual harassment complaints at Mitsubishi were filed in 1992. The womens' attorney thought the alleged harassment would stop. Instead, it got worse, she said. The women in the lawsuits were treated to retaliation and intimidation.

Management should have been hearing warning sirens when the EEOC launched a fifteen-month investigation in April 1994. Mitsubishi refused to cooperate, not letting the EEOC interview management-level personnel accused of harassment. The director of the EEOC Chicago district office said, "Companies under investigation not only cooperate, they also improve their practices to make certain they are in total compliance with the law. Mitsubishi didn't take any such steps."

To review some of the essential crisis management guidelines covered so far:

- Get bad news out fast.
- Tell the truth.

- Take responsible action.
- Fix the problem.

Mitsubishi did the direct opposite. Instead of quickly addressing the harassment suit and explaining what it intended to do to make amends, the company extended the negative story by denying it. The denials were false, making the company look even worse. Mitsubishi began fixing the problem, but only after it was forced into doing so.

Some may argue this was a cultural problem. True, there are few women in the Japanese workplace. There are certainly not any working on automobile assembly lines.

No excuse. There are laws. The general counsel, an American, had to be aware of them. Even if Japanese colleagues did not understand the problem, other American executives should have been sensitive to the seriousness of the charges. A company operating in another country has to be aware of cultural differences and laws.

The Mitsubishi problem got out of hand, demonstrating how sexual-harassment claims require rapid company action and investigation. Fixing the problem goes without saying. A company should work with, instead of against, a government entity with which it is negotiating, especially when it has done something wrong.

- **It's also smart to keep a low profile.**

It's one thing when a company is innocent; it should go public and prove it. It's another matter when a company is not telling the truth.

Mistakes cost Mitsubishi $34 million, tons of bad press, lost business, and a negative work environment. Denial doesn't make problems go away.

Guilty Till Proven Innocent

There is another danger in the workplace. Not all harassment charges are true. Unfortunately, there is the growing problem of false claims. Besides these frivolous suits taking a lot of time, money, and negative press, it takes a terrible toll on those wrongly accused and makes it harder for employees who have legitimate complaints.

In one situation, a CEO's former personal assistant, who had been fired, was claiming sexual harassment. One of the things she alleged was she had to run around the desk to escape his advances. She was threatening to go to the press if the company did not settle for a large sum.

Since I had never met the CEO, it came as a surprise when the man turned out to be in his late seventies, walking slowly into the room, using a cane. It would have taken him "hours" to get around his desk. After he left the room, I recommended calling her bluff. All the CEO had to do to damage her credibility was stand up in court. She never went to the press.

Not all false claims are so easy to squash. Virgin Atlantic Airways North America is an example of a company willing to unsheathe its sword and fight the dragon. Both Richard Branson, the founder and chairman, and David Tait, executive vice president, North America, found themselves on the "not guilty" end of sexual-harassment suits. Refusing to settle, they spent a great deal of time, money, and negative press taking these claims to court. They won. They decided to fight because the accusations were not true. Mr. Tait said the worst part was being presumed guilty until they could prove their innocence. But they felt settling the claims would have set a dangerous precedent.

If he has to fire or discipline a female employee, Mr. Tait now makes sure his office door stays open or has his assistant in the room.

One president at another company told me he will not conduct one-on-one interviews alone with women job candidates. Period.

Some top executives interviewed thought it was faster and cheaper to just settle claims, even if they aren't true. However, others applauded Virgin Atlantic's action. The whole issue of setting precedents for rewarding bad behavior is a weighty one, but it is up to the company.

A Brewing Crisis

Somehow, common sense seems to be getting lost along today's way. Miller Brewing proved this after a bad decision turned into a $26 million crisis. In a *Seinfeld* episode, Jerry Seinfeld's character didn't remember the name of the woman he was dating (Dolores), only that it rhymed with a female body part.

The next day, a manager at Miller Brewing Company was talking to a woman coworker, asking if she had seen the episode. He went on to say he thought it was offensive and couldn't believe the show had passed the censors. She said she couldn't guess what part rhymed with Dolores. About an hour later, they discussed the episode again with another coworker, who was also surprised the show aired. The woman wanted to know the rhyming body part. The man demurred, being sensitized enough to know not to say the word. The woman kept pressing, so he finally got a dictionary and showed her the word.

That night, she got married and was out of the office for a

long weekend. When she returned to work, she went to her boss and complained about the coworker's behavior, saying he had crossed the line. Her boss suggested she talk to the man. When she told her dictionary nemesis she found his behavior offensive, he apologized. He should have stopped there. He went on to express disbelief that someone who uses the vulgar language she used would be offended.

The company investigated the incident. The next day, the man was fired for sexually harassing a coworker by discussing the *Seinfeld* episode. This was a man who had worked at the company for close to twenty years. They said he showed "poor managerial judgment."

He turned around and sued the company, the allegedly harassed coworker, and his former supervisor. The suit went to trial, and the jury awarded him $26.6 million ($24.5 million from Miller, $1.5 million from his former coworker, and $601,500 from the former supervisor).

A judge later trimmed the jury award, dropping the punitive damages assessed to the woman and reducing the award against the vice president. He didn't touch Miller's $24.5 million judgment. Miller is appealing.

No matter. The jury's actions speak for themselves. They could be blunt because they didn't have to worry about being sued.

The irony of it all: the Miller folks probably fired the guy to avoid getting sued by the woman.

The fiasco should never have gotten so out of hand. As there is always more to a story, there are those who say someone in the company wanted him out and the complaint provided a great opportunity. It was still a stupid decision.

When Rights Aren't Right

What's going on here? How did things get so crazy? One explanation is we are seeing the fallout from the pendulum of social change, according to human resources expert Pam Banks. This change began in 1964 with the Civil Rights Act (Title VII) making it unlawful to "discriminate against any individual with respect to his compensation, terms, conditions, or privileges of employment, because of such individual's race, color, religion, sex, or national origins."

Then, in 1986, the Supreme Court affirmed that sexual harassment was a form of sex discrimination. As a result:

- **Today's employees are far more aware of their rights and self-needs than ever before.**

Those workers with the worst intentions have a new tool: the law. They know how to use it to get back at a company. In 1997, work-related claims made up one-third of all civil suits in the United States.

Some claims involve retribution or job protection. Let's say an employee was on probation, very close to losing a job. So, he or she dances with a boss at the company Christmas party, then goes to human resources the next day claiming inappropriate behavior. After that, even though the employee was not doing the job, it's unlikely the company would fire that person.

One industry experiencing a rise of claims is new media enterprises run by a number of young, inexperienced managers. A Silicon Alley attorney estimates 80 percent of the lawsuits filed against the New York–based new media companies alone have been brought by disgruntled employees. A lot of the suits are products of a casual, nearly rule-free environment at many firms.

Plus, many growth companies are amassing a huge amount of wealth. "People are making fortunes, so those who signed on early and now feel they didn't negotiate hard enough are likely to be upset," explained one attorney.

Sad but True

The climate has become more unsettled with the rise of violence in the workplace. In spite of the growing problem, it is often overlooked in "What If?" crisis planning scenarios. Most executives give me a blank look when I bring this up. That would never happen here. Forget employees kicking a trash can because they've had a bad day. Now, one person's bad day becomes everyones'. According to a Justice Department study, the workplace is the scene of almost 1 million violent crimes every year.

In addition to the event, the aftermath of a traumatic episode is fraught with the serious problem of internal post-traumatic stress disorder. This can lead to high rates of turnover, lowered productivity, absenteeism, and increased health problems.

Other alarming data show the number of bosses killed at work has doubled over the past ten years, with three to four bosses a month being killed by a disgruntled worker or former worker.

Adding insult to literal injury, if an employee gets violent, the company may be sued for negligent hiring and negligent retention.

Experts explain people in the labor force spend a very significant time at their workplace. For many, work is everything. Even the threat of job loss has become the threat of losing everything. When that happens, others may lose as well.

The Quick Fix

CEOs are facing such internal challenges as:

- Angry employees venting through the media and cyber-space.
- Employee violence.
- Discriminatory practices.
- Sexual harassment.
- Labor unrest.
- The misuse of legal protection.
- The loss of company loyalty.

- **All of these issues have the ability to damage a company's relationship with customers, shareholders, and the general public.**
- **They even affect a company's ability to recruit.**

There is no such thing as a quick fix, so don't try it. Lip service is not only useless, it can cause a lot of damage. Remember Smith Barney and its "boom-boom room" problem, addressed in Sin #1? The firm was accused of widespread discrimination and harassment. The original complaint concerned tawdry goings-on in a basement of its Garden City office known as the "boom-boom room." The lurid details attracted much media attention. Then, more women came forward with harassment and discrimination charges. The claimants said they went to the human resources department, but no one took any remedial action.

Quick aside: many human resource departments do not have the power or authority to take appropriate action. If that is the case, that is a serious problem in its own right. Regrettably, the human resources department is often brought into the picture after an incident happens—one that might have been prevented if the department was taken seriously. By the time trouble erupts, it is too late to contain internal anxiety and anger, as well as public exposure.

Back to Smith Barney. The firm settled the multimillion-dollar suit and announced it was instituting a number of "sensitized" programs. It said the initiative "focuses on effecting real change and progress." Smith Barney's lawyer even told the judge the settlement "set a new standard" that might be followed by the rest of the securities industry. "And this is not rhetoric," he said.

However, this commitment to "sensitivity" wound up exacerbating the situation. When a company makes a commitment like that, it has to follow through with it. Press reports said at least two programs were a sham, and once again, the company wound up in the headlines. Externally, this reinforced the perception of Smith Barney's "boom-boom" culture. Internally, women saw the company's statements as lip service, thus creating greater internal mistrust. With that kind of resentment, it is no surprise this story was leaked to the media.

It could be the story wasn't completely accurate. However, the company's past track record colored the perception of the story.

Game Effort

Internal problems are not easy to fix. That's why it's important to prevent them whenever possible.

- **The first line of defense is training, preferably for everyone and definitely for management.**

People have to know what to do and what not to do. Plus, they have to know how to spot potential problems.

To stop potential employee-liability issues, Tower Records takes an innovative approach. Every two weeks, human resource employees dress up as game pieces on a giant game board at corporate headquarters. Tower Records store managers then answer questions about a hiring or disciplinary situation.

With a correct answer, a staff member takes a step forward on the board. A wrong one and everyone discusses the best legal advice. Whoever has the most correct answers, the closer they get to the final winning space.

Since the training program began four years ago, Tower said company-wide grievances have fallen. All managers and supervisors are required to play the legal-training game.

Tower's Human Resources manager said, "Our managers just weren't spotting potential issues; they weren't documenting things that could have avoided suits." She explained the company wasn't trying to turn managers into lawyers but it wanted to "equip them with the resources and kind of knowledge they need to notice problems early on and deal with them effectively."

This game is an example of a company making a sincere, honest-to-goodness effort to eliminate or contain workplace-liability issues. Some may want to conduct training differently. Whatever works.

According to the American Society for Training and Development, the typical American company with fifty or more employees devotes 3 percent of training time to "awareness" training or issues affecting employee relations and workplace practices. With multimillion-dollar legal settlements and other damage, the percentage should be higher.

United Fates

The best way to prevent and contain problems in the workplace is to avoid doing anything that is going to make employees feel betrayed, confused or anxious or lose their dignity, advises Dr. Puder-York. Notice how such problems as sexual harassment, discrimination, and violence stem from those feelings.

How about happiness? Dr. Puder-York brought up an interesting point. She said in terms of the workplace, happiness isn't the issue because too many other outside elements come into play. All sorts of other things affect the way people feel. It would be nice if everyone was happy, but it is not management's responsibility.

A company's goal is to avoid making people angry. People don't tend to act out as much when the are unhappy or disappointed; they do when they're bitter.

Incidents are affected by employees' perceptions of their value to the company, regardless of its size. We're familiar with labor unrest on a grand scale; we've watched the impact of strikes on such companies as GM and UPS, for instance. But here's a tale of what happened to a small company when its employees felt undervalued. *Fortune* magazine ran a story about a mellow bookstore in Oregon said to be a book lover's Xanadu. The owner prided himself on his commitment to social responsibility. However, the owner's employees "un-mellowed." The store had been reorganized in a way that stripped workers of control over their sections. They got fed up with meager pay increases and the revised organization. As a result, the employees went union-hunting until they found one who would take them, the International Longshore and Warehouse Union.

In the employees' eyes, the owner had stripped them of their power and authority. He could have averted the problem by coming up with a compromise, but he stuck to the new system because it saved money. The result was a union drive, which played out in the media, to the detriment of the once tranquil bookstore.

Absolutely, Positively

When employees feel they are an important part of a team, they are bound to be loyal. When the Air Line Pilots Association (ALPA) wanted to disrupt Federal Express's business during an upcoming busy Christmas season to get higher pay, hundreds of nonunion pilots refused to join in. As one nonunion pilot explained, "I don't see how my future is being secured by scaring business away." In fact, some even volunteered to fly extra overtime.

- **Employees said they didn't want to support anything that might damage the company's reputation for reliable service.**

In a protest against ALPA, thousands of Federal Express workers gathered (at their own initiative) in a company parking lot and lined several blocks near the airport to bellow support for their employer. (Note the difference between this employee initiative and Mitsubishi's.) The gathering was described as part religious festival, part homecoming parade. Open convertibles sported pro-FEDEX posters. Employees lining the road cheered, and the master of ceremonies elicited "Amens" when he pronounced FedEx a "blessed company."

On November 20, the pilots backed down from their strike threat.

That same kind of spirit is pervasive at the Mercedes-Benz

factory in Vance, Alabama. The United Automobile Workers Union was trying to organize the factory, but most of the employees weren't interested. Many are making more money and receiving more benefits than they would in the union. Even more telling:

• **Employees said the company emphasizes teamwork and responsibility, and there's a collegial atmosphere on the factory floor.**

The turnover is about 1 percent a year. What a compliment to management.

Tech Happy

Unions need not apply in the high-tech sector either. The labor movement saw high-tech employees as ripe for the picking. After all, so many are pushed into working long hours without getting overtime.

Little did they know these workers are content. As one software developer at a start-up company explained, "Everything is offered to me here." He went on to say his job gave him stock options, an excellent medical plan, a sense of family, and the thrill of building something from scratch. In spite of the long hours, he said:

• **He loved working at a start-up, where he had a strong sense of making a contribution.**

On the other hand, unions have a shot at temporary workers in the high-tech industry. They don't receive stock options, sick days, or health plans. They are working side by side with others who are getting all the good benefits. One temp who claimed he liked his job said he did not think temps could have full-time benefits without a union. "Otherwise the companies will 'just blow us off.'"

Yes, money and benefits are an issue, but there is more going on here. The temps feel like second-class citizens; they are being left out of the culture.

One bank chairman saw a direct correlation between his employees' perceptions of their workplace and his customer base. Meaning:

- **If employees feel good about their company, they'll recommend it to customers.**

When making acquisitions to the combined tune of $1.4 billion, he said the bank's reputation depended on the new employees. While the bank views ongoing communications as a key component in successful transitions, it is also aware of the "people issues." For example, employees of one institution acquired earlier were asked to help with the transition efforts of the next one. Meanwhile, business is booming

Plucking the Grapevine:
How to Communicate Effectively

"We know that communication is a problem, but the company is not going to discuss it with the employees."

That logic comes to us courtesy of an AT&T supervisor. It happens to be very revealing. For some reason, the idea of internal communication falls into the "I'll begin my diet tomorrow" category. Employees are hungry for information. In fact, in some companies, they're starving. They want to know what's going on in good times and bad.

When Silence Isn't Golden

Think how it would feel if you were not able to attend your company's board of directors meetings and the members would not disclose what was being discussed. Of all the emotions it could arouse—anger, fear, embarrassment, rebellion—none of them inspire a sense of well-being.

- **Communication determines the way a workforce will act.**
- **Perception is every bit the vital issue inside the company as it is outside.**

Misconceptions, obviously, can be destructive. If employees don't understand and don't back company strategies, it's not possible to win their support.

- **Regardless of the problem, communicate.**

A member of the board of directors of a well-known non-profit organization called after a disgruntled employee "anonymously" sent letters listing a number of negative allegations about the president to board members and the press. The board, made up of the president's buddies, did not want to embarrass him by bringing the matter up, and it was not discussed at a board meeting. The press began probing, and the employee rumor mill churned out embellishments. The allegations were not true. However, the perception of wrongdoing persisted because the letter floated around without a response from the president. This began affecting the organization's fund-raising efforts.

The letter and its subsequent consequences were not the cause but the effect of the problem. The real issue was a lack of communication within this organization. If the employees had been kept informed on what the organization was doing, they wouldn't have felt ignored and alienated. A weekly news sheet was published. (This was before E-mail.) The president became more visible. Employees were encouraged to speak up on issues at regularly scheduled staff meetings. The problem wasn't solved right away, but the negative letter campaign ended. The employees were quite skeptical at first, but they slowly turned around when they saw the organization had made a long-term commitment to keep them updated and informed.

Communicating effectively with employees requires both information and the awareness that employees are people, not widgets. Used correctly, it can even become a form of "employer-of-choice" advertising. That was the case with the bank example where the chairman understood contented employees generate business.

Then, there's IBM. The company made a takeover effort against the steadfastly independent Lotus Development Corporation in 1995. From the beginning, IBM knew it was important to persuade Lotus employees the takeover would be a good thing. It took the battle onto the Internet. It posted press releases, speeches, and transcripts of analysts' meetings on the IBM home page, where Lotus's technologically sophisticated employees could read the material.

At the same time, IBM was communicating with Wall Street analysts and the media. The company wound up winning support from both Lotus employees and analysts. As a result, a $3.3 billion hostile bid turned into a friendly $3.5 billion merger. True, IBM was wooing employees who did not yet work for them, but it shows how much employees want to be included.

Providing information is the best way to let them know they are in the loop.

I Do/Don't Care

Depending on how a company communicates, its employees can be its best friend or worst enemy. Sometimes, they can be both. A prime example was a particular company with a young, enthusiastic workforce. Management had always been a big believer in internal communication, even in bad times. When the company began having financial problems, employees remained loyal. While observing one employee talking to customers, a couple asked him how the company was doing. The employee was upbeat, telling them the company was terrific and management knew what it was doing.

Then, a new management team came on board. Afraid of anything being leaked to the press, the president stopped all forms of communication, saying employees didn't need to know what was happening. A few months later, I happened to see the same employee with customers. One asked if the company was going to make it, and the agent said, "How the hell should I know what's happening at this damn company?"

Same employee. Look how fast his attitude changed. It was quite a lesson—sad, but instructive. Like falling dominos, employee enthusiasm and loyalty collapsed. The lack of communication indicated the current management did not value or trust them. They had once been treated as an asset, but no longer.

Ironically, the communication shutdown started leaks. Employees had never called the media before. In the past, reporters, half-impressed and half-frustrated, used to tell me how they could not get anything out of them. Now, reporters were flooded with calls.

The Cobbler's Children

There are times when even communicators fail to communicate. The following quote was included in a story about a company where a popular star employee was asked to resign. He refused to step down after he was accused of wrongdoing.

"People are really dispirited, they are upset, and a lot of people are angry that all they know about this is from what they've read in the paper. It's like the second death in the family in six weeks, and the head of the family hasn't got time to talk."

This quote came from a senior newspaper reporter at the *Boston Globe*. He spoke on the condition of anonymity after columnist Mike Barnicle was accused of plagiarizing from a book written by comedian George Carlin. Mr. Barnicle had been "less than truthful" when questioned about it. This incident occurred a couple of months after another columnist, Patricia Smith, was forced to resign after admitting she made up some of the characters in her columns.

The quote, though, is a pretty universal indication of how employees feel when left in the dark. Notice the word "angry" in the quote.

- **The anger was strong enough for a reporter to leak information to the competition.**

Front and Center

No one likes having to announce bad news. It may not be possible to have any control over circumstances, but it is possible to control how the news is best communicated. In a *Harvard Business Review* study, researchers found employees are eager to identify with their companies. They often feel embarrassed and left out when there's a lack of meaningful information. This falls into the "sense of diminished value" mental state, which leads to anger.

Quick quiz: When people hear about change, good or bad, what's the first question on their minds?

The answer: *"How will it affect me?"*

That's the answer that needs to be told both internally and externally. It has to be aimed primarily at the audiences' emotions. Don't placate. It is extremely annoying and insulting to those who are trying to get information that affects their lives.

When Honeywell Inc. merged with Allied Signal Inc., CEO Michael R. Bonsignore had the task of merging the two corporate cultures. He said he found employees were saying, "What about me?" He noted in times like these, "everybody's mind-set goes into 'me' from 'we' and stays there until the 'me' questions are answered." The goal was to answer questions and stomp out rumors. Mr. Bonsignore traveled through the merged company and talked face-to-face with about ten thousand employees. He said one of the employees' chief concerns evaporated when they were given the choice between the current pension plan or moving to a new cash-balance plan.

There's another aspect of "how will it affect me?" There are times when external problems expose employees to public backlash. When critics say something bad about a company, it can be taken personally by employees. They get interrogated by people outside the company. They get criticized. Others treat them with the sympathy reserved for serious diseases. It can get so bad employees won't acknowledge where they work.

Here is what one Microsoft employee wrote in the company's on-line magazine when it became embroiled in its antitrust suit: "A few months ago, everyone I met seemed to think that working for Microsoft was a pretty cool thing to do. Now, strangers treat us like we work for Philip Morris." For those on the top, it's very easy to get preoccupied with the problems at hand. However, this is the time to do some thorough communicating. Acknowledge the toll the problems are taking on workers and show appreciation for their efforts. The siege mentality during a crisis is going to be pervasive, no matter what is said. Communicating doesn't change the situation, but it goes a long way toward curbing hostility and maintaining loyalty.

Forget slogans, themes, and catchy phrases. I remember one executive pounding his fist on the desk urging a "can do spirit" to employees being told to paddle upstream. They looked at him as if he were crazy.

Say What?

Do not assume employees know what's really going on. They might be getting different versions of the problem at hand via the rumor mill, which travels faster than facts. It's like the game "Rumor," also known as "Telephone." A person says something to the next person, who passes it to the next person, and so on. When the last person in the chain repeats the message, it's different from the original. Everyone in the game has been provided information, but somehow, the actual meaning gets lost. That's why it's much safer to give the same message to everyone at the same time.

Employees have special radar that goes off when they suspect something is wrong.

• **Do not minimize the problem or promise anything that can't be delivered.**

• **Do not say things are going to get better if they're not.**

Raised expectations lead to feelings of betrayal. Continental Airlines chairman Gordon Bethune noted when he came to the airline, employees were hostile because they were tired of broken promises and lies.

• **Getting bad news out fast applies internally as well as externally.**

There are certain executive-stalling attitudes that are not helpful. Take, "They do not need to know yet." Never underestimate the grapevine; a little gossip goes a long way. Everyone will get a tidbit, true or not. One of the problems with the grapevine is it may be putting out a message different from the company's real message.

By the way, when reporters are covering the story and have to choose between the company's message or the grapevine's, they usually go with the grapevine.

Another inappropriate stalling tactic is, "We do not have the details, so we should wait." Wrong. When employees know something bad is happening but don't hear anything, they get frightened and resentful. If there are no details, say so and let them know they will get updates.

There are times when information is too sensitive to release and nothing can be said. Acknowledge employees' need for news and let them know they will be kept informed when the facts can be communicated.

• **Employees would rather hear management tell them there are no new developments than hear nothing at all.**

Your Turn at Bat

Think back to the days spent climbing the corporate ladder. What kind of communication problems were bothersome? As for most of us, it was probably the lack of timely or credible information. That's why answering the basic "w's"—who, what, when, where, and why—is so important. Use them as a guide.

- Who/What/When/Where:
  Provide specific information, explaining how it will affect both employees and external audiences. Otherwise, employees can read their own meanings into things.
  Let them know the scope of the change. For example, if there will be layoffs or the company is selling a division, say so.
  If a mistake has been made, admit it and talk about lessons learned.
- Why?
  This is the most important part. Explain the business reasons behind the change—or as much as you can. If possible, discuss the various options considered and rejected before coming to the final decision.
  There are times when executives think others know more than they do. Don't assume. Employees might not understand a decision if they don't know the facts behind it.

- **Credibility is key. Say what you have to do and do it.**

What Did They Say?

Sometimes it takes a while for a message to sink in, so keep repeating it. Once employees get back to their desks, they start having questions and concerns. Follow up with meetings so these can be addressed or assign someone to answer questions. Also, insure the same message is disseminated in as many ways as possible. It may be the best message in the world, but if it is not communicated properly, it does not do much good.

- **In bad situations, remember emotions overtake reason.**

Keep the human factor in mind and make sure the message is clear and understandable. Forget corporate-speak. For example, instead of giving numbers, explain what they mean. Often, what is said and what is perceived are two different matters. A cold explanation in a memo is not going to cut it.

- **Nothing takes the place of live interplay.**

Successful communication is not a one-way street. Employees should have the right and opportunity to ask questions. There may be problems that have not been addressed, or they may have some good suggestions the company had not considered. Their concerns have to be taken seriously by management.

Studies show employees prefer getting their information from, in order of preference:

1. Immediate supervisor
2. Small group meetings
3. Top executives

The last place: via the media or grapevine.

God bless technology. E-mail, teleconferencing, tele-meetings, videos, and audiocassette tapes are good ways for a CEO to communicate quickly and directly with employees. Memos, reports, and newsletters should be utilized as well. Cover all bases. However, it's important to stress:

- **These outlets should not be used as substitutes for live communication.**

Follow These Leaders

In a *New York Times* roundtable discussion about leadership with four top executives, each clearly believed in the value of ongoing communication with employees.

Lawrence A. Bossidy, CEO of Allied Signal, noted E-mail has made it easier to communicate. Not only does he issue E-mails, he gets them as well, explaining it's "essential that you do."

Shelly Lazarus, CEO of Ogilvy & Mather Worldwide, pointed out the importance of face-to-face communication. "Something happens when you are in the room with people with whom you work, trying to solve a problem together or just listening to them. And the E-mail becomes more meaningful after the face-to-face."

L. Dennis Kizlowski, CEO of Tyco International, which has 140,000 employees in eighty countries, also stressed the importance of face-to-face meetings. He said it took a lot of travel on his part to "articulate our goals and where we're going." He added he liked showing up and having dialogues.

Charles B. Wang, CEO of Computer Associates International, made the point ". . . as you get bigger, you still have to force the issue of thinking small, because otherwise you end up in a bureaucracy that can choke you."

Aware that employees are far more willing to critique CEOs these days, the four executives agreed open communication kept employees from venting in chat rooms on the Net.

These CEOs understand the importance of keeping in the information loop. That's why they're leaders.

Draino Might Help

General Electric CEO Jack Welch says his audience is the 250 senior managers who influence the remaining 300,000 employees. My only caveat is:

• **Senior managers have to communicate to middle management, who, in turn, have to communicate to supervisors.**

I have often seen information get clogged on the middle-management level. Information and the communication of company values somehow get stuck along the way. A Conference Board study of 130 companies showed only 5 percent of the employees said middle managers were very effective in communicating change to subordinates; 32 percent said their middle managers were not effective at all.

One of the reasons why information never gets down to the ranks is because many senior executives do a lousy job prepping middle managers so they know what to say. Employees are hungry for news. When they start growling, watch out. They can eat managers alive. Small wonder many stay safely in their offices.

Communication can be a manager's salvation. Sound information delivered with understanding brings the best results. That's not to say the internal lions will turn into pussycats, but they won't be out for blood.

It's up to managers, in turn, to insure their supervisors are equipped with the company's message and anticipated questions. In many cases, employees are afraid to ask senior managers questions and are more comfortable asking immediate supervisors.

• **Too often, those on the supervisory level are left out of the information loop, yet, they are the ones who are closest to employee concerns.**

When an offshore oil company was planning a restructuring that would mean layoffs, it was enlightened enough to ask supervisors for their input. Their anonymous responses went into an opinion report for the management team. They tried to include as many recommendations as possible. The final plan was then discussed with the supervisors, who explained it to their workers

Of course, the news was upsetting. However, by addressing the employees' concerns, their dignity was preserved. When the layoffs occurred, there was sadness, but no anger—or sabotage.

Up the Down Staircase

• **As important as it is for information to flow from the top down, it also has to go in reverse.**

CEOs who get the feeling they're out of touch with people probably are. Have open channels to get feedback from the troops. Deputies might not be telling their bosses what employees are saying, or they might not know either. To get the scoop on what is stirring within a company, go to assistants to get the real skinny on things. There is a saying that is dated, but the message still holds true: "An executive knows something about everything, an expert knows everything about something, and the switchboard operator knows everything."

While I was working with an executive vice president of a major bank, he was going through "What If?" scenarios with a pretend reporter. At one point, a scenario was presented where some women at one of the branches were claiming they were being sexually harassed and were filing a lawsuit. He blanched, but kept going. When asked how he could let that kind of thing go on, he paused and thought. Then he stopped the role-playing and said he really didn't think he would know if women were being harassed until after a suit was filed. He didn't have any idea what went on at branches beyond the financial data.

That was a wake-up call. This major communication problem is very common in large companies. Often, middle or senior management act as a filter and not only prevent people at the top from communicating directly with the workforce, but also block information from the workforce from getting to the top.

Continental Airline's CEO, Gordon Bethune, has illustrated the benefits of up-and-down communication. When he had to cut costs, it was clear the airline could save substantially by outsourcing the services of ticket agents and other ramp-service personnel at nineteen airports. He went to employees and pulled no punches. He told them they could keep their jobs if they came up with a way to match the economies offered by outsourcing.

Workers at seventeen of the nineteen airports changed their work schedules to save money, thereby saving their jobs.

Valuing Values

One the most dangerous practices is preaching one thing and doing another.

- **Executive action has to be consistent with its message.**

Otherwise, the message becomes a joke, and credibility is lost. Also, say good-bye to employee support. A new CEO, while treated skeptically at first, can change the environment. Continental's CEO, Bethune, was able to change the internal culture by bluntly telling employees the airline was in deep financial trouble and letting them in on decision-making.

What we're really talking about is values.

In a *Fortune* magazine article on value statements, Thomas A. Stewart wrote about an employee attitude survey. Workers were asked about their companies' values, which had been reviewed about a year before. These included such principles as quality, integrity, respect for individuals, and profitability. Nearly all the employees were aware of their companies' value statement, yet only 50 percent believed the companies meant it. He thought that percentage was low; I was surprised it was so high.

Upon taking a closer look, he discovered the list could be divided into "hard" values, such as profitability, and "soft" ones like integrity and respect. It turns out only 45 percent of employees believed the company lived up to its soft values. The top brass talked about hard values a lot, but rarely discussed the soft ones. In other words:

- **These executives didn't see soft values as a part of daily business.**

Soft values tend to wind up on a plaque near the front door. Yet, data show those are the ones employees care about most. If you were to take a survey within your own company, how many would believe the soft values were taken seriously?

A former client stressed all sorts of soft values to employees and paid high salaries, yet made them participate in questionable selling practices. The CEO was annoyed employees weren't motivated and couldn't understand the high turnover rate.

Values fit a corporate culture. For example, Warren Buffet had little success in making the Salomon Brothers hotshots show more respect for shareholders. The Salomon executives apparently didn't care much about soft values. Neither did the randy, stressed-out young men at Lew Lieberbaum, the extinct brokerage firm.

Sexual harassment was part of the "Astra Way" at Astra USA. The pattern started early, with female employees told during initial training classes their performance evaluations depended on their social skills and other socialization with senior management officials, according to the EEOC. The commission said its investigation showed:

• **When senior-management officials engaged in bad behavior, lower-management officials, employees, and agents followed suit.**

On the other side of the spectrum, such companies as Mercedes and Federal Express combine actions and values, thus winning loyalty and productivity. As one Federal Express employee said, "I have a lot of people that depend on me, that I care deeply about, and I will do everything I can for my customers to take care of them and take care of the people who depend on me."

- It's up to the employees to choose the culture in which they are the most comfortable.
- It's management's responsibility to uphold stated values.

In the Loop

Former CBS president Frank Stanton said, "Modern corporations are recognizing the high cost of impersonality." While he was referring to external perceptions, it's pertinent to internal ones as well. It's not that hard to turn an employee liability into an asset.

A good example of this comes from Southwest Airlines, one of the most admired airlines around. Also profitable. CEO Herb Kelleher believes when it comes to success, people are most important, noting the way employees are treated on the inside determines how they treat people on the outside. The airline is known for its tight-knit, family-minded culture even though everyone is expected to work hard. One of the reasons for the esprit de corps is inclusion. Employees are sent around the company to do other peoples' jobs—but not for cross-utilization. Mr. Kelleher explains, "We just want everybody to understand what everybody else's problems are."

The proof is in the pudding. This fast-growing, low-fare airline, founded in 1971, has become the nation's seventh-largest carrier.

When Everyone Wins

Companies spend millions of dollars on advertising and promotion. Yet, think which makes a better impression: a paid advertisement or employees saying terrific things about their company?

Today's work environment can either be a land mine or a gold mine. It depends on who's in charge. Although employee endorsements say a lot about a company, they are also a tribute to its top management.

7

React First, Think Later

There were two CEOs who were fierce rivals. They sold similar products, but one company (led by CEO A) was doing better than the other. CEO A knew his rival (CEO B) had a short fuse. So, he had his spokesperson leak the news they were going to drastically reduce the price of a certain competitive product similar to his rival's top seller.

The reporter who was the beneficiary of the tip called the other company for a response. This was the first CEO B had heard of it, and he hit the roof. He told his spokesperson to tell the reporter he was cutting CEO A's price by one dollar.

The price war was on.

CEO A's war wasn't nationwide; CEO B's was. If CEO B had waited to get more details, he would have learned his rival was cutting prices in limited markets.

Analysts following CEO B's company had a fit. The company couldn't afford to drop prices on such a massive scale. CEO B defended his actions, saying he was protecting market share. That didn't calm the market. The stock took a nosedive.

That Sunday, the newspaper's business section featured a front-page story on how CEO B had been duped. What a great story, thanks to CEO A, who helpfully supplied details. It spread to other publications like wildfire.

CEO B's board of directors was not amused. Funny how he suddenly resigned.

And so we have reached the Seventh Deadly Sin: "React First, Think Later." This happens when executives make decisions without thinking of possible consequences. Beware.Companies can be their own worst enemies. It's not that hard to open Pandora's Box, but closing it is another matter. Fear, anger, and vanity have made executives leap without ever looking.

However well intended, many unfortunate decisions have made a situation worse. In some cases, it's a matter of timing. In others, it's the mistake of not thinking it through.

• **Every decision has ramifications.**

This does not seem to be as obvious as it sounds. When there is a problem, many executives fail to consider both the unintended as well as intended consequences. Even seemingly minor decisions can have major repercussions.

• **There is no problem too small to be blown out of proportion.**

Caught in a Vacuum

Speaking of repercussions . . . file this one under "it seemed like a good idea at the time." To boost slumping sales of its vacuum cleaners and other household appliances in Great Britain, Hoover launched an attention-getting travel promotion. Customers who bought at least $150 in Hoover merchandise would be awarded two free round-trip tickets to one of several European destinations. Customers purchasing at least $375 in Hoover products would get two free round-trip tickets to New York or Orlando.

The programs were arranged in cooperation with two travel agencies. The agencies were to obtain low-cost space-available tickets and would help Hoover support the expense by earning commissions on land packages such as car rentals and hotels.

Hoover sold tens of thousands of appliances, far more than the company anticipated. The company went on overtime to produce canister vacuums. So far, so good. But wait.

About 200,000 consumers participated in one of the two promotions, which meant 400,000 round-trip tickets. That's roughly one for every 150 people in England and Ireland. Consumers quickly figured out the tickets were worth more than the cost of a vacuum cleaner.

Hoover and the two travel agencies couldn't meet the demand. In the understatement of the year, a company spokesperson said, "The response was much greater than anticipated." Inside sources said the company had projected redemption levels of about five thousand.

Hoover figured a lot of customers would drop out because they wouldn't want to fly on a space-available basis. The company also thought more consumers would buy land packages, thus helping to pay for the awards.

If this was not enough, a British television reporter caught the travel agents trying to talk customers out of taking the trips, or otherwise making it difficult to do so.

Hoover Damned

A bandwagon of anti-Hoover pressure started rolling into action in the small-claims court and television investigations. On top of that, the Office of Fair Trading and the Advertising Standards Authority got involved. Plus, ten thousand customers joined the Hoover Holiday Pressure Group.

The uproar from disgruntled Hoover users was so great, parent company Maytag Corporation sent managers from the United States to step in. The company assigned a task force to sort things out and set up a $30 million fund to pay for promised flights. The three top executives—the president of Hoover Europe, the U.K. vice president of marketing, and the European operation's director of marketing services—who were responsible for the plan were fired. Even this turned into a problem.

Hoover was forced to apologize to one of the departing marketing directors it blamed for the "free flights" fiasco. The company admitted the director left the company following a restructuring of its marketing department, which was apparently unrelated to the adverse publicity from the promotion. Hoover Europe issued a statement saying it regretted "any distress caused" to the reengineered-out executive.

Things went from bad to worse. The promotional effort wound up costing $48.8 million more than budgeted, and the company announced it would take a $30 million charge for the first quarter to cover unexpected additional costs linked to the "flawed" promotion.

The "flawed" plan ended up slashing Hoover's market share by up to 50 percent. In 1995, Maytag sold Hoover Europe at a loss to an Italian firm, Candy, for $170 million. Back in 1989, Maytag bought Hoover for $300 million. "Plan" was a misnomer for this fiasco. Planning involves thinking things through. Actually, it's pretty obvious because this mess wouldn't have happened otherwise.

- **When making a decision to go forward, focus on what could happen, not on what one would *like* to happen.**

"Scrooging"-Up

What's worse than disappointing adults? Disappointing children. What's worse is disappointing children on Christmas Day. That's what happened when Toys "R" Us couldn't fulfill all on-line Internet orders and get them shipped in time for Christmas.

During the week of December 13, 1999, Toysrus.com was the fifth most visited on-line store, with 1.6 million visitors, according to research firm Media Metrix. The CEO of Toysrus.com said it had taken them longer than expected to get through the complex process of filling orders. Toys, waiting to be hugged and flung about by excited children, woefully sat on shelves because the company's warehouse couldn't handle the orders. Customers found out two days before Christmas.

In November, Toys "R" Us mailed out 62 million catalogs offering free shipments of orders from its Web site. The conception of the idea should have been followed by a realistic "can we really meet the demand?" before the campaign started.

Considering the site couldn't handle a bigger-than-expected response to a promotion in November, one would think they would have been especially sensitive to their fulfillment problems.

When announcing the bad news, the company's chairman said the management team sat down the day before and realized "some" orders couldn't be filled. They came to that conclusion only days before Christmas. There had to have been an inkling all was not well in the warehouse prior to that point.

• **Face reality fast. Wishful thinking does not make a problem disappear.**

So, because some people at Toysrus.com were in denial over its growing crisis, parents who already thought they had completed their Christmas shopping were left with two days to fend for themselves in mobbed stores where popular toys were long gone.

Trying to make amends, the company sent customers free $100 gift certificates by overnight courier to be used at Toys "R" Us stores and offered to refund orders. Or, the company suggested, parents could give the certificates to their children. Certificates, in lieu of a present, are sure to make little ones clap their hands with glee.

Here's where customer anger comes in. At this point, whatever amends the company tried to make, they was not enough to appease those who didn't have presents for their children. That anger could have been assuaged by telling customers of the problems earlier and providing refunds. It would have given parents enough time to shop elsewhere while they had the time and a better chance of finding the toys they wanted. Instead, Toys "R" Us left their customers in untenable positions.

This mess became a national media story. It's hard to say who'd take a chance ordering toys for a specific date in the future. It's going to take a long, long time for the company to rebuild its credibility.

Besides the problem of not being prepared to meet the demand of any promotional offer, the Toys "R" Us example shows:

- **A company has to act swiftly, alert customers to the problem, and make generous—larger-than-expected—amends.**

They will be angry, but not nearly as angry as they would have been if told at the last minute.

"So we've decided we don't need your business anymore."

Trouble.com

• **Always consider which way the public-opinion wind is blowing before finalizing a decision.**

DoubleClick, an Internet advertising company, belatedly learned that lesson after setting off a firestorm over Internet privacy. The company announced plans to create a huge database containing personal data on Internet customers after it purchased Abacus Direct, an off-line marketing company. It would connect people's names, addresses, and other personal information to where they went on the Web.

This move set off howls of fury from privacy advocates, and the Federal Trade Commission (FTC) launched an investigation. Several lawsuits were filed. Investors fled. DoubleClick's stock dropped more than $30 in the last two weeks of February 2000. If that wasn't bad enough, the announcement was made before a scheduled secondary offering. The deal raised $677 million—$155 million less than before the brouhaha over privacy.

Trying to calm the furor, the company said it would allow customers to opt out of DoubleClick's surveillance and promised to hire a chief privacy officer. This did little to turn down the public heat.

In early March, DoubleClick backtracked, saying it would table the plan until privacy issues were ironed out. The company CEO, Kevin O'Connor, shows the value of a top executive apologizing when he said, "I made a mistake in moving ahead with these plans with no privacy standards in place." Upon the announcement, the stock went up nearly $3.

Sin #2 showed how the public's concern over Internet privacy landed Intel in hot water in 1999 when it introduced its serial-embedded Pentium III processor. By 2000, the fear of private intrusion had left Congress, the FTC, and privacy advocates debating the issue, with no clear solution in sight. Either DoubleClick was not sensitive to user privacy concerns, or perhaps it underestimated them. In any event, the company's experience shows how a plan, however profitable on paper, can backfire if the downsides aren't examined as thoroughly as the benefits.

Noting that the plan was only tabled, not scrapped, a reporter for one major daily newspaper said he was skeptical of DoubleClick's actions, and predicted reporters would be monitoring the company, "looking for slippage."

A Sour Note

Another example of acting before thinking comes from the American Society of Composers, Authors and Publishers (ASCAP), an organization that protects the rights of songwriters, charging royalties for copyrighted music performed by groups. Zealously, ASCAP decided to go after groups singing around campfires. They sent a letter to the American Camping Association, telling them their twenty-three hundred members had to pay for their right to sing ASCAP songs. Although this decision was widely criticized, a lawyer said ASCAP was within bounds, and the camping group had to shell out $250 per large camp each year.

In a letter, ASCAP explained the penalties for copyright infringement could be up to $100,000 per performance and a year in prison.

Enter the Girl Scouts. Out of 256 camps, only 16 paid. The San Francisco Bay Girl Scout Council director discovered 15 camps in her area would have to pay a total of $6,000 a year. She suggested campers sing only Girl Scout songs.

A group of "elves" at one of the camps wanted to teach the Macarena (that summer's dance craze) to the younger girls. The mothers in charge, concerned with legal ramifications, said they could as long as the "elves" didn't use the music. So, they danced the Macarena in silence. The media got wind of this and flocked to the camp. The pictures of little Girl Scouts silently dancing and the reason why made national news.

The perception: greedy songwriters were picking on little Girl Scouts. According to their public relations person, ASCAP descended into "p.r. hell." ASCAP wound up backing down, saying it had only meant to license music performed by professionals, even though their original letter stated otherwise.

Have you ever heard a professional musician say he had a gig at a campfire? Basically, we're talking about little girls singing "Puff the Magic Dragon." In ASCAP's fervor to collect more money, no one stopped to think how its actions would be perceived.

• **Always determine the downsides of a decision.**

When a Knee Jerks

Many a problem has been caused by knee-jerk reactions. The Miller Brewing Company case discussed in Sin #6 is one example.

Here's another instance of not taking consequences into account when making a knee-jerk decision. A new magazine, *Talk,* was going to celebrate its debut at the Brooklyn Navy Yard, with the glitterati of the publishing and movie worlds attending.

The yard is owned by New York City. Mayor Rudolph Giuliani, planning to run for the U.S. Senate, heard the rumor

Hillary Rodham Clinton, his probable opponent, was going to be on the magazine's maiden cover.

After plans were well under way, the request to use the Navy Yard was suddenly turned down. The Giuliani administration said it didn't want city facilities used in a way that could be perceived as being political.

For *Talk,* this decision turned into a gift from the gods. The cancellation became a national story, and the magazine wound up getting a great deal of attention it would not have received otherwise. The idea that Mrs. Clinton might make the cover gave the first lady cachet. Mayor Giuliani looked petty.

If the city had let them hold the party as originally planned, it would have been a molehill. The administration turned it into a mountain.

Up Close and Personal

It's important to make a distinction between personal and professional actions. An executive's controversial, private stand on an issue can negatively impact a company's image. An example is E*Trade Group Inc., an on-line investment brokerage. Its president and chief operating officer, Kathy Levinson, made a $300,000 donation to fight a proposed ban on same-sex marriage in California (Proposition 22). When the news of her contribution broke, E-Trade was deluged with angry phone calls, negative opinions on chat lines, customer cancellations, and even a call for Ms. Levinson to resign, according to the *Wall Street Journal.* At that time, polls reported a majority of voters supported Proposition 22, meaning E-Trade stood to alienate more than half of its potential market in California. (The proposal was later passed.)

The issue here is not Ms. Levinson's lifestyle and contribution, but the perception it was E-Trade's stand, not hers alone. Ms. Levinson said she thought there would be fallout from her pledge, but admitted she was surprised by the magnitude of the uproar. She had planned a public relations response, making it clear she didn't want to become a spokesperson for the cause, and told colleagues she wouldn't discuss the measure in business settings. The company said it would make it clear Ms. Levinson's actions were private, not corporate.

The plan didn't work. Enter the power of perception. The pledge was made in E-Trade shares, thus linking the contribution to the company even though they belonged to Ms. Levinson. Those who were angry concluded E-Trade stock was therefore an E-Trade donation. A cash contribution would have helped separate her actions from those of the company.

Another problem. Although a press release was being prepared, the news broke sooner than expected. As illustrated in Sin #4, news leaks wait for no man or woman. When dealing with a dicey issue, a response has to be ready to go as soon as the action is taken.

- **Warning: Actions can be misconstrued.**

That's why perception has to be factored in when a plan is being thrashed out.

The link between high-profile companies and their top executives is inevitable. This is not to say executives can't take a stand on personal issues. However, in these situations, they must make it clear the company is not involved. When Microsoft's Bill Gates makes huge philanthropic contributions, for example, it is clear they come out of his personal pocket, not the company's. True, these donations aren't as controversial as Ms. Levinson's, yet it shows private actions can be clearly defined.

An executive taking a controversial personal stand under a company's umbrella implies employees, customers, and shareholders hold the same views. The results could include internal and external embarrassment and anger for those who oppose the issue. While this might not hurt a company's bottom line in the long run, the question is how much more could it have earned if its top executive hadn't alienated some of its audiences?

A Fallen Rising Star

Some executives act before thinking and wind up experiencing unexpected ramifications. A fast-rising investment-banking star found this out too late. He returned to his company's headquarters in New York after heading the company's investment-banking business in Europe. Ignoring the firm's media policy (no interviews unless approved from the top), he set up an interview with *Investment Dealer's Digest*. The result was an article, "Top Banker Returns to Bolster Key Client Base." The article quoted him asserting he would "take responsibility for the firm's investment-banking clients," and said his role would overlap with the head of the firm's corporate finance business.

This came as news to the heads of the firm's corporate finance business and investment arm. According to an inside source, they went ballistic. Although this upstart was expected to work as an investment banker, none of his colleagues expected him to "take responsibility" for the whole business.

The next day, a curt interoffice memorandum from the company's chairman and president announced it had accepted the banker's resignation. In short, he was fired.

Not Funny

A business of any size has to be mindful of people's feelings. A fitness club in San Francisco didn't think about the consequences of its advertising campaign when it put up a new billboard that claimed when space aliens finally do encounter humans, "they will eat the fat ones first."

Not only was the billboard grossly offensive, it alienated a very important audience. If heavy people wanted to get fit, they would not do so at that club.

Not surprisingly, overweight protesters picketed in front of the club. The story ran on the newswires. In a written statement, the company said it knew how hard it was to lose weight, but "sometimes humor helps make things easier and can even be motivational." Try telling this to someone with a weight problem. An apology would have worked much better.

Just goes to show how any kind of business can create an unnecessary problem when it doesn't look at all aspects of an idea, including the human factor, before it's initiated.

Timing Is Everything

- **One of the most critical aspects in crisis management is timing.**

Different circumstances are going to determine when, how, or if a company responds. The key is always being ready.

Timing a response is like surfers waiting for a wave. They lie in wait until the wave comes before jumping into action. That takes patience, focus, and flexibility.

The Exercise of Jumping to Conclusions

One can get a lot of exercise by jumping to conclusions. This can be very dangerous. Stay grounded. When the "Hollywood Madam" Heidi Fleiss story became public, a Columbia Pictures executive released a statement saying he "never did business with Heidi on any level." Only thing is, nobody had accused him of doing so. His career was cut short.

The next case emphasizes:

- **An important part of timing is having the right information to make the correct move at the right time.**

There's a Cincinnati company that makes such products as cordless telephones and radar detectors. It was visited by a *Business Week* reporter who had some ticklish questions. Instead of waiting to see what he wrote, company officials decided to respond by issuing a news release, which went over the PR Newswire.

In great detail, the company listed and then denied a number of rumors and allegations, some of them not even raised by the reporter, including that the company didn't pay taxes and they inflated sales projections to boost stock.

The company's CEO said, "We assure everyone that there is no merit to the allegations made by the reporter."

Well, it turns out *Business Week* had not made any allegations because it had not made a decision to run the story.

The company should have held on and waited to see if *Business Week* published the article, and if it did, what it said. In this kind of situation:

- **A company has to prepare a response, then wait to see what happens.**

It could be the story was negative, but no one paid attention to it. Not all negative stories cause damage. If it is causing a problem, then the company should go on the offensive with its side of the story based on what the article is alleging.

According to the *Wall Street Journal,* the company's spokesperson said her relationship with the *Business Week* reporter was cordial. I guess she didn't see the irony when she said, "The reporter from *Business Week* told me that we had been one of the most cooperative companies he ever worked with."

• **Never volunteer to air dirty laundry if no one is asking.**

Actually, any information coming out of left field can look suspicious. It's like an airline pilot making an announcement saying, "There's nothing to worry about. Everything is fine" when everything is, indeed, fine. It's doubtful if the passengers would think so.

Something similar happened to Microsoft. During its antitrust trial, the company was expecting the government to play a damaging videotape in federal court. As a result, Microsoft executives held an early-morning press conference to offer an advance rebuttal with their own videotape.

Microsoft feared the government tape would demonstrate that Microsoft had, according to an Apple executive, "sabotaged" Apple's Quicktime multimedia player. A Microsoft executive played the tape and offered a whole bunch of technical details to show how Apple's own programmers were to blame for the fact that the latest version of Quicktime did not work well with Windows.

However, the Justice Department never showed the Quicktime videotape in court, making the sabotage issue—and Microsoft's tape—moot. In the courtroom, that is.

Sign on the Dotted Line

In another situation, an executive jumped the boat without realizing it. During a conference call with analysts, the president of Sensormatic Electronics announced it had just won a huge contract to install its security devices for drugstore giant Eckerd Corp.

A hedge-fund manager broke in on the call, reporting Eckerd said there was nothing in writing. The president snapped, "I wouldn't be saying what I'm saying if I didn't know it to be true." It turns out there was no contract, and the business went to a competitor. Sensormatic Electronic's stock dropped 4 percent that day. Even worse, the misleading announcement gave short-sellers an opportunity to expose (or exacerbate) Sensormatic's internal problems. This included an SEC investigation of whether the company held the books open at the end of quarters so they could get enough sales in the door to meet their earnings target.

The hedge-fund manager spread the news during the president's own conference call. It just so happens short-sellers profit when a stock's price plunges. . . .

* **Never announce anything unless it's in writing.**

One particular job required a press conference for a company who thought it had an interim financing agreement in place. The conference was scheduled to be held at 10:00 A.M. The time arrived with no CEO and bankers. They were still in a meeting, causing the reporters to wait until the conference was rescheduled for noon. Then 3:00 P.M. When I was checking the conference room where the negotiations were taking place, everyone was yelling.

The reporters were told to go home with the promise that information would be on the news wires if anything happened.

The next day's stories reported the announcement that never happened. Speculation ran rampant, and the stock was hurt.

The deal finally closed two days later. The bad press diminished the company's bargaining power; it walked away with less than it had anticipated.

Hold on until a deal is signed.

Lying Low

Mitsubishi was one example of the importance of taking a low profile when in trouble. This next example provides another aspect of lying low when a company is in trouble.

Often, a company knows when bad news is going to hit. However, occasionally, it forgets to pull its advertising. Deutsche Bank took out a full-page newspaper ad touting the combination of Bankers Trust and Deutsche Bank on the same day newspapers reported wrongdoings at both banks.

This kind of negative coverage couldn't have come as a surprise to top executives under investigation. It's only a matter of time before the news gets out.

Then, days later, a second full-page ad appeared for Deutsche Bank, even though it was still getting bad press.

People tend to think of pulling ads only after accidents. However, the same goes for those times when companies know bad news is going to become public. Clue in the advertising department so they can plan accordingly. In fact, make sure it has a crisis plan for pulling ads at the last minute if a problem hits.

Mad as Hell

"Speak when you're angry—and you'll make the best speech you'll ever regret."

Warning: Beware of anger. It is the source of many unfortunate, damaging decisions. Just ask cable giant Time Warner when it decided to block the Disney-owned ABC television network, affecting 3.5 million homes. During the thirty-nine hours, eleven ABC-owned stations were blacked out, Time Warner managed to anger customers and rile up local and national politicians. The company was bombarded by critical editorials and rebuked by the Federal Communications Commission (FCC) for violating FCC rules. Making matters worse, Time Warner's conduct hurt its efforts to win approval for its planned merger with America Online; the company's actions demonstrated how a big monopoly could become a threat.

The problem started when Time Warner and Disney were in the midst of a bitter dispute over whether the cable company should pay Disney for the use of three of its cable channels. The two titans clashed. Tempers flared and tension grew until hostility clouded Time Warner's judgment, causing it to yank the stations off the air, including those in New York, Los Angeles, and Houston.

Not only was this action calamitous for Time Warner's image, it helped Disney's. Ironically, the fiasco managed to turn the giant Disney into an underdog/victim. The company wisely utilized the situation to gain public and political support. It came out the clear winner in the dispute.

This story show how anger can lead to kamikaze-like decisions. *None* of this would have happened if cooler heads had prevailed.

Anger can also lead many companies into winning the battle but losing the war. McDonald's filed a libel suit against two anti-McDonald's activists in England for distributing leaflets attacking the company on nutritional, environmental, and worker-exploitation grounds. McDonald's wanted to defend its reputation.

Even though McDonald's ultimately won, it wound up losing. The company failed to look at the big picture. It spent millions of dollars going after an ex-postal worker on welfare and a part-time bartender who produced a leaflet, which reached a few thousand consumers.

McDonald's won after a two-and-a-half-year trial, the longest in British history, and it received negative coverage throughout.

- **The company wound up promoting the very claims it tried to squelch.**

The defendants set up a Web site with an expanded version of the pamphlet. Newspapers throughout the country published the information. Editorials accused McDonald's of bullying the defendants, and the two received more attention and support than they could have ever imagined.

This was a major blunder, which didn't have to happen if cooler heads had prevailed. True, McDonald's reputation had been erroneously attacked, but by whom? It would have been one thing if the accusations came from a powerful activist organization. However, McDonald's was attacked by two hapless individuals with no political clout. Yes, the situation should have been monitored to follow its effect, but it certainly did not warrant strong action.

In this kind of situation, there's a lot to be said for turning the other cheek. It's quieter and cheaper. No one likes a bully.

The Mouse That Slugged

Chalk this one up to "Why Smart People Do Dumb Things." FDR's coolie story, in which the one who hits first has exhausted all means, applies to feuding executives. Walt Disney CEO Michael D. Eisner and former studio chief Jeffrey Katzenberg came to blows in a very public courtroom in 1999. Their legal battle was just like a movie, complete with lies, back-stabbing, and bitter rivalry. The two, who used to be friends, were fighting over how much former-executive Mr. Katzenberg should get under a profit-sharing contract.

As the business dispute made it to court, one of Mr. Eisner's friends said, "It's like the messy property settlement in a divorce. Sometimes emotion gets the better part of you."

Too bad Mr. Eisner didn't compromise instead of letting a personal battle erupt in a courtroom. He was adamant about not settling. That animosity led to a display of Disney's dirty laundry. Disney leaked itself, and the media had a field day.

At the same time, the Disney company was losing steam businesswise. Its stock price had plunged 30 percent during the biggest bull market on record, and earnings were slipping. There were problems with skyrocketing film costs, dropping same-store sales, and ABC's stagnant ratings.

The mud-slinging might have been titillating for those watching from the sidelines, but it did not thrill shareholders, who felt Mr. Eisner should have been spending his time managing the company. The stock was depressed, and there was no Prozac in the kingdom. This public spectacle didn't do anything for Disney's image. In the middle of the trial, Disney settled.

Mr. Eisner created a situation that could have been contained if he had reined in his personal feelings.

As a result of this personal feud, this episode also opened the door for other people who share profits on Disney films and might want to sue.

This shows there are all sorts of crises that may not have a major effect on the bottom line, but are lousy for the reputation. The trial was an embarrassing situation, which reflected badly on the CEO.

Where's the Beef?

Did Oprah Winfrey slander American beef on her popular television talk show? That's what a group of Texas cattlemen claimed when they sued her for defamation.

Oprah had a show on mad cow disease and the safety of American beef. A guest said American cattle were fed ground-up meal made from dead livestock—a practice thought to cause mad cow disease in Britain. This prompted Oprah to say, "It has just stopped me cold from eating another burger! I'm stopped."

According to the cattlemen, her statement caused them to lose at least $12 million in business in April 1996.

Cattlemen were full of trepidation when they heard a very influential personality say she wouldn't eat beef again. After all, Oprah can get a book on the bestseller list by mentioning it on her show. However, what they failed to realize is people do not have long attention spans. If the beef industry had let the issue go, the audience would have gone on to the next scary crisis. Plus, the whole nation does not watch her show.

Like McDonald's, the cattlemen increased public attention on the very information they wanted to keep quiet. Mad cow disease is scary stuff. They could have taken a proactive route by talking about what they were doing to insure the safety of their beef. Instead, they yelled at Oprah, a beloved figure, who, in turn, used the publicity to her advantage.

When she was sued, she broadcast her shows in Amarillo, the cattlemens' own backyard, where the trial was being held. She was swamped with requests for tickets. Spectators shouted, "We love you, Oprah," when she entered the courthouse.

• **This is a great example of turning a situation around by going on the offensive.**

As it turned out, the cattlemen did not suffer as much damage as they originally claimed. Yes, cattle futures prices did drop more than 10 percent on the day after Oprah turned thumbs down on beef; it took weeks to recover. However, other commodities also took a sharp drop that day. During the trial, the sales damage estimates were lowered. In fact, economists say the industry slump was due to such factors as drought and high corn prices.

A federal jury ruled Oprah bore no liability for her television program exploring whether mad cow disease threatened the company's beef supply. The cattlemen were defeated in their own home cattle territory.

One cow proponent said the case demonstrated "the extraordinary financial and legal resources needed to defend against a lawsuit. Few organizations can afford to speak out if the cost of such speech is as high as in the Oprah case."

Although it should not have come as a surprise that lawsuits are expensive, a trial's cost is one of the factors that should be weighed *before* taking action.

Instead of containing the problem, the cattlemen raised national awareness of scary beef and turned it into a public relations bonanza for Oprah. It would have been smarter to just bite the bullet.

It's not easy to sit back and not defend a company, but the key lies in weighing the consequences. A couple of years after one client experienced a tragedy, it became the subject of a made-for-television movie. When it aired, there were many inaccuracies. The question was should the company go public and point out the errors? In doing so, they'd be keeping the story alive. It just so happened the movie was not very good. If the company had gone public, the resulting controversy would have only drawn more attention to the tragedy and would have rehashed the events.

Worth the Cure?

Often, a "solution" can make matters worse. Just ask Robert Citron, the former treasurer of Orange County, California. Under his management, Orange County's investment portfolio lost $1.6 billion, and the county went bankrupt.

Before the debacle, Mr. Citron was charged with maintaining a high level of service without raising taxes. California had enacted Proposition 13, which cut property taxes, and as a result, municipalities had to seek new sources of income. So, Mr. Citron invested $7 billion of public money in complex derivative securities. It seemed to do the trick until interest rates dropped with the fund's value. The rest, as they say, is history.

When Sears Roebuck & Co. was looking to cut costs, it's too bad the company didn't think of all the ramifications of switching its mechanics' compensation plan from salary to commission. The results of the decision backfired, and, now on commission, employees began forcing unnecessary repairs on customers and were caught. As a result, Sears paid $15 million to settle charges for foisting unneeded repairs in 1992. It was also disclosed that Sears auto centers overcharged customers from California and New Jersey. In 1997, Sears paid $580,000 to resolve a Florida attorney general's investigation of complaints that Sears charged customers for tire-balancing services that it never performed. In June 1999, Sears was hit with another lawsuit reviving allegations that the company charged customers at its auto-service centers across the country for tire-balancing services, which were not performed between 1989 and 1994. The suit also claimed the company then destroyed the machines that held evidence of the practice.

That one commission decision turned out to be pretty expensive. Besides the lawsuits, sales plummeted nearly 25 percent after the public learned about the goings-on, thanks to all the bad press.

After the company's admission of consumer fraud, the president lost his job. Sales commissions were abolished. The staff went back on salary. They wound up right back where they started, only in sorrier shape.

Part of the "seat-belting" concept introduced in the first chapter (Sin #1) includes checking corporate policies to safeguard a company. For example, at Exxon, why wasn't there a policy prohibiting people treated for alcohol abuse from piloting a tanker? Values also have to be examined. It appears Burroughs Wellcome Co., the maker of the AIDS drug AZT, didn't think of the implications of making the drug so expensive. The perception was the company was making money off critically ill people. The consequences included consumer complaints and negative press for price gouging.

The negative ramifications of decisions are not always immediate, so a company is often caught by surprise and unable to respond fast enough to avoid or control the damage.

Time Will Tell

By steering clear of the Seventh Deadly Sin, "React First, Think Later," CEOs are in a good position to save themselves from committing this book's other six "sins" as well. Many unnecessary evils can be avoided by first examining the consequences of a company's conduct. With careful thought and actions, CEOs can turn sins into blessings.

Deliverance

- What if Intel had recalled its pentium chip and provided customers with replacement chips when the flaw was discovered?
- What if Ashland Oil had refused to claim responsibility for its oil spill?

If those two suppositions had occurred, Intel would not have experienced a crisis, and Ashland Oil would have been vilified. As a company's action, or inaction, determines the ultimate outcome of a crisis, it's crucial for a CEO to know how to perform well.

It's important to point out most of the CEOs mentioned in this book are highly intelligent, articulate, accomplished, and dedicated. The problem with every mismanaged crisis example was bad execution.

Each of the "sins" in this book have been based on incidents and attitudes of the CEOs I've encountered or observed. To review, these include:

- Denial.
- Not taking responsibility for a mistake.
- Putting a company's financial interests first.
- Responding too slowly.
- Taking a "no comment" stance with the media.
- Not communicating with employees.
- Making decisions without thinking of consequences.

Sinners and Winners

As I review the crises discussed in this book, it is apparent how the "sins" played a part in getting a CEO in trouble. By committing any of the foregoing mistakes, the CEOs became their own worst enemies.

It's important to remember:

- **It is the attitude toward events, not the events themselves, that can be controlled.**

The following crises could have been avoided all together:

Hoover
QE2
ASCAP
Miller Brewing
Royal Caribbean
Eisner Versus Katzenberg
Intel
Time Warner Versus Disney/ABC
Mattel
Toys "R" Us

The next cases faced crises that grew when they could have been contained. Even though the CEOs might not have had control over the cause, they certainly could have reduced the length, severity, or criticism, depending on the problem.

CSX
Audi
Ford Pinto
Exxon
Mitsubishi
President Clinton's prolonged scandal
Jack in the Box
Coca-Cola
Shell Oil
Nestlé
TWA Flight 800

Then, there were some decisions based on unethical practices. These problems would not have occurred under different corporate cultures.

Archer Daniels Midlands
A.H. Robins
Roche
Cendant
Livent

Although they have already been mentioned, CSX, Royal Caribbean, and Ford Pinto also fit in this category.

The good news is there are companies that managed to maintain and enhance solid reputations, thanks to their CEOs:

Ashland Oil
Luby's
Proctor & Gamble
Johnson & Johnson
Xerox
Continental Airlines
The coffeepot maker
All the others we've never heard about

Also, there are companies who can get up from a mishandled crisis, brush themselves off, learn their lessons, go forward, and redeem themselves. One example:

•   **Jack in the Box**

Self-Preservation Tips

This book has shown how problems could have been averted or contained if the right actions had been taken. Also, note the CEO was held accountable in each case.

So, to maintain a good standing, always remember the basics when determining a crisis response:

1. Rules of Response:
   - Focus on the victims as well as the cause.
   - Take responsible action.
   - Communicate.
   - Reemphasize concern.
   - Provide ongoing updates.
2. Think Things Through:
   - What are you doing?
   - What are you trying to accomplish?
   - Do you have all the information?
   - What are the benefits?
   - What are the alternatives?
   - How will your decision be perceived?
   - What could go wrong?
   - What could really, really go wrong?
3. Get Feedback:
   When the Catholic Church used to decide if someone should be sainted, twenty of the Church's most important people convened. One was always appointed to give an alternative view—hence the term *devil's advocate.*
   - Bring in devil's advocates—and listen!

4. Cool Off:
    *   If you're angry about something that is ultimately not damaging: count to ten, breathe. If that doesn't work, keep counting and bring back the devil's advocate.

What's the Big Deal?

Some may point to companies that didn't perform well during a crisis but still regained healthy bottom lines. However, we don't know how much more they could have earned if they hadn't alienated customers. A crisis may fade away, but perception doesn't. Villains remain vilified. The public has raised the standard for company accountability. We're seeing a growing amount of shareholders seeking socially responsible companies. And, a majority of consumers say, if given a choice, they will take their business away from unethical companies.

Public expectations apply to a CEO performance as well. As a result, one who ignores the need to take effective crisis action has to be ready to go though the decades serving as a good example of a bad manager.

So, if we're judging the aftermath of a crisis strictly on the basis of financial results, that's not the best way to keep score. To this day, there are some executives who think Johnson & Johnson should have kept a low profile during the Tylenol crisis, believing that the company would have been better off financially.

Think what would have happened if J&J had heeded their advice.

An Ounce of Prevention

In the book *Art of War*, written twenty-five hundred years ago by General Sun Tzu, there is a story about an emperor who called in the general to discipline his army of concubines, which was acting up. The general ordered the women to do something. They giggled and didn't move. Then, the general pulled out his sword and whacked off one concubine's pretty head. The others began behaving instantly.

All too often, companies react like those concubines who didn't move until they understood the dire consequences of not doing so.

- **Effective crisis management means taking action before the first head rolls.**

After all, if the concubines had moved, the headless one would have kept her head.

Steady at the Helm

Boston Celtics president Red Auerbach said he never kidded himself he had all the answers. He would delegate some jobs and discussed new plays with assistants and players during practice and let them select the ones to use. When someone had a suggestion, he would always listen and consider it.

However, "when the game was on the line, when we only had time for the last play, I'd always make the decision. I said who should take the shot, who should put the ball in play, who should set the pick, who should stand in such and such a spot and what to do if the play didn't work.

"When winning or losing is on the line, the job can't be delegated."

That's the essence of crisis mastering. The general perception of crisis management is that it is a public relations problem. It's not: It's a CEO's problem. Regardless of how much talent a company has, it won't perform well in a crisis unless it's being directed by someone at the top who knows what to do.

Mastering a crisis is like going on a trip. One packs before leaving, not after. It's also important to have directions.

There's a story about an American couple who were vacationing in Scotland and wanted to go to Aberdeen. They rented a car and wound up getting very lost. They finally stopped a sheep herder and asked directions for the shortest route to Aberdeen.

"Shortest route? You can't do it from here," he replied.

There may be few short routes to mastering a crisis, but the destination can be reached successfully. The talented CEOs in this book who succeeded in managing their crises have provided excellent guides. A smart CEO will follow them.

The CEO had a dream. He was facing a problem that could hurt the company. His job was in jeopardy. He tried to hide, but the media glare kept finding him. Then, he was blinded by a flash of light. He realized he could manage the problem by biting the bullet and taking responsible action. Utilizing nimbleness and common sense, coupled with an understanding of perception and a commitment to responsible action, he surprised even himself by successfully managing the crisis.

Somewhat shaken but relieved, the CEO awoke and thought, "I never realized I was so wise. I must do that if it ever happens here."

Index: